The
Queens and I

COMMODORE GEOFFREY MARR DSC RD

The
Queens and I

The autobiography of the captain of the Queen Mary
and the last captain of the Queen Elizabeth

Adlard Coles Limited   London

Granada Publishing Limited
First published in Great Britain 1973 by Adlard Coles Limited
Frogmore St Albans Hertfordshire AL2 2NF and
3 Upper James Street London W1R 4BP

Copyright © 1973 Geoffrey Marr

ISBN 0 229 11526 8
Printed in Great Britain by
Northumberland Press Limited
Gateshead

Contents

First steps

When I joined HMS Conway on 11 September 1922, only few days after my fourteenth birthday, she was lying in that part of the River Mersey known as the Sloyne, about half a mile from Rock Ferry pier, and she looked very imposing in her distinctive black and white paintwork. Built just after the Nelson era as a 92-gun ship of the line, she had been HMS Nile, a typical example of the old wooden walls that had served Britain well before the age of steel. She has been too well described in the wonderful history of the ship written by John Masefield, the late Poet Laureate, an old Conway boy, to require any further description from me.

There were thirty-five other new boys making their first acquaintance with the ship that day, amongst whom I had the doubtful honour of being the youngest and smallest, and few sailors can have come from a more unlikely background than mine.

I was born six years before the beginning of the First World War, in the ancient market town of Pontefract between the plain of York and the South Yorkshire coalfield. For two generations my mother's family had been in business in the town, at the same time indulging in a little politics here and there, my grandfather having been mayor of the ancient borough just before I was born. My father on the other hand, came from a farming family, my paternal grandparents having lived in and farmed Flotmanby Hall, near Scarborough, before moving to Barton Manor, just outside Cambridge. To a family with this background, sailors were on a par with actors, and my insistence, when possible careers were being discussed, that I was interested in nothing but going to sea, astounded my parents.

The sea had held an irresistible attraction for me since early childhood and the long, happy summers I had spent at my maternal grandparents' cottage on the North Yorkshire coast: this early love persisted into adolescence. Although they were sceptical and still somewhat disapproving, my parents put no obstacles in my way, but rather doubtfully put my name down for a cadetship on HMS Conway, the Mercantile Marine Service Association's training ship for Royal Navy, Royal Naval Reserve and Merchant Navy officers.

As most new boys at a boarding school do, we soon found that life on HMS Conway was not all spanking new uniforms. Indeed, it seemed as though our fate was to provide amusement and sport for the two hundred or so other cadets who had already endured one term or more of the tough discipline that prevailed. I was already feeling very much alone in strange circumstances, and what little courage I had left completely evaporated when I discovered just how tough life on board was. By modern standards it was positively brutal.

We soon found out that every time we moved from one place to another we were expected to do so at the double, or faster, and the cadet captains placed in charge of us appeared to feel that they had a moral duty to smarten up the new chums in the shortest possible time. After we had been on board a week we were considered to have had enough time to learn the ship's routine and know the appropriate bugle calls so, as part of the smartening-up process, a sadistic custom known as 'bumming up hatches' was put into operation. This involved two cadet captains stationing themselves at the foot of the after ladder leading to the orlop deck (the lowest inhabited deck of the ship, where the new boys slung their hammocks and had their sea chests) armed with teasers—short lengths of rope with a loop at one end, the other end of which had been back-spliced and heavily whipped with spun yarn to make the last eight or ten inches quite stiff. When any important bugle call involving the whole ship's company such as Divisions, School, or Cookhouse was sounded, they would be waiting there, and the first dozen or so of the unfortunate new boys to arrive would be allowed up the ladder, which quickly became jammed as the main body reached it. Then as the late arrivals struggled to get a foothold they would find their rear ends smarting under repeated applications of the teasers accompanied by cries of 'This will teach you to be late, you lazy little devils.' The result was that for much of their first term the new chums tended to run like a flock of frightened sheep at the first notes of any bugle call, only to find that it was something like 'Away No 1 motor boat's crew' which did not really concern them—much to the amusement of the old hands.

Another sadistic custom was the one designed to teach you to lash up your hammock, with eight evenly spaced round turns and two half-hitches, in the shortest possible time. After breakfast the officer of the day would call the ship's company to attention, before giving the order 'Lash up and stow. Dismiss!' On hearing this, you turned smartly to your right; then you raced like a mad thing along the main deck, down two lots of hatchways to the lower deck and the orlop deck to your bunk, where you feverishly tried to roll up your bedding, which had been spread out along the ridge rope to air, stow it inside the hammock, lash the whole thing up and have it off the hook before the bugler sounded the 'Carry on' exactly three minutes later. Every boy who did not have his hammock off the hook before the bugle went automatically qualified for one stroke of the teaser, plus another if, when the officer of the day inspected the hammocks, he found the turns were not evenly spaced, or that he could get his fingers under any of the turns, or that any bedding was visible. With the new chums having the greatest distance to cover to reach their sleeping place, and finding the art of lashing up hammocks under stress a difficult one to master, I found myself collecting two strokes every morning, as a matter of routine for most of my first term. With similar punishment meted out for every minor breach of discipline, and bumming up hatches, the tenderest part of my anatomy started to take on many of the colours of the rainbow, as weal was superimposed upon weal. During our weekly bath night, in a communal bathroom containing a dozen baths, we compared our battle-scarred posteriors, and mine was voted the most colourful.

Coming from a home where corporal punishment had been reserved for the most outrageous offences, and a school where a caning by the headmaster was looked upon as something so serious that one talked about it with bated breath, all this was a terrible shock to my system, and night after night I silently cried myself to sleep in my hammock. Yet each Sunday when we wrote our more or less compulsory letters home there was little I could say because I knew my parents had the instant answer: 'We told you so. We knew you wouldn't like it, but you thought you knew best and you would have your own way!'

One can of course get used to almost anything in time, and I suppose it can be argued that in spite of the brutality the strict discipline did us good: it certainly left us no time to think of ways of defying authority. But even after fifty years I can find few memories of my two years on the Conway to look back on with pleasure.

Being small, and not particularly good at games, I became a mizzentopman (the division reserved for the smaller boys) at the end of my first term, and I never grew sufficiently while I was there to be promoted out of it; and because I failed to reach the coveted rank of cadet captain there were very few highlights during that period.

The ship herself was most uncomfortable. She had virtually no heating, such as on HMS Victory, which many people must have visited in Portsmouth; she was just a series of long, low decks, with big, square gun-ports along each side. Although all her guns had been removed and double windows fitted, these were our only ventilation system and some of them had to be kept open even on the coldest days. This seemed particularly noticeable on Saturday mornings in mid-winter, when all hands had spent the morning scrubbing the decks, and the only way of drying them was to let in as much cold, foggy Mersey air as possible.

As I lay in my hammock at night during that nightmare first term, I secretly vowed that wild horses would never drag me back to this awful place again, although I was not very clear in my mind how I could avoid coming back, without losing face. But like all nightmares this one ended, with the approach of the Christmas holidays. It was surprising how quickly the memories of all the horrors faded in the thrill of getting home again to all that wonderful warmth, comfort and good food, plus the feeling of being something a little bit special walking around a little country town, wearing the fore and aft rig of a cadet in His Majesty's Royal Naval Reserve, looking, one hoped, every inch a sailor. I couldn't spoil such a happy atmosphere by worrying people with my problems, so I found myself answering their questions evasively, and saying, 'Oh, I suppose it's not too bad.'

Then all at once Christmas, with its parties and presents, was over, and my spirits sank as the days flew past, and I knew that I had to go back and face it all again. This time, however, one wasn't a new chum any more. At least we knew what we were going back to, and could feel superior to the thirty frightened sheep who just didn't know what was happening to them. Then, after a couple more terms, one became a senior hand and would be allowed to remove the stitching that closed the trouser pockets, and even put one's hand in them discreetly, a great comfort on cold days. And I suppose, as boys will, I did my share of making life uncomfortable for the new boys coming along.

With slight variations, this I imagine is the story of nearly everybody's schooldays. We are all in our turn told: 'You had it easy, you should have been here two years ago, the discipline was twice as tough.' During my second year, as the result of a new boy's father writing to Captain Harvey Broadbent, the time allowed for lashing up and stowing hammocks was extended to four minutes, and the practice of bumming up hatches was officially banned. This, many old hands felt, was the beginning of the end, and could only result in those who followed us becoming a race of effete softies.

Cadets who wanted to try for direct entry into the Royal Navy were given special coaching in what was known as the Dartmouth class. But the Navy was cutting back after its wartime expansion and the standard required was so high that few attempted it during my time. However, the six brightest boys in each term, if they wished to do so, automatically qualified as RNR cadets and left the ship to do a further period of training with the Royal Navy before they started their Merchant Navy service. This left about thirty of us in my term for whom the main preoccupation of our final year was choosing the shipping company with which we would serve the last three years of our apprenticeship (the Board of Trade allowed two years on the Conway to count as one year of the normal four-year apprenticeship). There were long discussions among the boys about the relative merits of the various shipping companies. Since we had been moored at the Port of Liverpool, most Conway cadets tended to favour those companies which had their headquarters in that city, while cadets from our rival establishment, HMS Worcester—moored in the River Thames off Greenhithe—were more inclined to join London-based companies like the great P&O group. But to me, as I suppose to most of the boys of my time, the feeling of the glamour of the sea came from seeing the great Cunard and White Star liners alongside the Princes landing stage every Saturday, waiting to start their Atlantic crossing.

During the months of better weather, those of us who wished to do so were allowed to go swimming at the Guinea Gap baths in Wallasey on Saturday afternoons. This involved going by ferry to Liverpool and then catching another ferry to Wallasey. While we were on the landing stage, because we were in uniform, a friendly policeman could usually be persuaded to let us through the gates leading to the north end of the stage. These were the days when the Cunard liners Scythia, Samaria and Laconia were brand new ships, and the White Star Line still had its famous 'Big Four': the Adriatic, Baltic, Cedric and Celtic.

We stood in awe and watched the rush and bustle of embarkation as the special trains came into Riverside Station and the passengers' baggage was hoisted aboard. Sometimes we had the additional thrill of seeing the lines let go, and the tugs tow the ships off the stage and swing them into the river.

In those days very few passenger ships carried apprentices, so we could not hope to sail in one of these great ships until we had obtained our masters' certificates; but most of the big liner companies had their associated cargo companies (in the case of Cunard, they were Brocklebanks and the Port Line) where one could serve one's time. With a cadetship in one of these one had a foot on the bottom rung of the ladder. This made the competition for these places very keen. Not being in the First XV, and about halfway down my form scholastically, I knew I did not stand much chance; but I hopefully filled out a lot of application forms, and was accepted by Elders and Fyffes. They were a firm of banana importers, whose trim, white yacht-like banana boats had become part of our lives, for nearly every weekend would find one of them anchored in the Sloyne close to the Conway, waiting for suitable tidal conditions for its trip up the dredged channel to its unloading berth in Garston Docks.

CHAPTER TWO

Elders and Fyffes —
banana specialists

When I joined Elders and Fyffes Ltd in August 1924, they were a wholly-owned subsidiary of the United Fruit Company of Boston, Massachusetts. The ships were under British management, but as far as we could see the British board of directors largely carried out the policy laid down by the American company. It was a small concern then, with only twelve ships, more than half of which had been built prior to the First World War, during which they had suffered heavy losses. There was a strong family atmosphere within the company, with nearly everybody knowing everybody else. A tremendous expansion programme had just begun, which was to build up their fleet to thirty-six ships within the next ten years. In all departments this resulted in extremely rapid promotion for those officers who held the necessary certificates, making it a company of very young captains and senior staff. Carrying its own insurance for everything except total loss, Elders and Fyffes followed a policy of paying wages well above the average to attract a better type of officer. However, most of the chief officers were still of the older and tougher pre-war school who believed that young apprentices should learn their job the hard way, from the bottom up. They had no time for boys who came from the Conway and other training establishments, full of ideas about being officers and gentlemen, so my first sea voyage was to prove almost as rude a shock to my system as my first term on the Conway.

My joining instructions had said that I should report on board my first ship, the SS Greenbrier (a ship which had made a name for herself during the war, as the German raider Moewe), before noon on a certain date. Since there was no train from Pontefract that could get me to Garston so early in the day, I arrived the evening before, to find the ship under the coal tips, with ten-ton coal wagons being lifted by a hydraulic hoist and then tipped from a height of about fifty feet, down a chute, into her bunkers. The noise and dirt were almost beyond belief. An old nightwatchman helped me to get my gear on board before taking me to the second officer, who appeared to be the only other person around. The second officer had been drowning his miseries in beer, and was not the least bit pleased to see me. He gave me the key to the apprentices' cabin, which was alongside the bunker hatch, in a filthy state, with no bed linen on either of the two bunks. There was nothing I could do but lie down fully clothed on one of the bunks, pull a blanket over myself, and just listen to the thunder of the coal down the chute and, as the whole ship shuddered, wonder how I had got myself into such a mess.

The following day the ship started to come to life as, with the bunkering completed, the shore gang came on board with high-pressure hoses and started to wash off some of the soot. After I had washed some of the dirt off myself, the second officer called in, apologized for the previous evening and showed me the way to the docks canteen for breakfast. Later the other apprentice arrived, and with other members of the crew I went up to the shipping office to sign on ready for sailing the next day. But I still felt so lost, dirty and miserable in these unfamiliar surroundings that I sat down that evening and wrote a really desperate letter home.

The excitement and bustle of sailing day lifted my spirits a little, as did an interest in the mechanics of getting the ship out of dock, down the River Mersey, past the Conway and out into the open sea. But I was still feeling very much a stranger in a strange place when, at 06.00, with the other apprentice, I reported to the chief officer, wearing my new and still rather stiff dungarees, ready to start my first day's work. I was presented with a shallow square tin with two lids, containing colza oil, bathbrick and a couple of pieces of dirty waste, and told to polish the brasswork on the docking bridge, at the after end of the ship. From there I could look forward and appreciate to the full the rise and fall of the ship on the choppy sea, in what was now becoming a most uncomfortable motion.

Just how many hours I spent in this personal Garden of Gethsemane I shall never know, but between trying to polish the brass with the evil-smelling oil, and rushing to the ship's side to be sick, then getting utterly filthy wiping my face with oily hands, I certainly suffered for my folly in going against my parents' wishes. The other apprentice came along and told me it was time for breakfast, but when I showed little enthusiasm he must have told the chief officer, who ordered me to stow my things away, get myself cleaned up and go to bed. I felt a little better lying in my bunk, until the ship's motion increased, and fresh waves of misery swept over me.

By the time the apprentices reported for work the next day things not only looked, but felt, very different, although I was still a little taken aback by the menial tasks the chief officer found for us to do. I couldn't see how spending hour after hour on my knees, chipping and red-leading scuppers, was helping me to be a better officer. However, once I found my sea-legs I settled down into our daily routine fairly quickly, and the warm sunny days on the long leg between the Azores and Turks Island Passage made even the more unpleasant tasks bearable.

Kingston, Jamaica was much hotter than anywhere I had been before, but I found it fascinating, with the hissing and clanking of the slow-moving banana trains which brought the fruit down from up-country, and the monotonous, sing-song chant of the tallyman at each shell door as the stems were passed through. Then we completed our loading at the outports—Bowden, Montego Bay, Ocho Rios, and Port Antonio—before sailing for home. Once our perishable cargo was loaded, the ship made the voyage home at her best possible speed, between 15 and 16 knots, far different from the economical 11 to 12 knots of the outward voyage. When we docked in Garston, I was given five days' leave and an hour later my parents and I were on our way home in the car together. I was not sad and dejected as they had expected from my letter, but bubbling over with excitement as I told them about all the places I had seen and the things I had done.

Elders and Fyffes had by this time evolved two types of ship suitable for their highly specialized cargo—a 5,500 ton freighter carrying twelve passengers, and a 10,000 ton passenger/cargo liner carrying a hundred passengers, all first class; although the standard company joke was to tell passengers that they were only travelling second class, because our first class passengers were the green ones down in the holds. This meant that with a few exceptions, such as the Greenbrier and Miami, both ex-German banana carriers taken over as reparations at the end of the war, and the few pre-war ships that were still in service, most of the fleet tended to be identical. This enabled the company to follow a policy of moving captains and officer personnel from one ship to another at will, to fit in with leave and other requirements. They did this to such an extent that it became a matter of comment for an officer to remain in one of the cargo ships for more than five consecutive voyages, and led to suggestions that it was time he arranged to have his cabin painted out, usually a sure way of getting moved. This resulted in everyone getting to know nearly everyone else in the firm, and also in a fantastic amount of gossip. People tended to talk about those who had been with them in their last ship, or about the people who had just left this one, and often preconceived opinions of someone were formed before you actually sailed with him.

The ships were basically on a fine-weather trade, so a four-week trip to the West Indies on one of the twelve passenger cargo ships made an attractive family holiday for many people in both summer or winter. Not only did the fact that we were carrying passengers keep the standard of food high, but most captains encouraged all their officers, including the cadets, to play their part in helping to entertain the passengers, which made some voyages very enjoyable.

As far as the cadets were concerned, our great ambition was to be appointed to one of the six passenger ships, based on Avonmouth, which maintained a regular scheduled passenger service to Trinidad, Barbados and Jamaica, with occasional calls at Bermuda. Jobs on these were reserved for the more senior apprentices, usually those in their last year. We knew they meant an end to chipping and scraping and other jobs we had been given to keep up out of mischief, because each of the ships carried four officers, and the two cadets acted as junior officers of the watch, on the 8–12 and 12–4 watches. My turn came about eight months before my indentures expired, and I was sent to Avonmouth to join the SS Bayano (a ship which had served for a time as an armed merchant cruiser during the war) as her senior apprentice.

My indentures expired in August 1927. Then came all the count-
ing up to see if I had enough actual days at sea to allow me to sit my
examination for my second mate's certificate; fortunately, there
was enough seatime, and I passed the exam at my first attempt.
I rejoined Elders and Fyffes, and was soon tasting the joys of being
in charge of a watch, with a bright new single gold stripe on my
sleeve.

This process repeated itself a couple of years later, when I had
been in charge of watches long enough to allow me to sit for my
first mate's certificate; then there followed a longer gap before I was
able to take the final hurdle, my master's examination, in 1933. But
by then many things were changing: the wave of prosperity that
had swept the company along ever since I joined had started to
recede; and during a spell of sick leave I had met the girl I was
eventually to marry.

We knew we could not marry until I had my master's certificate,
because when a young officer came ashore to sit for his certificate
his pay stopped and he had to live on his savings until he was
successful.

To complicate the situation, Dorothie was having doubts about
whether she really liked the idea of a sailor husband, so I seriously
considered a post ashore. As I was on leave from the company to sit
for my certificate, this seemed the perfect opportunity. Besides ships,
my other great interest was cars, and with my father's influence
as a director and shareholder in a chain of garages, I was able to get
a job as an assistant salesman. However, with the country just
coming out of the Depression it was difficult to persuade the farmers
around Bourne that they needed to buy a new car. After about
three weeks I realized that it would be a very long time before I
would earn enough commission to support a wife and family in the
world of a car salesman. So, it was back to Captain Robert's
Nautical Academy and some really hard studying.

The master's certificate examination consisted of written and oral
sections. After successfully completing the written part, the senior
examiner called me in to take the verbal section. He asked me a few
questions, then gave me a pencil and paper and posed a simple
draught calculation. After I had worked it out correctly he said
'Mr Marr, can you write down five nines so that they equal one

thousand?' Immediately I wrote down 999 9/9 and handed it to him. I should never have known the answer had I not come across it in a book of puzzles a few weeks before. After such a lucky break, all the rest of the questions were easy. On 19 July 1933 I received my master's certificate, that piece of black pasteboard which represents to every officer in the Merchant Navy the culmination of years of effort, entitling him to take command of any British ship. With it I could finally think about my future, and my fiancée and I went ahead with our wedding plans.

However the atmosphere at Elders and Fyffes was very different when I returned. By now Hitler had come to power in Germany, and had forced the company—if they wished to continue importing bananas into Germany—to put six of their ships, including the Miami and the Greenbrier, under the German flag, and to man them with German crews. The building programme ceased, and most of the pre-war ships had by now either been sent to the scrapyard or taken out of service and laid up. Because of the earlier rapid build-up from twelve to thirty-six ships within ten years, it was now a company of young masters, with only a small age difference between them and their junior officers. When the same process was put into reverse, and the fleet was reduced to twenty-four ships within a couple of years, for each ship that went out of service one master had to revert to chief officer, two chief officers found themselves reduced to second officers, and so on down the line, with four third officers becoming redundant. With no immediate prospect of the fleet being increased in size again, the only hope of promotion for the juniors was the masters retiring, which most of them were not likely to do for about thirty years. I had reverted from second officer to third officer, and although I was still well up the third officers' seniority list, and not in any immediate danger of being fired, my prospects looked doubtful when Dorothie and I were married on 28 April 1934.

Unfortunately, things got steadily worse in Elders and Fyffes, and in the winter, when the consumption of bananas always falls off, they laid up half a dozen more ships temporarily, and gave all their third officers three months' leave on half pay. As my salary at this time was £20 per month, this meant that during our first winter in our new home we had to manage on fifty shillings a week for everything, rent and food included.

By the time the next winter arrived the slump was easing a little and there was no more half pay; but because all the officers who were senior to me were so near my own age, my prospects for promotion looked grim, and I appeared to be faced with the prospect of remaining a third officer for years and years. However, in the autumn of 1936, with the help of an old family friend, I was granted an interview with the Cunard Line's principal marine superintendent in Liverpool. This was wonderful luck, and as I waited outside the office for the fateful interview I examined all the pictures of the great Cunard liners on the walls, whose comings and goings I had watched so enviously as a young Conway cadet. The superintendent was very pleasant, and after a few routine questions, he said that if the directors accepted his recommendation, and I joined the Cunard White Star Line, I would be the first new officer he had engaged for almost eight years, and one of the first officers to join the new merger company. I came away from the office elated; I could scarcely believe my good fortune. When after a medical examination my appointment was confirmed, and I was able to sit down and write my letter of resignation to Elders and Fyffes, I could scarcely believe that it wasn't all a dream.

CHAPTER THREE

Joining the Cunard Line

I first joined the Cunard liner RMS Andania in Huskisson Dock, Liverpool, where she was preparing for a winter voyage to Halifax, Nova Scotia, and New York. Although she was one of the smallest ships in the company's passenger fleet, being only 14,000 tons, she certainly looked big to me that day; yet her top speed of 16 knots was not as fast as some of the banana boats I had sailed in. Joining her was an introduction to a new way of life, because in nearly a hundred years of operating passenger vessels on the Atlantic, Cunard had built up its own traditions, not only of service to passengers, but also of the duties and responsibilities of its officers, and there was a code of conduct and behaviour to which they were expected to conform. The temperament and behaviour of the captains and senior officers under whom he serves can often have a considerable effect upon the character formation of a young officer, and the chief officer of the Andania certainly had an effect on mine. He was an elderly, stout and very choleric man, a regular martinet of the old school, who could tell someone off in a manner worthy of a regimental sergeant-major for some minor slip in writing up the log, and then come over and greet him warmly in the wardroom at lunchtime and insist on buying him a beer.

Naturally I encounted problems in transferring from a small company, in which after twelve years I knew nearly everyone, and as a third officer felt able to talk freely to the captain, to a larger ship, with many more officers in all sections and where relationships were much more stiff and formal, with little mixing between departments. Also, due to the merging of Cunard and White Star and the subsequent reduction of the fleets, promotion had been slow for many years, and most of the deck officers were almost double my age.

But the biggest difference was in the weather, because even in the winter the banana ships had been in warm, sunny weather for at least fifty per cent of each voyage. However, on the Liverpool–Halifax–New York service, the winter gales were so continuous that we never knew where one ended and the other began, and for days on end never caught more than an occasional glimpse of the sun, and then it was low in the sky, through rapidly scudding clouds. With the temperatures in both Halifax and New York often well below freezing, we frequently had to use the hot salt-water hoses to thaw out the ropes before we could make fast alongside. At our ports on this side of the ocean—Greenock, Belfast and Liverpool—the weather wasn't usually so cold, but the low grey clouds just seemed to go on dumping their loads of moisture all winter long.

The coming of spring brought longer days and slightly less frequent gales, but at the first opportunity, usually about the middle of April, we were pushing our way through the ice of the St Lawrence and up to Montreal on a trade which, while it may well be a little less wearing on the nerves of the junior officers than those of the master, is still, I think, one of the toughest in the world.

Then, early in June 1937, I found myself transferred to the London 'A' boats, first to the Ausonia and later to the Ascania. These ships were exactly the same size as the Andania but just a little bit more modern in design. While the London service was even more exacting than the Liverpool service, the move was welcome. Now that Cunard had decided that there would be more ships sailing from London and Southampton in the future, it gave us the chance to move our home, and in the late summer of 1937 we bought a home at Ashurst, in the New Forest.

In the early summer of 1938 I was appointed junior third officer of RMS Queen Mary—the ship that during the previous two years had fired the imagination of everyone in England who loved the sea. I shall always remember standing on the dock gazing up at the sheer bulk of her enormous hull, almost a fifth of a mile long, which John Masefield described as 'Lofty as a tower and longer than a street'. Up to this time, I had never sailed in a ship of more than 14,000 tons, or a ship with more than one funnel, so I was tremendously impressed by the sheer size of everything.

I was very much the new boy, and glad to be given the job of night officer for my first two voyages, to get a chance to learn my way around the ship. Not only did I have this feeling of awe about the size and power of the ship, but I had similar feelings of respect for her captain, Commodore Sir Robert Irving, the Laird of Bonshawe, who was in my opinion not only a great seaman but a gentleman. Even in moments of great stress, when he must have been suffering from physical exhaustion due to long hours on the bridge—there were many in those hectic pre-war days, driving the ship across the fog-shrouded Atlantic with no radar at record-breaking speeds—I never saw him when he did not have both voice and temper under perfect control. He had a very pleasant and friendly manner, and a facility for making young, and sometimes very nervous junior officers feel relaxed and comfortable.

Looking back, one finds it almost impossible to understand how we managed to maintain such very high speeds on a North Atlantic which had just as much foggy weather as it does today, but which was then being used by a large number of passenger liners of all nationalities. It simply meant that captains and senior officers were prepared to gamble their professional reputations on the mathematical improbability of two ships arriving at the same spot on this large ocean at the same time. We all knew then, from near-misses (or rather near-hits) when the visibility was only slightly reduced, how very close a ship had to be before her whistle could be heard. This was particularly noticeable on board the Queen Mary, because when she was running at high speed there was so much extraneous noise on the bridge from the whistle of the wind through the rigging and superstructure.

There were older and wiser heads than mine to deal with the risks of collison, and when we ran into fog there was a standard procedure. Two extra look-outs were posted, the watertight doors were closed and the engines put on stand-by. This meant that extra engineer officers were on duty, steam was put on the astern turbines and the captain reduced the speed to what he considered prudent, considering the circumstances. The captain and the senior officer on watch then stationed themselves on opposite sides of the bridge and every one listened intently. If a ship's whistle were heard and its direction confirmed, course was immediately altered 45 degrees away from it. This new course was held for ten minutes, when, provided the whistle could no longer be heard, the original course was resumed. My main worries came when, as so often seemed to happen, we were approaching the coast in foggy weather and I had the responsibility of trying to fix the vessel's position with our two navigational aids: echo-sounding machine and the radio direction finder (usually called the DF). While the echo sounder is a most useful aid to navigation in shallow water, as it tells instantly the amount of water under the ship, the method of fixing a ship's position by taking a line of soundings at regular intervals and then comparing them with the soundings printed on the chart has generally been found to be unreliable, because in many parts of the world the charts are based on old and inaccurate surveys. This left us with the DF, with which in theory a position could be fixed within about 200 miles of the coast stations, by taking DF bearings of two stations as near 90 degrees apart as possible. Then two small corrections were applied, one from a calibration scale and the other for half convergency, and the bearings laid off on the chart. Their intersection was the ship's position. This system had many drawbacks and it is little used today. It is possible in daylight under good conditions to get a reasonably accurate fix, but at night and particularly during electric storms it became quite difficult, often with the most fantastic signals being picked up. As we approached the Nantucket light vessel on foggy nights there I was sitting for hour after hour with the headphones on, feeling sick with apprehension and worry, trying to get a decent cross bearing between Nantucket and the Pollock Rip light vessel or the shore station on Cape Cod. Added to this was an anxious commodore looking around the door about every twenty minutes, and saying 'Have you managed to get anything yet, Marr?' while the ship ploughed steadily on, covering a mile every two minutes, towards that ill-fated lightship which only a few years before had been rammed and sunk by the White Star liner Olympic, with a heavy loss of life among her crew. Then gradually I would be able to pick up her signal through the static crashes, and by the time the commodore said, 'We should only be about thirty miles from the lightship now, Marr; can you confirm that her bearing is opening on the starboard bow?' I would be able to say with reasonable confidence that it was. But nobody was more thankful than I when, eventually, the loom of its powerful light through the mist or the almost animal-like grunt of its diaphone fog signal on the beam to starboard told us that we had passed it safely once again.

Still, in spite of all these worries, they were exciting and exhilarating days, particularly during that voyage, shortly after I joined, when the ship made a record crossing in both directions and took the so-called Blue Riband from the French liner Normandie, although Cunard never made any official claim for the Atlantic record. Indeed they tried to maintain a polite fiction that this had just been a routine crossing which the ship could repeat at any time if the circumstances justified it. To give an air of verisimilitude to this statement the schedule was altered to allow the ship to do crossings at over 30 knots on two or three voyages after this, although our normal service speed was only about 28.5 knots.

In the early spring of 1939 the ship arrived in New York during a tugboat strike, and as one of the junior officers on duty on the bridge I watched Commodore Irving dock the huge ship without tugs, a manoeuvre I had to repeat twenty-eight years later with the Queen Elizabeth. As this was the first time this had been done, the operation—which led to the collapse of the strike—received worldwide publicity.

As the war clouds continued to gather over Europe during the summer, our passenger lists for the westbound crossings continued to build up, until on our 30 August sailing from Southampton every available bed was taken, and special liferafts were put on board to allow us to take passengers in excess of the number shown on our passenger certificate, in temporary berths in the swimming pools and libraries. By the time we sailed, things were already looking so grim that our portholes had been painted over and our upper deck lights blacked out. Instead of following our normal route we sailed under sealed Admiralty orders, and Commodore Irving had been warned that at least two of the German pocket battleships might be in the Atlantic.

When war was officially declared on Sunday, 3 September 1939, we were just starting our Sunday morning church service as Mr Chamberlain was making his famous speech. The ship was at the time steaming down the coast of Nova Scotia. At about noon there was a flurry of excitement on the bridge and the lookout reported the masts and funnels of two warships on the horizon. We wondered if these were the German pocket battleships. But our fears were soon set at rest by the wink of long-distance signalling lamps. They were two British cruisers, HMS Exeter and HMS York, racing out of Halifax to try to intercept the German liner Bremen, which had slipped out of New York harbour the previous night. However, she managed to give them the slip and finally reached the Russian port of Murmansk before sailing down through the Norwegian fjords back to her home port of Bremerhaven, where the Allied bombers eventually ended her seagoing career.

Monday, 4 September saw us gliding slowly up New York harbour to land our passengers and cargo and then settle down to a long period of inactivity. In those early days of the war nobody had decided what to do with the Queen Mary: she was regarded as too large and too valuable to bring home to England, where she would have been a prime target for Göring's Luftwaffe, because damage to her would have been a boost for German morale. It wasn't until the spring of 1940, after the brand new Queen Elizabeth had made her famous secret dash across the Atlantic, that it was decided to make the two ships into 'super troopers', a job they did with outstanding success for the remainder of the war. Our orders were to put the ship into a state of readiness to go anywhere in the world that we might be required, so we perfected our blackout arrangements and painted the whole ship battleship grey.

Once the larger part of the crew had left us there was little that the rest of us could do but settle down to make the best of our long spell of enforced idleness, listening avidly to the war news from home. Of course, we were not suffering any hardship; our ship had all the facilities of a luxury hotel and, berthed at Pier 90, we were only about ten minutes' walk from Broadway and Radio City. The English-Speaking Union made it their business to see that we were adequately entertained, and most of the crew had a circle of American friends. Joking about it afterwards, I used to say that while my poor wife was having a miserable time at home with blackouts, rationing, and working long hours in a local hospital helping to cope with evacuees, I had spent the first five months of the war living in comfort, if not luxury, and being lavishly entertained by my American friends. But I was a lieutenant in the Royal Naval Reserve, and in January 1940 I was informed that a relief was being sent out in the Scythia and I was to return home in the same ship. On 9 February I landed in Liverpool on a cold wet day, to start my war service with the Royal Navy.

CHAPTER FOUR

Contraband control and the Dunkirk emergency

On 13 February 1940 I was appointed to HMS Fervent, the contraband control station at Ramsgate. Not one of the most impressive of the Navy's 'stone frigates' (the sailors' name for shore bases), the station was just a collection of wooden huts that had only come into being with the war. All foreign merchant ships entering the North Sea from the English Channel were forced to anchor in the Downs between the Goodwin Sands and the Kent coast and submit to an examination of their documents, and sometimes their cargo, by officers of the RN Contraband Control Service, before being allowed to proceed to their destinations in Continental or Scandinavian ports. Ramsgate, with its small tidal harbour, was the most convenient place from which to do this. Working with the Contraband Control Service might have been rather a pleasant job during the summer months, but in February, March and April, especially with an easterly wind, it was as uncomfortable as almost anywhere in the world outside the Arctic Circle, for small boat work.

Much though I love the sea, I have always been a big ship sailor, and although I never reached the point when I couldn't feel rather squeamish in rough weather, especially at the start of a voyage, I don't remember any prolonged periods of discomfort from *mal-de-mer* since my agonizing introduction to it on the Greenbrier. But any illusions I may have had of being physically a good sailor were to be shattered for ever by this tour of duty at Ramsgate.

The boarding parties worked in teams of three: two officers and one petty officer or senior naval rating, the most senior of the officers being called the boarding officer, and the more junior one, as I was, the witnessing officer, with the PO or rating going along to carry the papers and to stand guard to see that no funny business went on while the officers were closeted with the ship's master. We reported for duty at 08.00 daily, and were then given a list of the ships that we were to deal with during the day, in the order in which they had anchored. We went down to the harbour to join our launches, which were twenty-five foot diesel-driven launches of the type used for taking pilots to and from ships at Dover, with a long flat foredeck and a wire stay running down the middle, especially designed for jumping on or off. Two or three of these little boats would steam boldly out of harbour together and then split up and each head for their designated ship. With a perilous leap and a scramble up a swinging rope ladder, we arrived on a deck that felt as solid as a rock, and were ushered into the warmth and comfort of the captain's cabin.

Provided the ship's papers were in order and she carried Navicerts (certificates issued by the British consul at her loading port to the effect that her cargo contained no contraband), our visit could be mostly a matter of routine. It would last about an hour, then our launch was called back alongside for the short run over to the next vessel on our list, where the process was repeated with minor variations, depending on how co-operative the neutral shipmaster was, and in some cases on how well he spoke English. We normally expected to do three ships before we took our lunch break. If the weather was rough, I had sometimes lost my interest in food by this time, and came in for a good deal of ribbing from my more robust companions. After lunch we followed the same routine until we had completed all the ships on our list. When we had finished and could no longer impose on the poor captain, who wanted to get the anchor up and get on with his voyage, we returned to our launch often as much as a couple of hours before we were officially allowed to put in to harbour. Our orders were to remain in the anchorage area until 16.00 to service any other ships that might come in and drop their anchors before that time. On the launch, the only place to get any shelter from the bitter east wind and flying spray was in the little cabin, full of the smell of the diesel fumes from the engine, which did little to improve my delicate condition. Fortunately, as I have said to many passengers since, there is no other disease I know of from which one recovers so quickly as sea-sickness, and by the time I had got back to our digs, and thawed out my frozen limbs in a hot bath, I felt completely fit, with an appetite like a horse.

In May 1940, when the Dunkirk crisis was about half way through, another RNR lieutenant and I were put in command of steam drifters, which were manned by civilian crews serving under a T124X agreement, a wartime arrangement under which merchant seamen agreed to serve under naval discipline, on merchant ships which were being used for naval operations. We also had an RNR sub-lieutenant, plus a small party of naval ratings, to man a Lewis gun which had been mounted on the bridge as our only armament.

My drifter was the Lord Collingwood, a ship which I knew from my time on the Contraband Control Service, and when I went on board I found that she had already been loaded with about 400 two-gallon cans containing petrol, and a small number of drums of diesel fuel. When we were briefed by the operations officer, we were told that many of the armada of small ships which had answered the government's appeal and sailed to Dunkirk to help ferry the troops off the beaches were now being put out of action because their fuel supplies were exhausted and they could not be supplied from the shore. Since the normal approach to the port of Dunkirk—a dredged channel which runs from west to east parallel to the coast—was protected by German artillery, making passage through it during daylight highly dangerous, our job was to try to find a passage in between the sandbanks, and approach the town just before high water, from the NNE. Shortly before 09.00 we left Ramsgate armed with the largest scale charts and tidal diagrams, but the navigational aids on a drifter are fairly primitive and less than three hours after we sailed my first command had grounded on a sandbank within sight of Dunkirk. We had only been going slowly, and as I was the leading ship of the pair, I was able to give three blasts on my whistle to give my companion sufficient warning to allow him to stop in time. Then he approached cautiously and threw us a line and was able with the help of the tide to pull the Lord Collingwood clear. Having moved our ships into deep water again, we held a council of war and decided that we could not fix our position with sufficient accuracy to attempt this approach from the north with any hope of success. But as ships seemed to be moving freely along the coast again we opted to try to get in by the normal approach route, and set a course for the entrance to the dredged channel.

What we did not know at that time was that a squadron of Fleet Air Arm Swordfish had divebombed the German guns and silenced them for the time being. So we were able to proceed without let or hindrance and arrived off the town in the late afternoon to find a very confused situation, and one in which all our efforts to get rid of our cargo of petrol, even though we were giving the damned stuff away, met with little success. The evacuation was reaching its closing stages, and German air activity seemed to be gaining in intensity, so many of the smaller boats which had come over had either run out of fuel or been abandoned because their engines had given out. The few that were still operational seemed disinclined to fuel by the slow process of coming alongside and having fuel passed over in two-gallon cans. So we cruised slowly up and down the beaches hailing every motor boat we saw, and finally managed to persuade one or two to come alongside and fill their tanks. During the remaining hours of daylight our attention was mainly concentrated on the skies, and as soon as we saw the destroyers back off the mole with their AA guns barking, we knew that another raid had started, and we waited hopefully for the arrival of the RAF. They didn't come every time, as by now their resources must have been pretty strained, but when they did arrive there were some magnificent dogfights, although we couldn't always tell who had won. The number of wrecked ships round the harbour mouth was, however, evidence that the German pilots were pressing home their attacks, and with our highly inflammable cargo we felt extremely vulnerable. I knew that our main armament—the solitary Lewis gun—had an effective range of only about half a mile, but I hadn't the heart to stop my enthusiastic gun crew letting off a few bursts at any hostile aircraft they managed to get in their sights, because while it may not have done the slightest harm to the enemy, the short staccato bark did a lot for the morale of all on board.

As darkness started to fall, all hopes of finding people willing to take any more of our petrol faded rapidly; but having brought it all the way over here it seemed wrong to take it back again if there was any possible use for it. By now, however, my fish hold was crammed with soldiers, mostly French, collected from various small craft during the evening. Then, in the gathering dusk, we came across another drifter loaded to the gunwales with troops, lying helpless with a rope round her propeller. We passed her a tow rope, made fast a couple of motor boats about the size of naval cutters whose engines were broken down just astern of her, and shortly before midnight set course for home looking like a mother hen leading a string of chickens. The whole scene was illuminated by the flickering light of flames leaping up from a blazing oil refinery behind the town, and as we threaded our way past the wrecked ships off the beaches by this eerie and ghostly light, we knew that we were still leaving thousands of men behind.

We seemed to be making desperately slow progress against the tide, when suddenly, ahead of us, we saw what looked like little green lights on the almost oily calm sea. These turned out to be the phosphorescent bow waves of a flotilla of British destroyers coming up the channel at high speed towards us, so we hurriedly switched on our navigation lights and they altered course to avoid us. Just after they had passed, they opened fire with their twin four-inch guns. The Germans promptly illuminated the area with starshell and, for the second time that day, we felt very vulnerable as the sub-lieutenant and I tried desperately to remember just how many channel buoys we had passed and to work out from the chart whether, at our draught, we could safely turn away before we reached the end of the dredged channel. But being stuck on a sandbank the previous day I decided not to take any chances, so we turned in the correct place. Fortunately the remainder of the trip proved uneventful and early the following morning we were safely back in Ramsgate harbour. After reporting to the duty officer I crawled wearily into one of the fishermen's bunks, pulled the sliding doors across, and had my first sleep in forty-eight hours.

All that day we stood by in case we had to make another trip, but by now the Germans had closed in around the town, so that only high-speed naval craft were being sent in, mainly under cover of darkness. By the next day the evacuation was officially over and

I was sent back to Portsmouth to continue a series of training courses.

Getting down to my studies again on Monday seemed a little difficult after all that excitement; but with German daylight raids we also had quite a bit of liveliness in Portsmouth that summer. I was at Whale Island, the Royal Navy's gunnery school, when it was decided to shoot the lions and other dangerous animals in the Navy's private zoo there, in case they got free during a raid.

CHAPTER FIVE

HMS King George V

In September 1940, the Luftwaffe carried out a series of raids on our airfields and then began round-the-clock bombing of London's dockyards. At the same time, the government, after studying the RAF photographs of German barges being assembled at ports along the coasts of Holland, Belgium and France; and after receiving reports of the damage to the destroyers HMS Esk and HMS Express, when they ran into a large force of E-boats in the southern North Sea, decided to send out the famous code-word *Cromwell*. This meant that they considered the danger of invasion to be imminent, and all the nation's defences were to be brought to the highest state of readiness against it. When the signal was received it threw HMS Excellent into a flurry of excitement, and at very short notice I found myself appointed company commander of C Company, Anson Battalion, a naval division made up of officers, petty officers and ratings from shore establishments.

Deputizing for the sick RN lieutenant who had trained them, I was ordered to take C Company—consisting of four RN sub-lieutenants and about 120 petty officers and men—to guard the outer defences of Fort Wiley at the top of Portsdown Hill. It was my first command and a proud moment for me, but although the Army decided that we sailors had a good deal to learn about modern ground warfare, and organized a series of combined exercises to teach us, we saw no action. A fortnight later my relief arrived and I returned to Whale Island. By now the Battle of Britain was getting into its stride and as the Luftwaffe losses rose, it gradually became obvious that if the Germans were going to invade it wasn't likely to be for some time yet. So, one by one, the precautions were relaxed.

But for me big things were afoot when I was appointed to HMS King George V, Britain's newest battleship, the first of a new class of five 35,000-tonners then nearing completion on the River Tyne. Not only was she one of the most talked-about ships in the Navy at that time, but also in this relatively early stage of the war the dilution of naval officer ranks by reservists had only just begun, so it was considered quite an honour to be one of the two RNR officers among her large officer complement. When I joined her on 9 October 1940 her manning was almost completed and her commissioning date was drawing near. The captain decided that I was to be the assistant navigator, the only lieutenant on board in full charge of a watch at sea.

To me, the best thing about being made assistant navigator was that I automatically became the 'Special Seadutyman OOW', which meant I was always on the bridge entering or leaving harbour or in pilotage waters, conning the ship except when relieved by the navigator. Also, it gave me a very special action station, which was to take charge of the secondary conning position. On board the King George V this was an emergency bridge about two-thirds of the way up after funnel, where I had all the controls necessary to enable me to take over temporary control of the ship if the main bridge were hit by an enemy shell. In such a case, if the captain were killed or seriously wounded, I should be joined by the commander, who always remains inside the citadel when the ship is in action, against precisely such an eventuality.

At this time the German battleship Bismarck was in our thoughts, and shortly after we had moved to Rosyth dockyard to complete our fitting out, Winston Churchill visited the ship to check on our progress. Before leaving he climbed up on one of our big quarter-deck capstans, and gathered the ship's company around him. He left no doubt in our minds as to how vitally important for the country it was for us to get our ship into fighting trim as quickly as possible. He told us that Germany's new battleship, the Bismarck, had already completed her sea trials, and was doing working-up exercises in the Baltic. Then he concluded, in his inimitable manner: 'Gentlemen, your great task is to seek out and destroy the Bismarck.'

But for us, there were still many weeks of trials and tests and seemingly interminable exercises, as equipment was checked and rechecked, very necessary on the first ship of a new class; especially important as we were fitted with a new type of rapid-firing, high-velocity, 14-inch gun. Important too, because it is told that the first time they tried the telegraph from the director to Y turret, the telegraph to 'Open fire' showed on the indicator in the turret as 'Abandon ship'.

We welcomed Winston Churchill again, in Scapa Flow, when he and Mrs Churchill, accompanied by President Roosevelt's special envoy Mr Harry Hopkins, came north to see Lord and Lady Halifax off to Washington when Lord Halifax was appointed as the new British ambassador there. The fact that we had been selected to take them meant for us a chance to settle down to normal sea routine for the first time. It was significant that in December 1940, when the Navy was so desperately short of ships, the government attached such a great deal of importance to the success of Lord Halifax's mission in those critical days, that it was prepared to send one of Britain's largest and most valuable ships to ensure his safe arrival.

We did a high speed dash across the Atlantic, unescorted but routed clear of areas of high U-boat activity, to Cape Charles at the entrance of Chesapeake Bay, followed by a 150-mile inland water-way trip to Annapolis, where we dropped anchor off the American Naval Academy. President Roosevelt came alongside in the Presidential Yacht Williamsburg to receive Lord and Lady Halifax. After a stay of less than thirty-six hours, during which our midshipmen were entertained by those of the Academy and returned to the ship with boatloads of American magazines, we sailed down the Chesapeake Bay again and up the coast to Halifax, Nova Scotia. However, we were to see very little of it, because within a few hours of docking news was received that the German pocket battleships Scharnhorst and Gneisenau were attacking British convoys on the Atlantic, so we left again as soon as we had refuelled and taken on essential stores, to supplement the escort of a homeward-bound convoy. I think most of us found this trip rather boring, stuck in the middle of a large convoy plodding along at nine or ten knots, so there was a sigh of relief when off the south coast of Iceland we were ordered to proceed independently back to Scapa Flow to resume our working-up exercises and trials.

During one of these trials, when we were checking the accuracy of our pitot log by running the measured mile along the north shore of Scapa Flow, I was conning the ship under the orders of our navigating officer, who said that he would take over as we approached the turn on to the measured mile. As I stepped down, the Captain asked me to check the chart to see that there was plenty of water, which I confirmed that there was, except for the shoal off Veeness. When I looked ahead again, it seemed to me that the ship was swinging far too slowly, but the navigating officer thought it all right as he didn't want to check our speed by using too much helm. He then asked me to stand by to get an accurate log reading as the marks came on, and I was bending down to do this when I felt a slight shudder and the ship heeled very gently over to starboard. What had evidently happened was that in using such a small rudder angle the navigator had not made sufficient allowance for the ship's advance and transfer, and in her swing she grazed the edge of the shoal. We were on our way to Burray Range for an AA practice shoot, so we proceeded there and as soon as we had anchored a diver was sent down to examine the hull, propellers and rudder. His report was that there was no damage apart from a certain amount of missing paint, except that the pitot tube which projects through the hull had been completely sheered off, something that could easily be replaced at the next drydocking.

However, a full report had to be made to the Admiralty, which found that had the incident not taken place, as it did, at the top high water, Britain's newest battleship might have been seriously damaged. They took a serious view of this, and a court-martial was ordered to convene on board the destroyer depot ship HMS Tyne. At this, the only naval court-martial I ever attended, I had the unenviable position of being one of the principal witnesses for the prosecution, which embarrassed me greatly, because not only was the navigating officer highly thought of as a navigator (indeed, his being appointed to the King George V showed that the Navy considered him one of its best), but he had also been a good friend to me and taught me a great deal about ship handling and naval methods of navigation. But because the court found against him and ordered that he be censured and also dismissed his ship, this one mistake, even though it had caused only minor damage, was to mean the end of his career. As we went in the boat together to HMS Tyne, he recited a verse from the Laws of the Navy.

> Although the strength of her armour protect her
> The ship bears the scars on her side.
> It would be well if their Lordships acquit me,
> But would have been better had I never been tried.

Apart from this our working-up continued uneventfully. Then in March we went on another operation, providing part of the covering force for the Commando raid on the Lofoten Islands, but apart from being persistently shadowed by Focke Wulf aircraft, which went round and round the horizon keeping just out of gun range, we saw no action on this trip.

Shortly after we returned from this operation we were inspected by the commander-in-chief, Admiral Sir John Tovey, and following this we were officially considered sufficiently well worked up to take the flag. The main difference that I noticed was when I found myself on duty as the officer of the watch in harbour. The pace was hectic for the entire four hours of a daytime watch, keeping the boat situation under control and making sure that the right boat was in the right place at the right time. At any time the C-in-C or his chief of staff might appear, and one had to be ready with the salutes and ceremonies due their rank, and to extend the same courtesies to all the other admirals and post captains who visited with them. Then, whenever ships were moving in the harbour, they had to be watched carefully so that we made the proper reply as they made their salutes to the flag.

Another of the events in our lives at this time was the visit that His Majesty King George VI paid the Home Fleet at Scapa Flow, accompanied by the youthful-looking Duke of Kent, who was to die tragically in an air crash the following year. He lived on board the flagship for two days, and they both came down to the wardroom for a drink before dinner one night, staying for over an hour chatting to everyone with complete informality. But as far as the officer of the watch was concerned, having the monarch on board for two days, paying official visits to the other major fleet units, was anything but informal; if we thought we had trouble when we took the flag it was nothing to this. I know that when I had the 8-12 watch on the last night of the royal visit, and His Majesty had entertained all the officers of flag rank to dinner on board the King George V, I felt more like the doorman at Claridges, except that he didn't have to consult the Navy List as carefully as I did to ensure getting all the barges alongside in the correct order of seniority.

Then as the spring advanced we found we were spending more and more time at sea, making sweeps down to the Bay of Biscay in hope of catching the Scharnhorst or Gneisenau if they dared to poke their noses out of Brest. During these sweeps I became aware of the delightful difference between being the senior officer of the watch of the flagship, and doing exactly the same job when we were a private ship. Then I had had to concentrate the whole time on keeping station; in other words, I had constantly to adjust my speed to keep the exact distance behind my next ahead, and every time we altered course on a zigzag I had to put helm on at exactly the right moment to keep our bows inside his wake. But once we became the flagship we couia relax a little in the knowledge that everyone else was keeping station on us.

CHAPTER SIX

The Bismarck chase

Wednesday, 21 May 1941

As far as the sailors on the mess decks and
the ordinary officers in the wardroom—who did not attend staff
conferences—were concerned, this was the day when things started
to happen. When a general signal was made cancelling all leave
and bringing the whole fleet to one hour's notice for steam, closely
followed by another which ordered all flag officers and captains of
major war vessels to report on board the flagship forthwith, nobody
had any doubt that something very serious was brewing. But I
think most of us knew before this, as there had been an air of
steadily mounting tension in the wardroom for two days; also
we had had several alerts as German reconnaissance aircraft
attempted to overfly the anchorage.

Then, during the day, it was learned that the Bismarck, accompanied by the heavy cruiser Prinz Eugen, had been sighted moving
up the Norwegian coast with a convoy of nine merchant ships, and
the RAF had later photographed them lying in a fjord near Bergen.
One didn't have to be much of a strategist to realize that there
could be no point in the Germans bringing these two valuable
fleet units out of the Baltic (which at this time was still a German
lake) unless they intended to use them for offensive operations in
the Atlantic. And since minelayers of the Royal Navy had been
busy for more than a year laying a deep minefield between the
south coast of Iceland and the Faroes and Shetland Islands (the
Germans called it the 'rose garden'), the most probable route for
the ships to take would be round the north coast of Iceland—where
in the month of May there is usually between twenty and fifty
miles of open water between the coast and the edge of the polar

icefield—and then down through the Denmark Strait.

This route had been so popular with the Germans for getting their surface raiders and essential materials in and out—since the Bremen had first used it to give the Royal Navy the slip in the opening days of the war—that we usually had at least two cruisers on patrol in the area. Currently these were HMS Norfolk, flying the flag of Admiral Wake Walker, and HMS Suffolk, but these two elderly cruisers, with their 8-inch guns, could obviously be blown out of the water by Bismarck's 15-inch guns before they could get close enough to inflict any serious damage. So the C-in-C and the Admiralty decided that they must be reinforced by heavier ships and that evening, in an air of growing excitement, we stood on deck and watched the battleship Prince of Wales and HMS Hood, the battlecruiser affectionately known on the lower deck as the Mighty Hood, flying the flag of Vice Admiral Holland, the second in command of the Home Fleet, steam out of harbour with their escort of destroyers.

They made a brave sight, but we knew that they were likely to have a rough time if they did meet the Bismarck because one ship was too old and the other too new. The Hood, for all her enormous bulk, was a relic of the First World War and had never been modernized. She had been built in the days when the speed of battleships was around 20 knots, and her high speed of 32 knots and her 16-inch guns were her main protection, as she had only light side armour and no deck armour. Her real Achilles' heel, though, was her fire-control gear, which was still the old Dreyer type table to which all corrections had to be applied manually. But to fit a new system would have meant putting the ship out of action for at least six months, which was something the Admiralty had been reluctant to do. Her companion, the Prince of Wales, was the second ship of the King George V class, and technically similar in nearly every respect to ourselves. But while we had spent more than six months in making ourselves battleworthy, she had left the builder's yard only three weeks before, and she still had 200 civilian shipyard workers on board, working to finish off the electrical systems of her fire-control equipment as she steamed to the westward to meet her enemy. As her ship's company had not had time to complete many of the normal working-up exercises, she was really too new for the tasks she was being called upon to carry out.

Thursday, 22 May 1941

When we all learned that a lone reconnaissance aircraft had managed to get below the cloud base of the fog-shrouded fjords and confirmed that the German ships had gone, we awaited orders to join the two ships that had left the previous evening. But our main interest centred upon the aircraft carrier HMS Victorious which had just arrived from the Tyne. She, like the Prince of Wales, was almost a brand-new ship, and not fully operational. However, as she was the only available carrier in home waters and the C-in-C felt it was essential to have a carrier with him, she was pressed into service, and a Fleet Air Arm training squadron was flown on board. Apart from their CO these were mostly young and inexperienced pilots and aircrew, and the flight deck party to handle the aircraft were an assortment of petty officers and ratings from the ground staff at Hatston. However, by that evening she was ready to sail, and we watched the remainder of the Home Fleet leave one by one until we finally slipped from the flagship buoy. From now on we could only break radio silence under special circumstances, and we should have to depend for all our information on cipher messages transmitted by the Admiralty.

As we formed up outside the boom defence the Home Fleet consisted of ourselves and Victorious with eight assorted cruisers and about twenty odd destroyers; the battlecruiser HMS Repulse had already left the Clyde and was to rendezvous with us the following morning to the west of the Outer Hebrides.

Friday, 23 May 1941

Most of us felt a sense of relief to be at sea again, and to settle down to sea routine after the mounting tensions of the past few days. Our first important news from HMS Suffolk told us that she had sighted the two German ships to the north of Iceland, steaming to the west at high speed, and she was shadowing, all that she could do because of her size and age. During the night, the Norfolk joined her, because there was no point in these two ship preserving radio silence now: the Germans knew where they were, and their information about the enemy's course and speed was vital to Admiral Holland, who was going to be very close to them by daylight next morning. However, even if the German ships turned towards us when they cleared the Denmark Straits it was going to be Sunday morning before we were anywhere near them.

Saturday, 24 May 1941

At breakfast on board King George V we heard the absolutely staggering news that, in one of the shortest and most disastrous actions in British naval history, the Hood had blown up and virtually disappeared in a flash, with the loss of all but three of her 1,200 man crew, and the Prince of Wales had been badly damaged and forced to retire under cover of smoke. This cast a terrible gloom over the whole ship because, ever since we had been in Scapa, Hood had been our 'chummy' ship; there had been intense competition with her in all forms of sport and, particularly among the officers, a lot of intership visiting and wardroom entertaining. We found it hard to believe that all those men we knew so well had just been wiped out.

The general opinion was that Admiral Holland had been wrong in keeping both ships in close order, because this meant that once the German gunners saw the Hood explode they knew they had the range exactly, and two salvos later they had four hits on the Prince of Wales. Two of these exploded outside the ship, although one passed through the bridge and injured both the captain and his navigator, putting the ship temporarily out of control. The third shell exploded at the base of the after funnel, doing considerable damage at the top of the engine room. A fourth shell which penetrated the ship near Y magazine, had failed to explode, and was removed in Rosyth. Had this shell gone off the Germans could have destroyed two of Britain's largest fleet units with three salvos: incredible gunnery by any standards, and speaking highly of the skill of the men who designed and constructed those huge guns, because the amount of spread on each salvo must have been remarkably small. Fortunately, in spite of the fact that her captain had been injured, the ship was able to make an emergency turn and retreat into the fog bank from which the two ships had emerged only a few minutes earlier to see the two German ships ahead of them. One of the great mysteries to me of this part of the action is why the German admiral, Admiral Lutjens, after his fantastic success, did not follow his obviously badly wounded adversary for the coup de grâce.

Once the stunning shock of the news had worn off we realized how drastically the Germans had, in a few brief minutes, altered the balance of naval power on the Atlantic. It now was imperative that the Bismarck and the Prinz Eugen should never join up with the Scharnhorst and Gneisenau, because these four ships together would constitute a faster and more heavily armed battle fleet than anything we could presently muster to oppose them. Our navigational problem, now that we knew the position of the German ships exactly and could plot their positions for the next twenty-four hours, was that if they continued their present course and speed the earliest that we could intercept them was at first light the following morning. The C-in-C had evidently decided that the most imperative thing was to try to reduce the enemy's speed, because shortly before noon, when we altered course to the south-west, HMS Victorious was detached with an escort of four cruisers and ordered to proceed at maximum speed, to make a torpedo attack with her six Swordfish aircraft before dark.

As the King George V steamed away to the south-west we waited anxiously for news, knowing that as the enemy was still being shadowed by the two cruisers their reports should help Victorious to locate her target. She launched her planes just before the light faded, and her young pilots pressed home their attack in the face of heavy anti-aircraft fire. They reported one possible hit, which appeared to be confirmed by the reconnaissance plane reporting that the Bismarck was leaving a trail of fuel oil. But in the German accounts of the battle they state that their loss of fuel was due to a hit by the Prince of Wales during the early morning encounter. By the time the Swordfish were able to return it was almost completely dark, but by switching on all his lights, a most unusual thing to do in wartime, the captain of Victorious was able to guide all his young airmen back safely.

Sunday, 25 May 1941

When we closed up to our action stations long before dawn we saw nothing but swirling mist, and when dawn finally broke it showed a lead-grey sea and sky with light winds and an oily swell. The fog, which in these latitudes at this season of the year is never far away, had shut in shortly after the Victorious had made her attack. Then, as we know now, after ordering Prinz Eugen to act independently, Admiral Lutjens turned on his two shadowers and, using some primitive form of radar-controlled firing, drove them off. When he turned again, HMS Suffolk, the only ship of the pair fitted with the latest surface radar, reported that she had lost contact. After reaching our expected rendezvous point, we turned to SSW, the course the enemy had been steering, and by the time we were stood down from action stations visibility was improving, but nobody had any idea where the Bismarck was, or what she was doing.

Among the amateur strategists drinking coffee in the wardroom, there were three main schools of thought as to what Admiral Lutjens would probably do now that, after nearly thirty-six hours, he had got rid of his shadowers and was once more able to take the initiative.

The first group thought that he would be satisfied that the propaganda value of his victory the previous morning would more than justify the risks he had taken, and he would head back towards the safety of the Norwegian coast and then back to Germany. And it was thought that he would now cross the deep minefield to use a route south of Iceland. (This in fact seemed to be the C-in-C's idea at this time, because shortly after, we felt the ship alter course towards the NE.)

The second was of the opinion that neither of the German ships could carry sufficient fuel oil for a high speed dash twice across the Atlantic, and the reason they had maintained a SSW course for so long after passing through the Denmark Strait was that they were trying to rendezvous with a German fleet tanker somewhere in that desolate part of the Atlantic south of Greenland. (History has now revealed that this theory was correct for the Prinz Eugen, but not the Bismarck.)

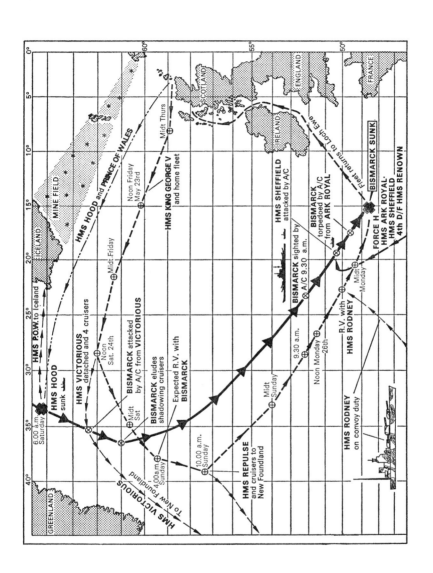

The third idea, which eventually turned out to be the correct one, was that Admiral Lutjens, once he had got rid of his shadowers, would head direct for the port of Brest. In doing this the two fleets must have passed relatively close to each other during the dark foggy hours of that early morning, neither of them being aware of the other's presence.

While these various ideas were being discussed, not only in the wardroom and on the messdecks, but also probably round the admiral's conference table and at the Admiralty, much valuable time was being lost, and more might have been had not the German admiral broken radio silence, thus enabling the high frequency direction finding stations to get bearings on him. These stations, of which the Navy maintained a large number in all parts of the world, could only get very approximate bearings, but they gave enough information to convince both the Admiralty and C-in-C that the third of the three ideas was the correct one; so we altered course again, but not before enough hours had been lost to turn it into a stern chase.

As we turned towards Brest we had no idea where the Bismarck was, but we did know that, excepting ourselves, all the ships that had made up the Home Fleet when we sailed had now reached the point of no return. The destroyers had left us some time before, and gone to Iceland to refuel, and now Victorious and Repulse had to make for the American base at Argentia in Newfoundland: only King George V had sufficient oil left to get home and—as we were to find out later—that was only with a very narrow margin of safety.

So as we ploughed across the empty ocean for the rest of that Sunday the only good news around was that the Admiralty was bringing ships into the search from all quarters. The most important of these was the famous Force H, which had sailed from Gibraltar, commanded by Admiral Sommerville, flying his flag in the battlecruiser HMS Renown. She was the sister ship to the Repulse which had so recently left us, but following the loss of the Hood the Admiralty was anxious to avoid bringing battlecruisers into direct confrontation with the Bismarck except as a last resort. Our main interest lay in the fact that Admiral Sommerville had with him the fully operational aircraft carrier HMS Ark Royal (carrying two full squadrons of torpedo bombers, with highly trained and very experienced crews), plus the cruiser HMS Sheffield (a modern vessel carrying 6-inch guns) and the Fourth Destroyer Flotilla, commanded by Captain Phillip Vian, of Altmark fame. As they steered to the north-westward at high speed, their job could best be described, in the language of American football, as 'running interference'; in other words, they had to try to get in between the Bismarck and the port she was trying to reach. Then the Ark Royal's aircraft would be used to locate the Bismarck and reduce her speed to allow us to catch her.

Monday, 26 May 1941

I think that the Bismarck was one of the finest fighting machines of her type that the world will ever see. At 42,000 tons displacement she was considerably larger than the 35,000 ton King George V and almost as big as the American Missouri-class battleships, while her 15-inch guns had a greater range and threw a heavier projectile than our 14-inch ones. But her greatest strength lay in her subdivision into a large number of watertight compartments, and in her armour. The Germans contend that her citadel (the part of the ship which contains the engine rooms, magazines, and other vital places), was protected by twelve inches of nickel-chrome steel armour plate, which had been specially developed by German scientists for the purpose, and this made her, as we were shortly to find out, virtually unsinkable.

That Monday, our first lucky break came in the middle of the morning when an American-built Catalina flying-boat of the type known in the American Navy as a PBY, flying a reconnaissance patrol from its base at Limavady in Northern Ireland, managed to spot the Bismarck through a hole in the clouds. At least, he sighted a large warship which suddenly threw everything she had in the way of anti-aircraft artillery at him; so, having decided that the natives were not very friendly, he scooted into a cloud and sent out an enemy report.

This vital piece of information provided the answer to the question that hundreds of senior officers ashore and afloat had been asking for more than thirty-six hours: 'Where is the Bismarck?'

And it sent everyone to their charts, anxiously measuring off distances. But although we were glad to know just where she was, no matter how often we measured it the 200-mile gap that she had put between us seemed almost impossible to close. We knew that if she kept up her present speed, in a little over twenty-four hours she would have reached a point close enough to the enemy-held coast of France to receive air cover from the Luftwaffe. Also, it was an open secret on board that our fuel stocks were now getting dangerously low. So in spite of the need to close the gap our speed had to be gradually reduced to conserve fuel, and the general impression one got was that, unless Force H could reduce the enemy's speed, shortly after midnight that night King George V would have to abandon the chase and head for home, as there is no quicker way to end a major war vessel's useful life than to allow her to run out of fuel in submarine-infested waters.

Yet another factor on this fateful day was the rapidly worsening weather situation, as a deepening depression in mid-Atlantic was bringing south-westerly gales, with low clouds and driving rain, into the area in which we were operating. So, although the information received from Coastal Command did enable Admiral Sommerville to position his ships to launch his first torpedo bomber attack that afternoon, operating conditions for aircraft were far from good.

The first British warship to sight the Bismarck was HMS Sheffield, who after she had made her enemy report settled down to shadow her in the same way that the Suffolk had done, while, on board the carrier, preparations for the attack continued. But apparently, due to some mix-up in signals, the Sheffield's enemy report had not been received in the briefing room, and the pilots had been told that the only large warship they were likely to see was the Bismarck. With a cloud base of 200 to 300 feet, and reduced visibility, it is probably very easy for a pilot flying at about 150 knots to mistake one warship for another. So the Ark Royal's aircraft must have come out of the clouds and attacked the first ship they saw, HMS Sheffield, who was shadowing the Bismarck from a position about fourteen miles astern of her! Waiting anxiously for news of this air strike, on which so very much depended, we were amazed first to get an emergency signal from Sheffield that she was being attacked by British aircraft; then listening out on the fighter direction frequency to hear Ark Royal's fighter direction officer's orders to his aircraft: 'Return to base. You are attacking British cruiser.' This news shattered our spirits again, because of our fuel situation; but we were relieved to receive another signal from Sheffield shortly afterwards reporting that she was undamaged. The reason for this, we were to learn later, was that the torpedoes used for the first attack had been fitted with a new type of magnetic pistol designed by the Admiralty Research Laboratory after they had cracked the secrets of the German magnetic mine, to allow torpedoes to be set to run deep, and then to explode as they came within a ship's magnetic field. Thus, it was hoped, they would cause the maximum damage to the ship's soft underbelly. But like so many things developed under the pressures of war, it had probably been rushed to sea before all the bugs had been ironed out of it. The incident proved that the pistol's delicate mechanism was still not sufficiently robust to stand up to the strain of being dropped into the waves set up by an Atlantic gale.

But on the bridge of the flagship as the news came in, the question in everybody's mind was whether the Ark Royal could get her aircraft back from this abortive sortie, land them in the heavy seas that were now running, and refuel and re-arm them in time to allow them to make another attack before darkness fell. If she could not, the Bismarck was probably home and dry.

By this time we were joined by the HMS Rodney, a powerful ship carrying nine 16-inch guns in triple turrets. But she was only able to make between 22-23 knots, which we estimated to be about the speed Bismarck would be doing at this time: so the gap was not being closed, and the following morning the enemy would probably be too close to the French coast for safe pursuit by big ships. Not that this would concern King George V because shortly after midnight that night we should be compelled by the fuel situation to head for home.

This was the situation when I arrived on the bridge that evening at 20.00 to take charge for the 8-12 watch. For much of the time the commander in chief and his chief of staff stayed on the bridge talking to the captain as the signals came in from Ark Royal reporting her preparations for the attack which she hoped to launch at about 22.00. As the minutes ticked away with the vital deadline approaching the feeling of tension and strain increased.

Then relief, almost exultation, as the aircraft on the fighter direction wavelength reported one and then two probable hits, to be followed by reports from Sheffield that the Bismarck appeared to be circling, and then that she had stopped. The whole situation had suddenly, dramatically and, it seemed to us at the time, almost miraculously changed. Instead of having her tail well up after sinking the Hood and damaging the Prince of Wales and knowing that by the following morning she could look for shield and protection from the Luftwaffe, the Bismarck was now a badly wounded ship, surrounded on all sides by hostile forces intent on her destruction. Her only hope of survival depended upon the power of her guns and what support she could get from the U-boats in the area.

Then, towards the end of my watch, a signal from Sheffield reported that the enemy was under way again, making about 10 knots, and gave her course as 290 degrees. This was later confirmed, and we knew that the situation had changed from a stern chase to one in which we were converging with the enemy at more than a mile every two minutes. The C-in-C was anxious to avoid a night action, because with so many British ships converging, and with methods of identification at night notoriously unreliable, there was grave danger of what had happened to the Sheffield being repeated and ships opening fire on friendly forces. It seemed at that time, though, that we might easily have a night action thrust upon us.

When we later learned the full extent of the damage inflicted on the Bismarck by the lucky torpedo hit which damaged her steering gear, it was easy to understand her dramatic change of course. When a ship is running before an Atlantic gale the heavy seas hitting her rudder put enormous strains on her steering gear, but a ship which is heading into the wind and sea has her rudder protected by the bulk of the ship, and it operates in the smooth water astern of the ship. Admiral Lutjens, finding his steering compartment flooded, and having only been able to make partial repairs to his steering gear, had evidently decided that he dared not risk losing his ability to control the ship completely, which he might have done if he had continued on his course towards Brest.

Tuesday, 27 May 1941

At about 03.00 the alarm gongs rang and sent us racing to our action stations. Yet we were to have a long, weary wait, first for the slow arrival of the dawn, then nearly three hours more for our first sight of the enemy. But there were many things happening during this period, which I was only to hear of later.

First Captain Vian led his Fourth Destroyer Flotilla in to make a series of torpedo attacks on the Bismarck. But as these gallant little ships closed in to get into firing range they were met by very heavy fire which, considering the darkness of the night, was surprisingly accurate. One can only assume that the enemy was using the same type of elementary radar she had used to drive off the shadowing cruisers. Several of the destroyers suffered casualties.

But sitting up in my draughty emergency conning position, trying to get what shelter I could from the fierce rain squalls that marked the passage of the cold front, I anxiously swept the horizon with my binoculars. So far as could be seen, the Rodney and ourselves were all alone. But as the daylight strengthened we saw the two big battleships running before the gale, with their decks cleared for action and their big silk battle ensigns streaming from every masthead, like knights in armour riding out to meet their adversaries on the jousting field. For the last time two battleships were preparing to fulfil the role for which they were designed and built—to fight a gun duel to the death with one of their own kind.

As the sun rose we couldn't understand why there was still no sight of the enemy we knew to be so close. Then at about 08.30 the whole ship was suddenly electrified by the cry 'Enemy in sight', although, even as high up as I was, there was very little to see and I had to sweep the horizon very carefully before my binoculars were able to make out the two little sticks that were the tops of her masts.

The two British ships turned towards her and, to avoid the mistakes of the Denmark Strait action, we had already opened out to put the Rodney about two miles on our port beam; a few minutes later the signal to open fire was flying from the starboard yardarm. The range appeared to close quickly, and soon her guns and the main part of her superstructure were visible. Shortly after the open fire signal came fluttering down, the fire gongs rang 'Ting! Ting!' and then the whole ship shook with an ear-splitting roar as the first salvo went on its way. The battle had begun.

I was trying to observe all the details that I could for my periodic reports to the commander, and I soon noticed that, while she was still firing at the Rodney, the Bismarck's fire was becoming more sporadic. The great advantage that we had over our opponent was that we had one of the first radar sets to go to sea with the Royal Navy, specially designed for gunnery control. It enabled us to get the enemy's range with great accuracy from over 30,000 yards, which was far beyond the capabilities of the German optical range-finders, until then considered the best in the world. Thus we made hits with our first few rounds, one of which seriously damaged the Bismarck's main director (the heart of her elaborate gunnery-control system). Afterwards her guns had to fire in local control, which is like changing to bows and arrows from a modern rifle.

After about twenty minutes or half an hour we had closed the range to a little over 10,000 yards—almost point-blank range for heavy guns firing on a nearly flat trajectory. This did quite a bit of blast damage to our wardroom below the quarter-deck when the gyro-controlled sights came on as the ship was pitching. But blast damage was the only damage we had. I could see scenes of almost indescribable devastation and destruction on board the Bismarck. She was still moving slowly through the water, but all her guns were silent and she was a blazing inferno fore and aft. A dense pall of black smoke covered her and dozens of her crew appeared to be jumping into the sea, probably only to be killed by the concussion from the shells still exploding round her. Shortly after, the signal for King George V and Rodney to cease firing was given, and as the two big ships turned away we were once more in a strangely silent world. Then another signal was made to HMS Dorsetshire, another county class cruiser, who had come up from the south to join the party, to close the enemy and try to sink her with torpedoes. As we steamed away to the north, towards home, we were still close enough for me to watch through my binoculars as the explosion of the Dorsetshire's torpedoes shook the Bismarck, and then to see her slowly roll over and slide below the waves. A sad end to a very gallant adversary, who had come out to fight against impossible odds, hoping only to take one or more British ships with her to the bottom of the ocean.

Like, I suppose, most of the Royal Navy personnel present, I assumed that she had been given the fatal blow by the Dorsetshire's torpedoes, but the Germans who survived claim that no British shell or torpedo managed to penetrate her specially armoured citadel, and that her engineer commander blew scuttling charges when he knew all was lost, to prevent the ship from falling into enemy hands.

But the effect was still the same, and when the House of Commons started its business that day Winston Churchill was able to stride in with a smile on his face and throw down a signal on the dispatch box, before announcing that the Bismarck had been sunk.

That evening Sir John Tovey came along to the wardroom before dinner to thank his officers for the way they had done their jobs and to discuss various aspects of the action. One point he stressed repeatedly was that he would have liked to have been able to give the cease fire order long before he did, in order to save as many lives as possible, once it became clear that the Bismarck had no more offensive power. But the tactical situation had demanded both that the action be decisive and that it should be quick, because from German signals which the Admiralty had deciphered it was known that all U-boats within range had been ordered to rendez-vous with the Bismarck to try to sink us before we could sink her—a likely possibility, as it was not until after the action that King George V and Rodney received anti-submarine protection from escorting destroyers. Actually, the one U-boat which did reach the scene caused many Germans to lose their lives unnecessarily, because after the Dorsetshire and about three of the destroyers had pulled about one hundred men from the very rough seas, an Asdic (an underwater device used to detect submarines) contact was made and all ships were ordered to leave the area at high speed, leaving many hundreds of men, who could not be picked up by the U-boat, to drown. Ironically, this boat, returning from patrol, had no torpedoes.

After all the tension of the preceding six days and the excitement of the engagement, our leisurely voyage home with a large destroyer escort, at the nearest we could get to an economical speed to conserve our rapidly dwindling fuel supply, was rather an anti-climax. Everybody felt tired and nobody thought of celebrating until after the ship reached Loch Ewe. But getting the ship to Loch Ewe was to prove no easy task, because even with a comparatively new ship there is always an element of doubt as to exactly how much of the oil in her tanks is actually pumpable, and how much has become so thick and tarry that it almost needs to be dug out with a shovel. At one point, it looked as if we should have to put into the Clyde to fuel; then it was decided we could just make Loch Ewe, but after that decision had been taken we ran into dense fog approaching the narrowest part of the Little Minch. Our surface radar was still suffering from the effect of the gun blast in our recent action so we had to stop for a time, but we eventually managed to crawl through.

Within a week of the ship's return to her home base at Scapa Flow, my request to do a long navigation course, with the idea of becoming a specialist navigator, was granted. It had not taken me very long after assuming my duties as navigator's assistant on board King George V to realize that Navy officers who specialized in navigation not only had an interesting and fascinating job, but also had somehow managed to invest their work with all the mysteries of a black art, whose secrets are revealed only to a very select few. Since navigation had been my main occupation in the Merchant Navy, I felt that I could give my best service to the Royal Navy as a specialist navigator. But the Navy was very strict about admission to this select band: even if one had handled the Queen Mary, to handle a major war vessel, a six-week training course at HMS Dryad, the Royal Naval School of Navigation at Portsmouth, had to be completed and it was to this establishment that I had now been appointed.

CHAPTER SEVEN

The convoys

When I first joined HMS Dryad I had hoped that I could live at home and commute to Portsmouth for classes, but on the third morning, when I arrived at the station on my bicycle to catch the early train to Portsmouth, I was told that there were two unexploded bombs on the line and they couldn't say when the next train to Portsmouth would run. This left me no alternative but to pedal the whole thirty-three miles to Dryad, where I arrived stiff, sore, and very hot, half an hour late for the start of the day's classes. Being rather out of training for long cycle rides, I decided that once was enough, so I became a weekly boarder, and after those long months in Scapa Flow I found getting home every weekend a delightful change.

When my next appointment came out, it was to HMS Ibis, a new, improved Black Swan class sloop, then building at Haverton Hill on Tees. She was not due to commission for another four months, so my wife was able to close up our home and come up and join me in digs in Middlesborough for the rest of the summer and part of the autumn. This was a very pleasant interlude between two periods of fairly extended sea service.

The commissioning of an 1,800-ton sloop is attended by a lot less ceremony than that of a battleship, especially in wartime. But for weeks before our commissioning date the first lieutenant and I went round armed with long lists of uncompleted jobs, quite convinced that the shipyard would never be able to finish the work in time. Then suddenly things started to come together, and on the appointed day the crew arrived, all very new and unfamiliar, but somehow they made the ship come to life. A couple of days later she moved out into the river to start her trials, and in spite of our forebodings most things actually worked.

In wartime, the builder's acceptance trials were kept to a bare minimum. Within a few hours we were back alongside, the captain had signed for the ship, the red ensign came down, to be replaced by the white ensign, hoisted with all appropriate ceremony, prayers were read, the captain addressed the ship's company, and another unit joined the fleet, as HMS Ibis started her naval career. Unfortunately it was not to be a very long one, as in a little over a year she was sunk by German aircraft off the coast of North Africa during the Allied invasion, with the loss of more than half her company, including her captain.

There is, of course, a vast difference between just getting a ship to sea and being ready in all respects to meet and engage the enemy. A lot of hard work and many dull and boring exercises, repeated time after time, go to make up what the Navy call the working-up period, before the admiral in charge of training and his staff officers are finally satisfied and the ship is classified as operational. The Ibis did her working-up exercises, first at Scapa Flow and later at Loch Ewe, all through the short, cold and damp days of a Scottish winter, so we all felt a sense of relief when we had passed our last test and were ordered to proceed to Londonderry to become the leader of the newly formed 41st Escort Group. This group—which included another sloop, HMS Aberdeen, the ex-Admiralty yacht HMS Enchantress, two ex-American Coastguard cutters and an ex-American destroyer which had been in mothballs since the First World War—was employed escorting convoys from Londonderry to Freetown in Sierra Leone and back. In fact, in the early days, due to the limited range of some of the ships in our group, we only took the convoy as far as Bathurst in Gambia, where we handed over to the ships of the Freetown Escort Force, and spent a week or ten days swimming and enjoying the tropical sunshine while waiting for the northbound convoy to arrive.

Later on, the Ibis and other ships which had sufficient range had to go all the way to Freetown, and it was on one of my visits to this port that I caught malaria. Fortunately I had the type known as sub-tertian, which is not supposed to recur, but it was a most unpleasant experience at the time. We did, of course, meet some bad weather on the Atlantic once we were north of the Azores, but the Ibis was fitted with the then very new Denny-Brown anti-roll stabilizers, which in theory were to make the ship steadier and to improve the efficiency of her twin 4-inch guns.

After I had been with her for nine months, Ibis was ordered to London for a refit in August 1942. I wasn't too happy when, shortly after we docked, after a lively trip down through the North Sea along what used to be called 'E-boat alley', I received the news that I was to be relieved. I felt, at the time, that I should have liked to stay in the ship, but I felt better when I heard that my next appointment was to be to a new aircraft carrier being built in Dundee. When, a few months later, I heard the sad news that the officer who had relieved me was among those who were lost when the ship was sunk, I made a silent resolve to be more philosophical about my appointments in future.

After the success of the first of the small aircraft carriers, HMS Audacity, which had been converted from a captured German ship, the government was looking around for other suitable merchant ships to convert. At this time the Blue Funnel Line, officially the Ocean Steam Ship Company of Liverpool, had a fast 10,000-ton cargo liner which was to be called the Telemacus being built in Dundee. She was to have been powered by two Burminster and Wain diesel engines, which were being built in Copenhagen, and the engines had got as far as Norway on their way to Scotland, only to be captured when the Germans invaded that country. As a result construction was held up until another firm could produce a set of engines for her.

This gave the Admiralty naval architects time to cut off all her upperworks one deck above the forecastle and replace them with a 512 foot flight deck, complete with trip wires, a safety barrier, a lift and a small hangar; then to stick a bridge on the starboard side, plus gun sponsons, etc. They also fitted all the empty cargo spaces which were not required for other purposes with thousands of empty oil drums filled with millions of ping-pong balls, which they calculated should keep the ship afloat for a couple of hours even if she were hit by two torpedoes.

So on 24 August 1942 I found myself joining this rather strange-looking craft, now renamed HMS Activity, in Dundee, and any unhappiness I had felt at leaving my little Ibis and the joys of Londonderry were more than compensated for by the fact that Dorothie and I were able to spend a delightful holiday together at a hotel in Broughty Ferry while the various problems involved in getting the first ship of a new class ready for sea were solved. Because the converted Activity was urgently required to provide air cover during the forthcoming Allied invasion of North Africa, she had been given top Cabinet priority, and work went on around the clock to get her to sea as soon as possible.

Not only were these small carriers odd-looking ships; they had, to ease the Navy's shortage of manpower, been manned in what seemed to us at the time a rather odd manner. All their engineering staff, engineer officers, electrical officers and ratings, and all their catering staff, supply officers, paymasters, cooks and stewards, and a few of the seamen required for maintenance work, came direct from the Merchant Navy, serving under the T124X agreement. In fact, several of them were old shipmates of mine from Cunard. The executive officers were a mixture of RN, RNR and RNVR, the bulk of the POs and seamen were RN, while all the people on the flying side—air crews, flight deck crews and maintenance personnel—were Fleet Air Arm.

In many of the ships that were to follow us it did not work too well, as it proved difficult to weld three groups of men, all with different backgrounds and training, into a harmonious ship's company. However, on board Activity we had one priceless asset in her first captain, who at the time was one of the youngest captains in the Navy List. Captain Guy Willoughby, RN, who was to go on to be the first captain of Britain's largest aircraft-carrier, HMS Eagle, and to retire with the rank of Admiral (air), was a Fleet Air Arm officer with an impressive record, who therefore understood the problems of our young aviators, as well as those of running the ship. He threw himself into the task of getting the ship operational with tremendous verve, and I think that he, more than any other man I have ever met, realized that the crew and their morale are more important than the ship. Captain Willoughby let it be known that whenever conditions permitted he liked to be invited to join his officers in their wardroom for a drink before dinner; but when he did so, he never just joined the commander and a small group of senior officers. Instead he made a point of getting to know every young engineer officer or FAA pilot and bringing them into a group. So our wardroom never tended to divide, as did the wardrooms of many ships manned in this way, into the executive officers in one group, the T124X officers in another, and the FAA officers in yet another. Long after Guy had left us to go on to bigger things the spirit he had engendered persisted, and Activity remained a happy ship right up until she reverted to her original role as a merchant ship.

Everyone was pressing as hard as they could to get the ship away to sea. The bulk of our crew arrived by special train from Devonport at 23.00 one night, and by 06.00 the following morning, before it was properly daylight, they were on stations for leaving harbour, and as the ship made her way down the narrow and twisting channel of the River Tay she had a CPO coxswain at the helm, because we had not yet had time to find out which of our seamen could steer!

After very curtailed engine trials we sailed straight for the Firth of Forth, where we went into Leith to drydock. As we entered the locks we found that, while the ship's hull fitted in quite easily, nobody had reckoned on the projection of the gun sponsons below the flight deck, with disastrous consequences for some of the ornamental lamp standards along the side of the lock.

When we left Leith we carried out more trials during our passage round the north of Scotland to the Clyde, where we embarked our squadrons for a short but intensive period of flying training. But time was now running out and too many things were still not working as they should when the admiral (air) came on board to make his inspection.

After a long conference with the admiral and his staff, Captain Willoughby emerged looking very grave and told us that our squadrons were to transfer to HMS Argus, an elderly carrier left over from the First World War, which was employed on deck landing training, and that Argus would be going on Operation Torch instead of us. We would be taking over her job of training young pilots to land on a carrier. I think the ship's company were mainly disappointed for the captain's sake, because they knew how hard he had worked to whip the ship into shape, and nothing is more likely to prejudice the success of a naval operation than a ship which has not had time for proper preparation.

As a navigating officer, the next few months while the ship was doing deck landing training were to give me more practical experience in ship handling than I would have got in years in the normal way, and I used to boast that I had steamed Activity nearly 10,000 miles without getting out of sight of the Ailsa Craig, the big rock which sticks up in the middle of the Firth of Clyde.

During the war, the only area of sea of considerable size round our coasts where a carrier could operate reasonably free from the risk of air or submarine attack was in the Firth of Clyde, just south of the island of Arran, between Campbeltown on the Mull of Kintyre and Turnberry on the Ayrshire coast. Naturally, always being so close to the land did impose a strain on the navigator's nerves at times, because so often the ship appeared to be rushing straight at the forbidding-looking cliffs of the Mull of Kintyre as some poor trainee pilot struggled to put his aircraft down on the deck, with the captain saying rather apprehensively, 'How much longer can we hold this course, Marr?' Even when he was finally down and the order went to the helmsman : 'Port twenty degrees of helm,' the advance and transfer effect, at 20 knots, caused the ship to move still closer to the danger before the effect of her rudder overcame her forward motion. Then, as she finally came round to her new course, the optical illusion of looking down from the bridge over the end of the flight deck made it look as though her stern was almost touching the rocks.

All through that winter and spring, almost into early summer, we operated from Monday to Friday as long as there was sufficient daylight and weather conditions permitted, anchoring for the night in Lamlash harbour, a small port on the south-east corner of the Isle of Arran. At the weekends we returned to Greenock, for stores and to give the ship's company a run ashore. To me it was one of the most interesting jobs I have ever had, because there was always something happening and every landing was different— some were so highly spectacular that we had to return to harbour and have the wreckage lifted off with a crane! The best part was that in all the thousands of landings made on our decks there was no loss of life, nor any serious injury; and, as the pilots used to say: 'If you can walk away from it, it was a good landing!' The long hours of daylight in northern waters as the summer approached sometimes meant some long hours on the bridge for the captain and his navigator. On a fine day we would fly from 07.00 to 21.00, and our only chance to have a meal or put our feet up was during the runs down wind. But a very good personal relationship developed between Captain Willoughby and myself, and I cannot remember either of us being overtired or overstrained. When the weather was unsuitable for flying, we either remained in harbour or found a quiet spot and left the officer of the watch to cruise up and down at slow speed until the front had passed and the weather cleared.

Eventually the Argus was ready to take up her old job again, and we were sent round to Liverpool to have a new mast fitted, one heavy enough to carry new radar and other electronic equipment. This meant a welcome leave for the captain and myself, then back to the Clyde again to work up with our squadron. This time it was for real, and I think everyone felt a thrill of pride when we finally passed the admiral (air)'s inspection, and proceeded to Scapa Flow to join the Home Fleet.

During this operational period we were employed on Russian convoys, Gibraltar troop convoys and sweeps out into the Atlantic as part of a hunting group, to close the gap where up to now the shore-based planes had not been able to give full air cover. Of these, the Russian convoys were by far the most spectacular. By the time we came to make our first trip to Russia, the fantastic losses like PQ17, the convoy that was decimated, were in the past and things were much better organized. Every convoy now had an admiral in overall charge, flying his flag in a cruiser, and two escort carriers to give fighter protection during daylight hours. The convoy usually had an inner screen provided by destroyers of the Home Fleet, and an outer screen provided by ships from Western Approaches Command. On the five convoys which Activity covered, shipping losses were very low and our aircraft managed to have their share in the twelve enemy planes which were shot down with no losses on our side.

One lovely morning in late spring our convoy was north of the North Cape, which is the northernmost tip of Norway, with the edge of the polar ice not too far away. But in spite of the sunshine the wind was cold and the sea temperature about freezing. The two carriers HMS Fencer and ourselves were operating a continuous fighter patrol (known as a CAP patrol) around the convoy, with both carriers acting independently astern of the convoy, each with a destroyer acting as a crash boat. At about 11.00 we had two Wildcats, small American-built fighters on our flight deck, preparing to relieve two of Fencer's aircraft which had almost completed their two-hour patrol. Then our radar reported a 'bogey' (unidentified aircraft) on the scan, so the commander (flying) gave the order to prepare to scramble two Wildcats, and the ship swung slowly into the wind. Unfortunately, a few minutes before this our destroyer had picked up a submarine contact on her asdic, so in accordance with her instructions she was carrying out a series of attacks, and was by now a long way astern.

The first plane took off beautifully and climbed like a bird with the throttle full open. But the second plane, piloted by a young New Zealand pilot who had had some trouble getting his engines to fire, was obviously in trouble as it trundled down the flight deck with its motor spluttering. However, having passed the point of no return, there was nothing he could do, and he did gain a little altitude before, about half a mile ahead of the ship, the motor finally died, and he did a perfect pancake landing right in our path. We altered course slightly to starboard and as we passed him we could see that he was quite unhurt, and as his plane sank we saw him climb out on to the wing, blowing up his Mae West. Normally our attendant destroyer would have scooped him up out of the water in a few minutes, but she was now almost out of sight and Captain Willoughby knew that the chance of anyone surviving for more than thirty minutes in such very low sea water temperatures was slim. He was now faced with the difficult decision of whether to stop and pick him up, thus exposing a valuable fleet unit with a crew of more than 500 men to the risk of being torpedoed in submarine-infested waters, or whether to steam away, leaving an obviously unharmed shipmate to an almost certain death. Within a few seconds this decision was made, and I received the order: 'Bring her round to port under full rudder, pilot, and warn the engine room we shall want to go astern.' Then he said to the commander, 'Get your port whaler manned and lowered to the water's edge.' Soon the bosun's pipe shrilled through the loudspeakers, and as the pipe 'Away whaler's crew' rang out every available man stood by to help. Taking over the conning of the ship from me, the captain brought her round beautifully in a big circle, gradually reducing her speed, until he finished up within about 200 feet of the man in the water, doing about 3 knots but with the engines just starting to go astern. The whaler was slipped while the ship still had slight headway and the seamen drove their oars like a racing crew to cover the narrow gap, while the ship's engines were bringing her up dead in the water. Willing hands soon pulled the pilot, still fully conscious, in over the stern of the whaler, and in less than five minutes the boat was back under her falls again and, thanks to the remarkably calm sea, was soon hooked on and about two hundred men stood by to run away with the falls. Then, as the commander gave a wave which told Captain Willoughby that the boat was clear of the water, the engine room telegraphs were put back to full ahead and a temendous cheer went up from the ship's company.

While all this was happening our bridge loudspeakers had been kept on the fighter direction wavelength, so we knew that one of Fencer's fighters, who had sufficient fuel remaining, had joined up with our other Wildcat to chase the Focke Wulf. On the horizon we saw the German aircraft go down in flames. Then it wasn't long before we were preparing to land our one Wildcat, and I think we all felt a thrill of pride as the aircraft landed safely and the pilot came walking up the flight deck with a big grin on his face.

After the convoy reached Murmansk, an inquiry into the incident was conducted by Admiral Roderick McGregor on board his flag-ship, and Captain Willoughby came under considerable criticism for what he had done. But no official disciplinary action was taken by the Admiralty, and it does not seem to have affected his career in any way.

But as far as his ship's company were concerned, things were never going to be quite the same again after that morning. There wasn't a man on board Activity who did not know that Guy had laid his career on the line to save one of their shipmates, and who wouldn't after that have been prepared to go through hell and

high water if his captain had asked him to. Field-Marshal Mont-
gomery once said, talking about discipline, that the first battle
every officer must win is the battle for the hearts of his men. Well,
I think Guy Willoughby did more to win the hearts of his men
in those few short minutes than many of us do in our whole lives.

We usually only had two or three days to wait in Murmansk
before the next convoy was ready to leave, and few of us were sorry
to say goodbye to that cold, inhospitable place. But starting our
journey so close to the German air bases in northern Norway meant
that the homeward convoys were sometimes even livelier than the
outward ones, because once the enemy knew that we had sailed he
could forecast with considerable accuracy just where we should be
at any hour of the day or night for the next four days. Then he
could direct submarines from their secure bases on the Norwegian
coast to lie in wait for us. The Germans also knew that our
carriers carried no night-flying aircraft, and that once darkness
fell all they could do was to tuck themselves into the middle of the
convoy until dawn. Sometimes they would send aircraft to drop
flares over the convoy, to light up the ships for the submarines to
fire their torpedoes. As we had many American ships in our convoys
at this time, with, it seemed, almost unlimited supplies of tracer
ammunition, these flare-droppers used to produce an effect
resembling an English Bonfire Night, as ships blazed away at the
planes they couldn't see, or the flares they could see but hadn't any
hope of hitting.

Considering that we were forcing these convoys through, along
a route which allowed little scope for evasive tactics, around the
perimeter of an enemy-held coastline, it was a remarkable tribute
to the way in which the C-in-C Home Fleet had these convoys
organized that in the later stages of the war they got through with
so few losses.

In spite of the low losses the Admiralty decided not to send any
convoys through during the continuous daylight of high summer,
so Activity now found herself on the 'sherry run', escorting troop
convoys to Gibraltar. Compared to the Murmansk run this seemed
like a pleasure trip, enabling us to get a little sun and have a swim
at Catalan Bay, while also allowing us to stock up with considerable quantities of Saccone and Speed sherry, which were disposed

The Cunard liner RMS *Queen Mary* on full-speed trials off the Isle of Arran in 1936.

Left Taken on board the drifter *Fairbreeze* off Ramsgate in March 1940 while I was a contraband control officer attached to HMS *Fervent*.

Below HMS *King George V* (35,000 tons), flagship of the British Home Fleet, involved in the action against *Bismarck*. The emergency conning position giving me a grandstand view of the action, can be clearly seen half-way up the after funnel. She carried 1,500 officers and men, and her armament consisted of ten 14-inch and sixteen 5·25-inch guns (*IWM photo*)

Above A German artists impression of the battleship *Bismarck* at speed in the rough weather like that experienced during the action when she was sunk. (*IWM photo*)

Below An official German photograph of the battleship *Bismarck* in harbour. (*IWM photo*)

Above HMS *Ibis*, a sloop of the improved Black Swan class, on which I served on Atlantic Convoy duty during 1941 and 1942. (*IWM photo*)

Below The Escort Carrier HMS *Activity* on which I served as Navigating Officer, from August 1942 until demobilization on 4 February 1946.

Left A boatload of survivors from an American freighter sunk by a Japanese submarine in the South Indian Ocean coming alongside HMS *Activity* after being adrift for three weeks. (*Taken by Sub-Lieut (E) Eric MacKay RNR*)

Above The Cunard liner RMS *Queen Elizabeth* (83,000 tons), the world's largest passenger liner and flagship of the Cunard fleet, entering New York Harbour shortly after I joined her for the first time in 1947.

Below The Cunard liner RMS *Scythia* (20,000 tons) my first passenger ship command. I joined her in 1957, and had the sad duty of delivering her to the breakers yard in Inverkeithing on 20 January 1958 after she had completed thirty-seven years' service.

Left The Cunard liner RMS *Carinthia* (22,000 tons) passing under the Jacques Cartier Bridge entering Montreal Harbour on the first voyage of the season with ice still in the river.

Below RMS *Carinthia* berthing alongside the Princes Landing Stage in Liverpool in a dense fog. This docking led to a headline in the *Liverpool Echo*, '*Carinthia*'s two mile fog crawl, leads to Captain's sunny smile'.

Above Riding a ship of the desert in Cairo, while commanding the Cunard luxury cruise liner RMS *Caronia* on a Mediterranean cruise in September 1962.

Below The Captain's Table on a Mediterranean cruise on board RMS *Caronia* which we used to call the 'Tiffanys of Cruising' in September 1963.

The Cunard cruising liner RMS *Mauretania* (35,000 tons) berthing alongside in the harbour of Santa Cruz Teneriffe, on an Atlantic islands cruise in 1964.

of to the wardrooms of less fortunate ships in Scapa Flow, to the benefit of our mess funds. Between these 'sherry runs' we did occasional sweeps into the Atlantic, the most famous of which was when HMS Nairana, another escort-carrier, and ourselves, accompanied Captain Wake-Walker RN when his flotilla of improved Black Swan class sloops accounted for seven German submarines in seven days.

But our halcyon days were coming to an end, because more and more of the slightly bigger American-built carriers of the new Ruler class were coming into service, and they could operate the new Avenger torpedo bombers. While on board Activity the size of our lift and our limited hangar space restricted us to Swordfish and Wildcats, so we found ourselves withdrawn from operations and relegated to the role of a ferry carrier, transporting aircraft out to India and then running between Southern India and Brisbane, Australia with replacement aircraft for the British carriers operating with the American Navy in the Pacific.

This run back and forth across the Indian Ocean and mainly in fine-weather latitudes proved a pleasant and comfortable way to spend a war, although the fact that there was still danger around was brought home to us on one passage when we picked up the crew of an American freighter which had been torpedoed, I assume by a Japanese submarine. The men had been adrift under the tropical sun for nearly three weeks and the look of relief on their faces as we hauled them on board was memorable.

Study of the charts and careful measurement of distances enabled me to convince those in authority that we could make faster passages and probably deliver our aircraft in better condition by going round the north of Australia, then through the Torres Straits and down through the Great Barrier Reef to Brisbane, rather than along the south coast, where one could meet rough seas and very heavy swells crossing the Great Australian Bight. When this change of route was approved it was to prove a very profitable one for me, because according to the Admiralty pilotage instructions the navigating officer of a major war vessel can claim a special pilotage fee for every passage his ship makes through the Barrier Reef. This passage does involve some fairly tricky navigation, such as passing between two unlighted islands only a little over a mile apart, and in those days it was normal practice for merchant vessels using this route to employ a Barrier Reef pilot and to anchor at night except at periods of full moon. However, being fitted with radar made an enormous difference, as it showed up the islands and beacons remarkably, so in spite of a few worrying moments, we managed to keep going night and day and at the end of the war I received a very useful little bonus.

The end of the war with Germany made little difference to us. In fact, we found ourselves turning round even quicker because of the demand for replacement aircraft; until the night the atom bombs were dropped on Hiroshima and Nagasaki, when we were anchored in the harbour at Trincomalee, Ceylon, where a large fleet was assembled preparing for Operation Zipper, the relief of Singapore. These arrangements were already so far advanced as to let much of the operation go through as planned, even though no serious opposition was expected. However, the plans for the reopening of the port of Singapore had to be considerably advanced, so Activity was pressed into service and we hurriedly embarked the advance port party, with all their equipment to get the docks operating again, and a large group of the Army paymaster branch, who had with them about fourteen tons of new currency with which to reopen the banks and restart the commercial life of the city.

We sailed twenty-four hours after the main body of the invasion fleet, with orders to arrive at One Fathom Bank light in the Straits of Malacca in time to pass through the swept channel before dark. But the adverse current proved stronger than expected and it was 16.30, with only ninety minutes of daylight left, when we entered the minefield. As we were the senior ship, I found myself leading two other carriers through. The minesweepers who had led the fleet through the previous day had laid buoys with flags on them at one-mile intervals to mark the centre line of the channel they had swept, but some of these had either sunk or dragged their moorings. When one was missed it was a nerve-racking time until the next one was sighted. Life became particularly difficult after darkness fell, looking for these pesky little things with two big 22-inch searchlights; but eventually we found and identified the last buoy and I began to breathe more easily.

The cruiser HMS Cumberland had already arrived at Singapore

(Lord Louis Mountbatten had accepted the Japanese surrender on board her), and the two big Dutch hospital ships, the Oranje and the William Ruys, were in to evacuate the most serious cases from the infamous Changi Camp. We were the next to arrive and were to remain alongside in Singapore for five days. Before our eyes, the great city fell into a state of anarchy and confusion when the Japanese occupation money which had been in use for nearly two years suddenly became completely worthless. Everything had to be done by barter, with American cigarettes as the basis of most transactions. Our first thought was for the people who had been enduring the hardships of Changi Camp for so long, particularly the women and children. Our first lieutenant managed to persuade the army to lend us a lorry, which we used to transport the entire contents of our canteen, and as many of the items of clothing in the purser's clothing store as we felt could be any possible use, up to the camp commissariat. There were many horrifying sights to see, but all the 'prisoners' were quiet and made no complaint on any account. Here were humans reduced to the level of brute endurance. Some of those who were strong enough managed to get lifts into town and came on board the ship looking for food and companionship, and one of our main problems was not allowing them to eat too much before their systems could adapt. A great thrill for me was being one of the officers chosen to accompany E J R North, RNR, the captain, to represent the ship when Lord Louis Mountbatten signed the surrender agreement on the parade grounds, and one of my most cherished souvenirs is a samurai sword from among those handed in by the Japanese officers that day.

After we had landed all the stores and equipment that we had brought, and the officers and men who had come with us to re-open the port had been accommodated ashore, there was no point in our remaining any longer. So, after embarking as many ex-prisoners not needing specialist medical treatment as we could, we set sail for England, and for HMS Activity the war was suddenly over at last. Our voyage home became a real peacetime voyage, with all lights on, portholes open, and a very relaxed atmosphere on board, as we all carefully studied the latest Admiralty regulations on demobilization and tried to work out who would still be required for further service.

When we reached home waters towards the end of November we proceeded up the Gareloch to a berth near the old No 1 Military Port, and when the time came for me to leave the ship, knowing that this would also be the end of my service in the Navy and the beginning of my return to civilian life, my feelings were very mixed. After those long years of war which had just ended it was going to be strange to feel free to do more or less what one pleased. I knew that I should shortly be returning to Cunard, and this was going to mean changes, and one would need to readjust one's values. While one would still be working in a world of ships, it would once more be a commercial venture, depending on profit and loss in the financial world, while the Navy lived, moved and had its being in a world of 'doing the right thing', with small regard for the cost aspect. This atmosphere tended to produce a well-knit team in every Navy ship which had a good man in command, for every man on board felt part of a family and was ready to pull his weight. The men were dedicated—loyal and true to their ship and their shipmates.

The moment at last came to leave the ship. After saying good-bye to the captain and officers, I went down the gangway and, turning to take a last look at the Activity, which had been my home for more than three years, I found that the ship's company had manned the rails and was giving me the traditional naval farewell of 'Three Cheers'. It was a signal honour, and I felt humble and deeply touched. Later when the announcement was made that I had been awarded the DSC, the congratulatory telegram from HMS Activity completed my day. I have always maintained that it isn't the ship, it's the men who really matter, and the men of Activity were a band of brothers. So, as I said my farewell to the Royal Navy, I made a secret vow to try to keep up to the naval standard for the rest of my life.

CHAPTER EIGHT

The stranded Queens

Back in my New Forest home by the end of November 1945, I settled down to enjoy a long overdue spell of leave, including the first Christmas with my family for several years. Then, early in the New Year, I was summoned to Queen Anne's Mansions for my medical checkup and the final formalities of discharge from the Navy at the end of my war service.

Once these were over, I felt it would be wise to let Cunard know that I was available again, although I still had well over a month of my demobilization leave to go. I was rather taken aback to receive a letter from Liverpool by return of post, appointing me junior first officer of RMS Mauretania and instructing me to join her in Liverpool on 14 January 1946.

Back in the old familiar surroundings, with familiar people, it was quite amazing how quickly one found oneself settling down into peacetime routine again. After the ship (still in her wartime grey, and operating under the orders of the Ministry of Shipping) had made a winter Atlantic crossing to Halifax, Nova Scotia, carrying Canadian war brides and their children, and a trooping voyage to Bombay (on the return part of which we had brought back the contingents of troops which were to represent the sub-continent in the victory parade in London, included in which were the prime minister of Nepal and his entourage), one found oneself looking back on the war and all its excitements as just another chapter, which had now closed.

On one of the Mauretania's visits to Bombay I was invited with her captain, G E Cove, to dinner at Government House. This was my first introduction to the full panoply of Oriental splendour which they still maintained at Government House, even in the closing days of the British Raj. The magnificent appointments, the military band playing a slow march as the governor, Sir John Colville, KBE, led his guests into dinner, the turbaned servant behind every chair; then, after coffee and cigars, back to the drawing room to join the ladies, with good-looking young ADCs discreetly circulating the guests so that everyone had an opportunity to talk to the governor and his lady—these are things which I never expected to see again, part of our nation's past which has now gone for ever; but I was glad to have had the opportunity to see and participate in them once.

After these two voyages the Mauretania returned to Gladstone Dock, Liverpool, to start her reconversion to passenger service, which was going to take several months and would mean the ship being completely shut down. I was very glad to learn that I was going to be relieved because standing by a dead ship can be a dreary business.

Following a spell of leave I was delighted to rejoin my old love, RMS Queen Mary, in Southampton on 22 June 1946. Still in her wartime grey apart from the familiar red and black Cunard livery on her three funnels, the Queen Mary was maintaining the transatlantic service to Halifax and New York, while her newer and slightly larger sister, the Queen Elizabeth, had returned to her birthplace on the Clyde for a major overhaul and to be fitted out as a passenger liner—a process which had not been completed when she had sailed on her secret voyage to New York in March 1940.

At this time the Queen Mary was commanded by Captain C Gordon Illingworth, a man whose affection for the ship was so great that when he was later promoted to commodore he made a special request to the board of directors to be allowed to continue to fly his flag in her rather than transfer to the Queen Elizabeth, which was regarded as the company's flagship.

On all of our westbound crossings at this time we still had a large contingent of Canadian war brides and their children, whom we landed at Halifax before going on the New York. And, in spite of the fact that we were still sailing under austerity conditions the number of ordinary commercial passengers steadily increased with every voyage we made. The most notable passengers we carried during this period were, I think, General and Mrs Dwight D Eisenhower, when he was coming to London to receive the approbation of the British people for the part he had played in the Allied victory as Supreme Commander of Allied Forces in Europe. On one evening the General and his aide came to the wardroom for cocktails, and with the relaxed, friendly manner for which he was famous he soon made us all feel at ease. Eventually, somebody steered the conversation around to his personal feelings about D-Day and the gales which followed it, and for almost an hour he held everybody in the room spellbound with his account of those difficult days.

In October 1946 we were steaming into Southampton, heading home and looking a little dingy in sombre grey after the rigours of an Atlantic crossing, when we passed our younger sister, RMS Queen Elizabeth, waiting to start her maiden voyage as a passenger liner and sparkling like a diamond as her brilliant new paint reflected the afternoon sunshine. This made one of the most dramatic pictures of the two Queens together, stressing the dual role they both played in war and peace. But unfortunately a shadow was cast over the Queen Elizabeth's inaugural voyage by the sudden and tragic death, the evening before she sailed, of Sir Percy Bates, the man whose brainchild the weekly service with two giant ships had been.

When the Queen Mary started her reconversion, I hoped that I should be one of the officers standing by her, because with my home only eight miles from the drydock I should have had part of every day at home, which is always a pleasant change for a sailor. But after only a few weeks I was transferred to RMS Aquitania, then the dowager of the Cunard fleet, as senior first officer. This wonderful old lady, one of the most popular and successful ships that the Cunard Line ever owned, did yeoman service in two world wars, and was still running on the Southampton-Halifax service at speeds not much below what she had done on her trials thirty-three years before. In spite of her fine lines she was a splendid sea boat, and her razor-sharp bow used to slice through the Atlantic sending plumes of spray over her foredeck. But there was one little triangle just abaft the knightsheads which remained dry, except in very bad weather, and it was usually assumed that so long as you could still see the dry spot on the forecastle there was no need to reduce speed. Another distinctive feature of this elegant ship was her four huge funnels, which really looked impressive, but they were also very useful in describing the thickness of the fog which we so frequently encountered off Halifax: it was either a two-funnel fog, or a three- or four-funnel fog, depending on how many funnels could still be seen from the bridge.

Before the end of February 1947 I was moved again, this time to the busy bustling world of RMS Queen Elizabeth, which at the time was scooping up the cream of the North Atlantic passenger traffic as the first of the big ships to resume normal peacetime sailings. These were indeed very exciting days to be with Cunard. Our sailings were booked up for months ahead, and there seemed to be every prospect that things would be exactly the same for the Queen Mary as soon as she was ready to join us. In addition to the two Queens, the Mauretania and the Britannic in Liverpool were being refitted by a grateful government, almost regardless of expense, and other ships in the fleet were to get similar treatment when they were released from war service. Up on the Clyde, a new 32,000 ton luxury cruise liner to be called Caronia was being built, and plans were being discussed with Brocklebank's, one of Cunard's associated companies, to take over two of the 14,000 ton cargo liners which they had on the stocks and convert them into passenger cargo liners, which eventually became the Media and Parthia.

This was the start of the most prosperous period in the company's history. For ten glorious years, until 1957, the Cunard Line had passengers clamouring to be able to sail in its ships, some of them quite willing to put down a deposit six months before they wanted to sail, in order to secure the cabin of their choice. Indeed, to the directors sitting around that oak table on the fifth floor of the very solid-looking Cunard Building at Liverpool's pierhead it must have looked as though they had found the secret of eternal prosperity. When the two Queens got into their stride each ship was showing a gross profit of over £100,000 per round voyage, and in 1949 the chairman, in his annual statement, was able to announce a gross profit of about £7,000,000, of which more than half had to be paid to the government as excess profits and other taxes. In 1957, with a magnificent fleet of twelve passenger liners, we were to carry the greatest number of passengers across the Atlantic and on luxury cruises than in any year of the company's 117-year history.

But also in 1957, the first of the big jets went streaking across the Atlantic in less than six hours, and although to us at the time it seemed like the proverbial 'cloud no bigger than a man's hand', this was to prove the start of a new era in travel history. During the next ten years the number of such planes steadily increased and by 1967 the once great Cunard company was reduced to only three passenger ships, and in grave danger of being forced out of business.

It says in the Bible, 'Where there is no Vision, the people perish', and one feels that someone ought to have written that out in letters a foot high and hung it in the Cunard boardroom, because it seemed that the elderly gentlemen who met there certainly failed to recognize any writing on walls.

The announcements that issued over the years from this boardroom deep inside what used to be known to seagoing staff as the Kremlin, in the form of chairman's annual statements, should make interesting reading for future students of maritime history. From business recessions to the war in Korea, every possible reason was found to explain the decline in the company's fortunes, but the right one. They also stubbornly refused to learn the lesson which their Scandinavian, Dutch and German counterparts learned early in the 1950s: that with the rapid decline of winter travel on the North Atlantic the only passenger ships that could hope to make money must be dual-purpose and suitable for luxury cruising in the winter months. They seemed incapable of realizing that, if crew wages and stevedoring charges continued to rise in the same spiral, it must inevitably become uneconomical to try to carry passengers and freight in the same ship. While ships were in port loading or discharging wages were paid out to a big catering department for doing nothing. As late as 1956, they were cheerfully building the last of four 20,000 ton passenger cargo liners with seven cargo hatches for their service to Canada, that were quite unsuitable for any type of cruising, having hardly any air-conditioning, few passenger cabins with facilities and no swimming pools.

To return to the spring of 1947, this was the year in which the first of two highly dramatic strandings of the great Queens occurred. I was very much involved in both incidents, and although they were widely reported in the world's press at the time, some of the reports, based on hearsay, were not strictly accurate.

The story of the first stranding starts on a lovely clear spring evening in 1947, when the Queen Elizabeth was due to dock at Southampton at about 20.00. As I was off duty on the ship's arrival, and anxious to catch the earliest possible bus to my home in the New Forest, after the ship passed the Nab Tower at about 18.00 I had completely changed into civilian clothing apart from my uniform jacket and cap and a navy blue raincoat, before going up to my station for entering harbour, the after docking bridge.

Normal practice for both the Queens was for one of the company's 'choice' pilots to cross to Cherbourg to join the ship there, so that the ship need not stop off the Nab Tower. But on this voyage, our pilot had failed to reach Cherbourg before the ship sailed. This meant we had to stop at the Nab and, as none of the company's pilots were on the cutter, we had to take the senior rota pilot, who had never previously handled one of the Queens. The weather was fine and the winds were light, so there was no problem until after the ship had passed Egypt Point, near Cowes on the Isle of Wight. There she had to make a 160 degree turn around the Brambles Bank and come out into the channel with the Calshot Spit light vessel right ahead as she left the Brambles buoy to starboard. With their huge (135 ton) rudders and powerful steering gear, both the Queens have been famous as good steering ships, but for a turn as tight as this it was usual to reduce the speed of the engines on the side towards which she was turning, and in this part of the Solent the way the tide is running across the Brambles Bank can affect the way she turns.

Not being on the bridge at the time, I do not know what orders were given or what action was taken by the pilot or anyone else. But either the action came too late, or it was not sufficiently drastic, because from my station right aft looking along the whole

1031 foot length of the ship, I probably became aware that she was not swinging nearly quickly enough before this became apparent to those on the bridge, which is only about 200 feet from the stem. About half way through the turn I became worried. The ship was coming closer and closer to the Brambles buoy and still heading well to the north of the channel course. I knew there was nothing I could do: to have telephoned the bridge would only have added to the confusion. Suddenly everything began to shake. The four big propellers started to thresh up the water as they checked her headway; but it was already too late. The ship must still have been making about 6 knots through the water as she slid past Bourne Gap's red flashing buoy on the wrong side and buried her bows, almost up to the bridge, in the mud, sand and shingle bank. Although the ship shuddered a little there was no great shock on impact and nobody was thrown off his feet. Indeed, there were a great many people inside the ship who had no idea at the time that she had grounded. But to those of us on deck it was all too obvious that, in spite of the maximum astern power that the chief engineer could develop, the propellers were just threshing the water and stirring up the mud and sand to no purpose: her bows were too firmly embedded. To avoid silting up the main condensers the engines were then stopped. The peak of high water was rapidly approaching, so there was going to be nothing we could do on this tide: it would be impossible for enough tugs to reach us in time.

Within an hour of the news of our predicament reaching the Southampton Docks, numerous harbour board officials, the London salvage representative and a host of Cunard managers and superintendents came on board the ship for a series of long conferences in the captain's cabin.

Although my station for entering and leaving harbour was the after docking bridge, for the actual operations of mooring and un-mooring I was relieved by the staff captain. With the senior third officer, I moved down to the after mooring deck to supervise the handling of the ropes and wires. As senior first officer I was responsible for making fast the thirteen tugs which had assembled round the stern of the ship by 06.00 the following morning. As we had only seven pairs of bollards, and because the Alexander and Isle of Wight tugs refused to use their ordinary towing wires but insisted in taking the ship's manilla ropes, in many cases the only thing we could do was to have the smaller tugs towing in tandem, with two tugs on one line.

When they were all made fast, and as the time of the next high water approached, they all started to tow together. The wash made by their combined thousands of horsepower, and that churned up by the ship's propellers, made an impressive sight. But, as the tide had fallen the previous evening the ship had settled herself even more comfortably into her bed of mud and sand, and in spite of all we had been able to do to try and lift her bows, by transferring oil and water, and filling some of our after tanks, she steadfastly refused to move. Not that this had been easy, because when the two Queens arrived at Southampton they had very little fuel oil or fresh water remaining, so all that could be pumped out to lighten the ship were the tanks that had been ballasted for stability or trim.

After half an hour of hard towing the attempt had to be abandoned, again because of the silting of the main condensers. The next tide, twenty-four hours after the stranding, was supposed to rise a little higher; but when our efforts once again produced no results, the situation began to look really serious, and arrangements were made to disembark our first class passengers, some of whom were by now getting a little restless at the delay. Indeed the late Randolph Churchill was furious, because the captain had refused to let him send reports to newspapers about conditions on board.

Our problem was how to break the suction and ease the ship out of the comfortable bed she had made for herself. The following morning we made the tugs fast a little earlier, and this time, on a a prearranged signal, they were all ordered to tow the ship's stern to port for fifteen minutes; then, when the whistle blew, to swing over together and tow the stern to starboard for a similar period. On the second change we felt a slight movement, and when, on the third change, this was more pronounced, the ship's main engines were put full astern. Finally, about an hour before high water, she slid off the bank into deep water. A cheer went up and we hurriedly let go some of the tugs to go forward and help control the bows. Then, surrounded by an armada of tugs, the ship made her stately progress to her berth in Ocean Dock. Once she was securely moored I went along to my cabin and changed into civilian clothes again, and took a taxi to the bus station. There I caught my bus home, arriving nearly two days late, and resolved never to tempt fate again by changing before the ship was actually in the dock.

The diver's examination of the hull confirmed that the plating was quite undamaged but in some places highly polished. The only thing that had to be done to get the ship ready to sail again was for the engineers to clean the silt out of the condensers.

I was not present at the company's official inquiry, but I understand that the captain was not found to be to blame. Indeed, a letter was sent by the management to him, thanking the whole ship's company for the way they had handled a difficult situation.

By the time that the second stranding happened, I had been promoted to chief officer and was back on the Queen Mary. She had just completed her annual overhaul and was sailing from Southampton on 1 January 1949. Her captain, Harry Grattidge, who was later to write one of the best books yet published about the Queens (*Captain of the Queens*), was making his first voyage in command of her.

After a late night to celebrate the New Year, I wasn't feeling too well at 06.00 the following morning as I trudged down a lonely forest road to catch the first bus to Southampton, being buffeted by a blustery wind and cold driving rain. Then, waiting in the wardroom with a small group of officers to start boat drill at 08.00, I found myself listening with more than usual interest to the BBC weather forecast at 07.55, though nothing that the announcer had to tell us made us feel any more cheerful. A rapidly deepening depression was approaching the west of Ireland and moving quickly eastwards, giving gales in all areas, with long periods of rain, followed by squally showers; exactly what we saw as we went out on deck in the grey half-light.

Our official sailing time was 13.00 and our embarkation had been completed shortly before noon, but all morning the question as to whether it would be possible to sail the ship in such weather had been under discussion. When we went on stations for the first time at 12.30, a fierce squall hit the ship and orders were given not to touch the moorings. But after that squall passed there was a definite lull, the sky cleared for a time and the sun came out. Two extra tugs which had been docking one of the Union Castle ships now became available and a quick decision was made. At 13.00 the order 'Make fast the tugs, and let go fore and aft as quickly as possible' was passed. This produced a rush of activity at both ends of the ship as the shore gang struggled to land our heavy mooring wires as quickly as they could, and we took the towing wires aboard from our nine tugs, while from all parts of the ship anxious eyes were being cast at the heavy black clouds building up over Hythe and the New Forest, heralding the approach of the next squall. But by 13.30 the tugs had moved us clear of the berth and we were on our way down the Channel with adequate steerage way on before that squall struck.

We had a rough cross-Channel passage, with the barometer still falling fast and, being the officer in charge of the 4-8 watch, I was on the bridge with Captain Grattidge and the Cherbourg pilot, who had joined the ship in Southampton, when we were discussing the weather prospects at 18.00 after listening to the weather forecast. This did not hold out much hope of improvement if we were to wait for daylight the following morning. I got the feeling that Captain Grattidge was not keen to enter harbour; but he was worried about the three hundred passengers who would be arriving shortly in the special train from Paris—for whom there was no overnight accommodation in Cherbourg if the Queen Mary remained at sea. The pilot, on the other hand, was quite optimistic, and pointed out that with the wind from the south, as it was at the time, we should get the maximum protection from the land as we approached the French coast. The decision was taken to go in, and the truth of the French pilot's words soon became apparent. Until we got to within about seven miles of the coast, the waves were breaking over the forecastle head; but by the time we had closed to about three miles north of the breakwater, we were able to get our men up there to clear away the anchors and lift the derricks.

In fact we were getting such a good lee that, entering harbour, putting two anchors down, getting the five tenders alongside and completing what seemed a fairly routine embarkation, presented no major problems. And when stations were called for leaving at 20.30, I put on my oilskins and wet weather gear to go forward and weigh the anchors, thinking only how good it would be to get away to sea and go to bed, because I was feeling so tired.

But as soon as I got up on the forecastle I realized how much the wind, which had now veered to the SSW, had increased in strength. The cables had a good weight on them, but the anchors were holding, and when the orders were received to weigh first one and then the other, there was difficulty in getting them in. But while we were doing this a violent rain squall hit the ship and the junior second officer and I, together with the two carpenters, the bosun and about twenty men, were having such difficulty in standing on our feet, and in managing to see anything more than a few yards from the ship in the blinding rain, that it was some time before I became aware that the ship was not turning as she should, and that she was in real trouble.

Cherbourg harbour, which is entirely man made, consists of an imposing stone breakwater about two miles long, running east and west at a distance equivalent to about three times the length of the ship from the shore, and this area between the shore and the break-water affords a reasonable sheltered anchorage in anything but the worst weather. But the depth of water shoals considerably at the eastern end of the harbour. The anchorage used by the Queens was midway between the shore and the breakwater, about a quarter of a mile inside the western entrance, and had only sufficient water to allow one of these ships to remain in the anchorage through low water at the period of neap tides.

For a ship lying, as we were, with our head to the south, the normal practice once the anchor was aweigh would have been to turn at rest, by going full astern on the two starboard engines and half ahead on the two port engines, until her head came around to the right heading to allow her to steam out through the break-water. But, in a gale like the one which was blowing that night, big ships, with their tremendous areas exposed to the pressure of the wind, do not respond to normal procedures. So Captain Grattidge and the pilot were now faced with a situation in which the Queen Mary was in irons, and nothing would overcome her natural tendency to seek the wind's eye until she had sufficient headway to feel the effect of her rudder. She could never do so in such a confined space; and while she was in irons the effect of the wind and tide would be to carry her down towards the shallow water at the eastern end of the harbour. In desperation, the pilot decided to drop the starboard anchor again, hoping it would stop her drift and perhaps enable him to swing the ship far enough round on her anchor to get her heading towards the breakwater. But it was already too late. Even with four shackles of chain out, the anchor would not hold; and as the ship dragged she was getting dangerously close to the buoy marking the edge of the shallow water.

With the French pilot now in complete despair, Captain Grattidge had to step in and take over, and as desperate situations can only be cured by desperate measures, he took one of the most courageous actions I have ever seen. Knowing that if the engines are going astern in a strong wind, the action of the propellers is to hold the stern, while the pressure of the wind on the hull tends to blow the ship round until she is stern to wind, he decided that the only way in which he could hope to get the ship out of harbour under such conditions was to make a sternboard (manoeuvre astern).

His first action was to pass word forward to weigh the starboard anchor. I attempted to carry out this order—and knew from the moment the capstan started that we had a foul anchor, because the cable was coming in so slowly. When we did eventually get the anchor to the water's edge, I could see that it had picked up two or three fairly heavy wire cables. These were the remains of the armoured section of the wartime PLUTO (pipeline under the ocean), used to supply invasion forces with fuel and abandoned at the end of the war. By the time I was able to pass the information about the foul anchor to the bridge, the engines were already going astern, and the order came back for the chief officer to put the brake on hard, to try to drag the anchor clear.

When the order to put the engines astern was first given the ship was still lying right across the harbour with her head to the SSW and her stern towards the breakwater, and even in a ship whose bows are held—as ours were—by the foul anchor, the turning effect produced by the engines is a slow process and the ship gathers sternway before she starts to turn. This brought those four threshing propellers closer and closer to the rocks which form the foundations of the breakwater, much to the alarm of the senior first officer, who was on duty on the after docking bridge and reported at one time that the ship's stern was less than 200 feet from the rocks.

By now the starboard anchor cable, which I had walked back a little, was stretched out like a bar, with such fantastic weight on it that I felt sure it would snap, so I had ordered everyone abaft the anchor capstan. I went to the telephone myself to inform the bridge, and said, very urgently, 'This is the chief officer speaking! Tell the captain we can hardly hold the starboard anchor. We have the brake on and the power on and it's still walking back.' In spite of the wind, I could hear my message shouted across the wheelhouse, followed by Captain Grattidge's cool reply, 'Tell the chief officer there is nothing we can do to help him now!'

Fortunately the anchor held until the stern started to swing away from the breakwater rocks and round towards the eye of the wind; then, just at the right time, the wires holding the anchor started to tear away from the harbour bottom and the ship began to gather sternway and move down the harbour, turning until her bow was pointing out towards the Western Fort and the safety of the open sea. The engines had been stopped for some time and were starting to move ahead, although the ship herself still had slight sternway, when suddenly with a bump right aft we knew that we had hit something. The ship stopped, and after putting the engines to half ahead to try and get her to move, Captain Grattidge decided to stop them—for fear of damaging the propellers. Cross bearings then pinpointed the ship's position, and showed that she had gone too far astern and grounded on a pinnacle of rock, just to the southward of the western entrance.

Although we had no means of knowing it at the time, the ship must have landed with the strongest part of her hull on a single pinnacle of rock not more than eight or ten feet across at its apex and standing clear of other rocks, just about twenty-five feet forward of her stern frame and midway between her two after propellers. A thorough examination at our next drydocking showed no sign of damage to the rudder or the propellers, and the only mark on that huge hull was one indentation, just abaft O tank, which required about sixty tons of iron-crete cement to stop the leak.

But at 21.00 on that dark and stormy night, all we knew was that we had grounded aft. Yet the bows still seemed to be swinging, so on the forecastle, where the starboard anchor was now clear of the water, and the bosun and his men were trying to get the trailing wires clear of it, I received the order to drop the port anchor underfoot, to stop the bow moving. Having done this, I made my way to the bridge, where I found Captain Grattidge, still remarkably calm, with the staff captain and the senior first officer, and we discussed what was to be done. Two local tugs had already arrived, with others, including a French naval tug, coming as soon as they could raise steam. But as the time of high water had passed, it was decided that no attempt would be made to refloat until the next high water, just after 09.00 the following morning.

There was, however, one problem we were not sure how to deal with: that was, what was likely to happen when the tide fell about fifteen feet, as we knew it must do, in the next six hours. We had no idea where the ship was held, but if it was under one of our bilge keels it could have produced an alarming list.

So an officer and a quartermaster were sent round the ship in one of the tugs to take soundings, and they reported fairly deep water down both sides, which made us feel easier. In fact, as the tide slowly ebbed, the ship remained perfectly upright, with the stern lifting until all four propellers were showing above the water and the ship was drawing forty-seven feet of water forward. Luckily the darkness of the long winter night drew a kindly veil over our proud ship's sad predicament, and the rising tide restored her to a more even keel.

As chief officer, my immediate problem was lightening the ship; but, unlike my previous experience in the Queen Elizabeth, this was not to prove difficult, because we were starting our voyage with most of our tanks full. We arranged to lift the stern two feet by pumping about 3000 tons of domestic and ballast water overboard and asking the chief engineer to transfer some of his oil fuel.

This evidently achieved the desired effect, because just before 08.00 the next morning, while we were making the tugs fast, we noticed that as soon as they started to put a strain on their wires, the ship moved, even though it was still more than ninety minutes to high water. As soon as we were sure that she was clear of the

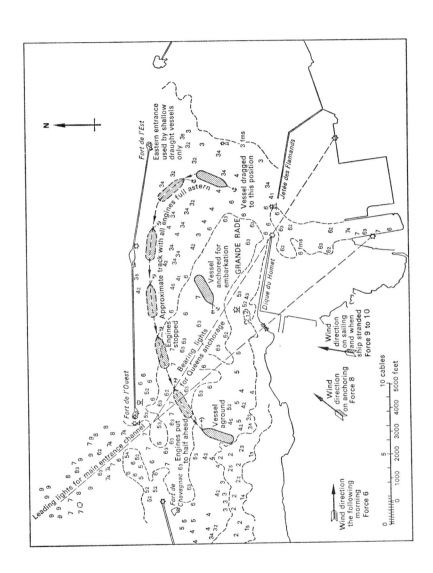

N

Leading lights for main entrance channel

Fort de l'Ouest

Fort de l'Est

Fort de Chavagnac

Approximate track with all engines full astern

Engines full astern

Engines stopped

Engines put to half ahead

Bearing lights for Queens anchorage

Vessel aground

Vessel anchored for embarkation

GRANDE RADE

Eastern entrance used by shallow draught vessels only

Vessel dragged to this position

Jetée des Flamands

Digue du Homet

Wind direction on sailing and when ship stranded Force 9 to 10

Wind direction on anchoring Force 8

Wind direction the following morning Force 6

0   1000   2000   3000   4000   5000 feet

0   5   10 cables

obstruction we weighed the port anchor, only to find that it picked up some of the wires we had so laboriously removed from the starboard anchor the night before. But, knowing that they were no longer attached to anything, we decided to tow them out of harbour as we moved slowly out and we passed the breakwater escorted by the tugs. The carpenter reported that his soundings showed no signs of leaking tanks, so all that remained was for us to thank the tugs who had stood by us all night and, after dumping our unwanted wires in deep water, to set course for Southampton, adjusting our trim as we went.

It was not until I got the chance to put my feet up for an hour during our run across the Channel that I began to realize how tired I was, having only had an hour's sleep the night before. But once we anchored in the Solent, we were inundated with marine superintendents, surveyors, salvage experts, repair managers and company solicitors. There was no peace until we finally berthed in Southampton at about 01.00 the next morning, when I locked my door and went to bed.

The next time she went into drydock, we were able to stand under the enormous hull and look up at that one tiny spot on which 82,000 tons of ship had been balanced all through one stormy night: and felt that if we hadn't seen it ourselves, we would never have believed it.

During my next three years as chief officer of the Queens, voyage seemed to follow voyage in rapid succession, and the memories that remain are of the personalities of the men who were commanding those ships at this period, many of them rugged individualists and seamen of the old school, with their roots in the closing years of the sailing ship era.

Then, during the winters of 1950 and 1951, I had an enjoyable break, making the first two post-war Mediterranean cruises as staff captain of the very popular Britannic, the last surviving relic of the White Star Line.

These were busy days, and happy days, with the whole fleet still sailing with full passenger lists; days in which one could still feel that the Cunard Line was as solid as the Bank of England. When I received my first command I think most of us still thought things would go on in the same way.

CHAPTER NINE

Staff Captain to the Queens

To every sailor there is something rather special about his first command. It usually means a farewell to watchkeeping or, as we used to call it, 'pounding the teak', for eight hours a day in fair weather and foul. Also, it seems to make a subtle difference to the way one is treated by the various officials who come on board the ship, and it is pleasant to be addressed as Captain Marr, rather than the Mr Marr one has grown used to over the years. But mostly, I think, it is the feeling of independence that comes from the realization that once the ship leaves the dock it is the captain who makes all the important decisions. It is no longer a case of knocking politely on the captain's door and saying 'What do *you* think we should do about so and so, sir?' Now the decisions and the responsibility for them rests on oneself.

The Cunard cargo liner Andria was one of a pair of two-funnelled cargo ships which had been built for the Silver Line's round-the-world service and later bought by Cunard. Both looked very smart in the Cunard livery, because of their prominent funnels, although these were more for decoration than use, as the forward one was a dummy and actually housed part of the captain's accommodation.

My first voyage in command was an uneventful summer passage to New York then down the coast to Baltimore, Newport News and Norfolk, which meant making my first transit of the Chesapeake and Delaware Canal—a rather alarming experience. Our pilot was a man with nerves of steel, who only seemed to blow for the bridges to open at the last moment, as the ship was bearing down on them at a speed which would have made it impossible for her to stop in time if the works had jammed. But each time, just when, to me, it seemed as though disaster were inevitable, the last car would straggle across and the bridge swing clear to allow the ship to glide through.

Our homeward cargo consisted mainly of strip steel, so after leaving New York our first port was Middlesborough on the north east coast, where we met some unpleasant weather in docks which seemed uncomfortably small for a ship of the Andria's size. So I was relieved to get round to London and hand the ship back safely to her regular captain, whom I had been relieving, and return to the Queen Mary again for a further short period as chief officer, before being promoted to staff captain of the same ship in April 1953.

The job of staff captain in Cunard is an unusual one and they were only carried in the Queens and in cruise liners. I have never been quite sure how the rank originated but I did hear the story that when they were building the Queen Mary the company realized the strain it would be for one man to drive this ship at 30 knots across an ocean where she was likely to meet some of the worst weather in the world. With fog, which in the summer months could cover thousands of square miles, and winter gales, such conditions could, in those pre-radar days, make it necessary for the captain to remain on the bridge for days at a time. So they conceived the idea that she should have two captains, of similar seniority, and one could relieve the other. But long before the ship sailed it was recognized that this arrangement would never work satisfactorily, because of the difficulty of trying to divide responsibility. In any potentially dangerous situation, who would decide when to hand over to the other? A successful and well-run organization can only have one head. So the rank of staff captain was evolved instead, whereby a junior captain was appointed to the ship to take over as much as possible of the social and administrative side of the captain's duties. This meant that, even if bad weather forced the captain to remain on the bridge for days at a time, the internal life of the ship could go on: all the drills and inspections would be carried out, defaulters would be dealt with promptly, and important and influential passengers suitably entertained.

In practice, the staff captain's job was an extremely pleasant one, and the years I spent in that post were about the most enjoyable part of my career at sea. Then one was able to enjoy the pleasures of the social side without the burdens of responsibility. And as 1953 was Coronation year, we seemed to have more of the top people in all walks of life, travelling by sea. I have always been aware of my good fortune in being able to meet and entertain so many delightful and interesting people whom I could never have met in any other way. One could, by thumbing through old diaries, produce long, name-dropping lists of the rich and famous who had accepted one's invitations to cocktail parties; but it would not really mean anything. They knew as well we did that we were only carrying out our social duties: dispensing drinks, paid for by the company, to those passengers whom the company felt should be accorded special treatment, to enable them to meet other important passengers travelling on that crossing in a friendly atmosphere.

During my first period of service as staff captain of the Queens I was ahead of my station, waiting for Captain E A Divers to return from a world cruise on the Caronia. In August 1953 I relieved him to start my tour of duty on board Cunard's specially built luxury cruise liner, then at the peak of her popularity and known as the Tiffany's of cruising.

While in the Atlantic service one only met people for about four days and, pleasant though this was, it could only be casual acquaintanceship, as there were 600 new first class passengers and 1,400 passengers in cabin and tourist classes every week. These could only ripen into friendship with those regular travellers who enjoyed one's company sufficiently to make the effort to travel again in the same ship. These particular passengers tended to become, through many meetings, a sort of special travellers' club, with a certain ship and/or a particular captain as the unifying link. They became close friends, and to this day many of us still meet and correspond, though the days which engendered this state of grace have now long gone, together with the splendid ships which have provided the backdrop for our meetings. However, on board the Caronia, which apart from the odd positioning voyage was permanently cruising, life was very different from the rush and bustle of the Atlantic ferry service. The passengers who join a cruise liner are sometimes going to be with her for as long as 105 days, and seldom less than a fortnight, and they have no interest in getting anywhere quickly;

they just want to settle down and enjoy the voyage. The atmosphere on board became that of a very expensive club and, particularly on the very long cruises, so many people used to come back year after year that they tended, like the senior members of a country club, to be jealous of their rights and privileges. In this relaxed atmosphere, I made more lasting friendships than at any other time in my life.

The long cruise that the Caronia made in 1954 was called the Great Pacific Cruise, and because of the vast distances involved it meant spending a great deal of time at sea. So when, with Captain C S Williams in command, we sailed from New York on 25 January 1954, we knew that the Cunard officials who had planned this cruise were worried that our 500 or so passengers, some of whom had paid as much as $32,000 to occupy the main deck suites, might be bored by the long sea passages; and in particular, by the one from Callao in Peru to Suva, Fiji, when they would not be able to set foot ashore for more than two weeks. Another unusual problem about the cruise was a housekeeping one, because for the six-week period between leaving New York and arriving in Auckland, New Zealand it would be impossible to buy any quantities of fresh milk or cream, or reliable salad vegetables; yet for more than 85 per cent of this time we would be cruising in tropical waters with passengers who would expect not only fresh milk and cream at every meal, but also crisp lettuce and firm tomatoes. Our chief catering officer and the chef put a lot of thought into solving this problem, and with strict control and refrigeration we got through without a single complaint.

Our route took us from New York down through the Panama Canal to Callao; then across the Pacific via Easter Island and Pitcairn Island—where brief stops were made to allow the natives to come on board the ship, although conditions were not suitable for our passengers to go ashore—and on to Suva. Between Fiji and New Zealand we called at Vauvau and Pago Pago. This involved crossing the international date line twice in the course of one week, so that we had no Monday, two Tuesdays and no Thursday. After a fairly extensive visit to ports in New Zealand and Australia, we passed through the Great Barrier Reef to Guadalcanal in the Solomon Islands and Port Moresby in New Guinea, then through the Torres Straits to Bali, Manila, Singapore, and Japan, where we were the first large cruising liner to arrive since the end of the war, and got a great reception, with bands, balloons and firecrackers. Then came another long trek back across the Pacific via Honolulu to Long Beach, and from there back to New York through the Panama Canal, with brief stops at Acapulco and Balboa.

The people who planned the cruise need not have worried about the long sea passages: our passengers used them as a chance to relax and settle down and seemed to enjoy them. What they should have worried about was that the ship was only air-conditioned in her public rooms. Between the Torres Straits and Bali, when we were cruising parallel to the Equator, and only between five and ten degrees south of it, in hot and humid weather with violent tropical rainstorms, it was difficult to get a good night's sleep. Yet, on the whole, this was one of the Caronia's most successful cruises, and perhaps the best testimonial to our passengers' enjoyment of the cruise came when, just before the end, the company announced the itinerary for the ship's world cruise in 1955. By the time we arrived in New York more than one hundred of our five hundred passengers had made their reservations for that cruise.

During the Pacific cruise, our visit to Melbourne coincided with that of Her Majesty the Queen and Prince Philip. Unfortunately, the port's tug boats were on strike, and Captain Williams had received orders from Liverpool not to attempt to enter the harbour without tugs, because of the very narrow channel. This meant that the ship had to anchor at the entrance to the channel, about three and a half miles from the town, in a completely unsheltered anchorage. It was like being out in the open sea and with unfavourable weather forecasts and a nasty sea running we tried to discourage our passengers from going ashore. But because of the royal visit everyone was keen to go, and once they had got into the launches the trip ashore proved quite pleasant, as they had the wind and sea behind them for the run in.

Normally, under conditions like these, I should never have gone ashore myself, but I had relatives living in Melbourne who had emigrated after the war, whom I had not seen for more than ten years, and I had written to them, inviting them to visit the ship that afternoon. The weather appeared to improve a little at about lunchtime, but it was still not good enough to allow visitors. So I was given permission to go ashore to visit them.

But I can't say I really enjoyed the visit, as I was listening all the time to the sound of the rising wind, and when we returned to the landing place my fears were confirmed. But there was nothing we could do now except wait until all our passengers returned and then make sure that we got them all into the six launches. Having made sure that everyone had embarked, I left in the last launch with the staff. We got everybody down into the two cabins, and the crew laced the canvas covers over. Although the coxswain kept his engine well throttled back, our trip out to the ship was like a ride on a crazy roller-coaster, and it took me back to those unhappy days at Ramsgate. There were people being sick all round me, but I did not feel too bad until we got out to the ship, with the waves breaking over the gangway and four of our launches waiting their turn to go alongside. The ship was yawing and tugging at her anchor cable, and it was only possible to get the passengers out of the boats when she swung far enough off the wind to give a temporary lee, so it took more than two hours to get them all back on board. We were the last boat to come in, and our coxswain had to stop and let the boat roll in the trough of the sea. Inevitably I was sick, which seemed to make everyone feel better.

Our Pacific cruise was followed by a spring cruise to the Mediterranean and the northern capitals and, just as we were leaving Lisbon on 29 May 1954, our agent came on board with a telegram from Cunard in Southampton which said: 'Inform Staff Captain Marr home damaged by lightning wife and family safe relief arranged at Dun Laoghaire.' As the ship was leaving for Glengariff a few minutes later there was nothing I could do but wait until we were out at sea and then book a radio telephone call to my home, but there was no reply.

When I was eventually able to contact my wife it was to learn that we were now homeless. Apparently some type of thunderbolt had struck our television aerial, and the electrical discharge had run around the electrical circuits of the house, setting the roof and the upper storey alight. By the time the fire brigade arrived the whole of the upper part of the house was almost gutted and, although they did manage to salvage things on the ground floor, they were nearly all either water or smoke damaged.

It was five days after the fire before I was able to get home. By this time my wife had found us a place to live, and had attended to many of the sordid details of dealing with the insurance company's assessors and so on, which have to follow such tragic events. But the roofless shell of what had been our home for sixteen years, and which had survived the wartime air raids with only minor damage, made a most depressing sight, and we both decided that even if it could be repaired, we could never live there again. So we started house-hunting, and before I had to join the Caronia again about three weeks later, we had found a new home and managed to choose a few bits of furniture together. However, it was nearly three months before the legal details were sorted out and my family were settled in our new house.

Fortunately, I now had quite a long spell of leave due, after which I returned to the Queen Mary as staff captain, much to my wife's delight. She always said that when I was sailing on the Queens it was like being married to a travelling salesman, who only came home every other weekend; but that when I had to go away on the Caronia it was like not being married to anyone at all.

It was during this tour of duty, on 17 November 1954 that Her Majesty Queen Elizabeth, the Queen Mother, joined the Queen Mary in New York for her journey home after her visit to the United States. She had made the westbound crossing three weeks before on board the Queen Elizabeth, the ship which she had sponsored and which had been commanded by Commodore Ivan Thompson, with Captain W E Law as staff captain. Then, as a compliment to Her Majesty, the company had decided that the commodore should transfer his flag to the Queen Mary for her homeward voyage. The decision had, however, created a difficult situation, because many of the Queen Mary's crew saw it as a slight to the ship's regular master, Captain Donald Sorrell, a man who was held in high regard by his ship's company.

For the five days Her Majesty was to spend on board the Queen Mary I was allowed to delegate many of my ordinary duties to the chief officer, leaving me free to act as the liaison officer with the royal party and to organize the details of what the Queen Mother wanted to do and arrange for her to meet those people she expressed the desire to meet. This turned out to be a wonderful experience although I was naturally a little apprehensive at first, having never done anything like it before. A special gangway had been arranged in New York so that Her Majesty could board at promenade deck level, clear of the main embarkation, which was taking place at the same time, and all the ship's senior officers were there to be introduced to her by the commodore. After this, the British ambassador took her along to the Verandah Grill, which had been turned into a television studio, with banks of klieg-lights and numerous cameras and microphones.

Following the official farewells, Her Majesty made a charming and gracious speech in which she thanked the American people for the warmth of their welcome, and said how very much at home they had made her feel. Then, after a long pause for the photographers and several of her characteristic little waves, she stepped down from the dais and said goodbye to the ambassador, who handed her over to Commodore Thompson and myself, and we escorted her down to her suite on the port side of the main deck.

Everyone who has ever met the Queen Mother for more than a few minutes remembers her wonderful ability to make those about her feel at ease, and I became aware of this even during the few minutes it took to reach her cabin.

Her household on this voyage consisted of Sir William Elliot, who was acting as her equerry, Oliver Dawney, her secretary, and two ladies-in-waiting, Lady Jean Rankin and Mrs Mullholland. After her busy time in the USA one would have expected that she would be rather tired and want to take things quietly; instead she appeared to be full of energy, and anxious to see as much of the ship as possible, and to watch the crew carrying out their various tasks. She also walked round some of the passenger decks, and she seemed to particularly enjoy meeting the mothers and children at our children's party.

On the second evening at sea she dined with Commodore Thompson at his table in the centre of the main restaurant, and it was a glittering occasion, with all the ladies present wearing their most lavish gowns, and Her Majesty looking very regal in a beautiful ball gown and magnificent jewels. But on three evenings of the voyage she dined with her household in the royal suite, because she is a keen cinema-goer and she wished to attend the 21.30 performance in the first class cinema. On each of these occasions I had to check with the operator the exact time that he would be starting the main feature as she did not want to see the cartoons or shorts. Five minutes before this time, I would tap on the door of the royal suite and say, 'This is the staff captain; we are ready now, ma'am'. Each night was like a command performance. As soon as the shorts finished, the operator would bring up the house lights, and the audience would stand as the royal party moved down to reserved seats on the centre aisle.

The highlight of the voyage for me was on Monday, 22 November, the night before we were due to pass the Bishop Rock light in the early hours of the morning, when I was invited to dine with Her Majesty. Sir William Elliot gave me the invitation, and said that he was arranging a table for ten in the Verandah Grill. In addition to myself and the members of the household there would be four other guests, Lord and Lady Knollys (he was at that time the chairman of Vickers) and an American couple, and I was to be at the royal suite for cocktails by 20.30.

After introductions, a martini, and a little general conversation, we moved to the Verandah Grill, where Lord Knollys was seated on Her Majesty's right and I on her left. We had a delightful meal, chosen by the Queen Mother, who was at the time very diet conscious, and she talked about the problems we must have, being always surrounded by so much rich food. The meal was served with all the flair and flourish our Verandah Grill manager and his staff could do so well, with a different wine for nearly every course. It was most enjoyable, and when the meal was finished the members of the household shepherded us back to the royal suite, where chairs had been arranged round the sitting room and coffee and liqueurs were served, and we settled down to a sort of family party which did not break up until nearly midnight.

The next morning—just before the ship's arrival at Cherbourg— the Commodore, myself and the rest of the heads of departments were invited in turn to a short private audience, during which Her Majesty thanked us all for what had been done to make her crossing so pleasant. She presented me with an autographed portrait in a leather frame bearing the royal cipher, and also with a silver cigarette box for my wife with the cipher in gold.

The Queen Mary was due to dock at Southampton at 21.00 that evening, and during my private audience the Queen Mother had said that she would like to be on the bridge to watch the ship coming to her berth. So, being freed from my normal duties, I had arranged to collect her at 20.30. It was a fine, clear, but rather cool evening, with the brilliant lights of the Ocean Terminal reflected in the calm water, as Her Majesty and I stood on the port side of the bridge, to keep clear of the commodore and the pilot, who were bringing the ship in, and I explained what the various tugs were doing and the meaning of the signals that were being given as the hauling lines were sent ashore and then carried up the quay by the shore gangs.

The official ceremonies next morning were very brief and then with another little wave she was gone, and I came back to earth and my normal duties with a bit of a bump.

In that same year (1954) which saw the Queen Mother on board, we also carried the beautiful and elegant Duchess of Kent, whose husband had been so tragically killed in a plane accident during the war. She was a lovely figure with a penetrating gaze and a most beautiful voice. Her daughter, Princess Alexandra, was with her, a young girl with her mother's low, sweet voice. Beautiful, amusing, and at this particular moment highly delighted with a brand new camera she had been given, she charmed the whole ship. I find it hard to understand, in these days, when the climate of public opinion has changed in so many ways, how those who question the need for a royal family can imagine that there would be any benefit to be gained by our having a president instead. We, as a country, are the richer for a family which can produce such warm and human people.

The Duke and Duchess of Windsor also travelled regularly in the Queens in those days, and although we never saw much of his wife, the Duke always liked to come onto the bridge for a few minutes before going to bed. He seemed to be happy in the quiet male atmosphere on the bridge of an ocean liner in the middle of the night.

Sir Anthony Eden, when prime minister and already not a well man, and his foreign secretary, Selwyn Lloyd, travelled with us in 1956, and as staff captain I had several encounters with him, and found him a gentle sort of person, genuine, and what one would call a good man. It was a pleasure to converse with him, and when later on in his career he came upon Suez and the incomprehensibility of it all, I always felt he was too good a man to be able to cope with the other figures in the drama. One must be a little devious oneself to be able to understand a devious situation, and it is a devious world we have to live in.

CHAPTER TEN

In command

My tour of duty as staff captain of the Queens was by no means over and I was to wait another two and a half years before getting a ship of my own. But during the spring and summer of 1955 I did get a break by doing voyages as relieving captain on the Franconia, Ascania, Parthia and Samaria.

My voyage on the Franconia was not to be a very long one; the ship was caught by an unofficial seamen's strike, her sailing had to be cancelled and all I was called upon to do was shift berth a couple of times around Southampton Docks. This meant that I made my first voyage in command of a passenger liner on the small (14,000 ton) RMS Ascania, affectionately known to her crew as the Ash Can. It was an early spring voyage from Liverpool to Montreal, a good baptism of fire for any newly fledged captain, because the ice was only just breaking up in the St Lawrence and navigation was far from easy. Also, she was rapidly coming to the end of her days, and her top speed in fine weather was down to about 14 knots. Yet she was a very happy ship, and her crew and the passengers all seemed to enjoy her.

In April 1957 I took over the command of RMS Scythia. She was over 20,000 tons, more than 600 feet in length, and to me, as the first ship I had commanded of my own, a thing of beauty. Built in Liverpool in 1921, the Scythia was the first of a new class of five ships with which the Cunard directors of that day hoped to make the company's fortune during the post First World War boom period. They were designed to carry a large number of passengers and cargo, at a speed of 16 knots, on a fairly low fuel consumption. They were good, steady plodders, capable of maintaining a monthly service between Liverpool and New York in competition with the White Star Line's Big Four, the Cedric, Celtic, Baltic and Adriatic. But most people thought that they were out of date before they left the builder's yard, because by this time the travelling public were showing interest in speed on the Atlantic service and the Germans were building the Bremen and Europa.

While in command of the Scythia I had to send the ship's lifeboats away twice on errands of mercy, not an easy thing to do on a ship of her great age, fitted as she was with old-fashioned radial davits, rope falls and electric winches which could be extremely temperamental. On the first occasion we were outward bound to New York when we received a radio request for medical assistance from a freighter of the Luckenback Line which had a sick captain. We arranged to rendezvous with him at first light, which would be at around 04.00. As the dawn broke, I was delighted to see that although there was a rather heavy swell it was a lovely morning, with no wind. Having sent a message to the chief officer of the freighter asking him to stop his ship, I was able to close to between half and a quarter of a mile from her before dropping my boat. But after the big, heavy, clinker-built wooden lifeboat was in the water, pulled by eight seamen and with Dr H D Smith and his little black bag in the stern, the freighter started to go ahead on her engines, presumably to provide a better lee for the boat to come alongside in the swell. Every time the lifeboat started to climb one of those long swells, it seemed to lose ground, and at times the bow would come right out of the water, causing the bow oarsmen to catch crabs. They must have made progress eventually, because slowly and painfully the gap closed, and after more than an hour of back-breaking work the boat was at last close enough to catch a line thrown from the stern of the freighter.

She was hauled alongside and Dr Smith climbed on board. His diagnosis was that the captain would have to leave his ship and return with us to New York. But apparently the captain was reluctant to do this, so it took time to persuade him and more time for him to hand over to his chief officer the cash, the accounts and all the other papers. The precious minutes continued to tick away, and our chances of arriving in New York at our scheduled time were looking pretty dim; but after a wait of about eighty minutes we eventually saw that the boat was alongside again, and a man was being lowered into it in a stretcher. Calling on the Morse light, we asked the freighter to tell our boat to stay where it was, and then to steam away herself and allow the Scythia to come around in a big circle and pick up the boat. But by the time we had done this and the boat had been safely rehoisted, it was 08.00 and four hours had been lost. The ship had no reserve of speed, so instead of docking at 17.00 as we had expected, we could not now arrive before 21.00. This meant we had to offer our passengers the option of remaining on board overnight and involve the company in a big overtime bill for stevedores and customs and immigration officials.

There is an international code of the sea which requires ships which carry doctors to answer radio requests for medical assistance, even though at times they may have to steam many miles off course in order to do so. This often leaves the ship master who receives one of these calls in rather a quandary because he knows that answering it may involve the owners in unrecoverable additional costs running into thousands of pounds, as it did on this occasion.

My other sea rescue came later in the summer, while we were homeward bound from New York. The morning after sailing the purser mentioned that a man had called at his office and asked to see me. I naturally asked why he or one of his staff could not deal with the matter. But the purser said that the man seemed rather odd and had insisted on speaking to me, so I agreed to see him. At about 11.15 there was a knock at my door and a rather stocky middle-aged man who spoke with a northern accent was introduced to me by the purser. I asked both of them to come in and sit down, but the man said that he must see me alone. Without any preamble, the man, who appeared to be in a nervous state, burst out: 'Lock me up, Captain!' Then he added: 'If you don't, I'll go over the the side.' This really took me aback. Here was a situation I had never met before, and I had no idea how to deal with it. I asked him if he had seen the ship's doctor. When he said that he hadn't I reached for my telephone and asked the doctor to come to my cabin at once. A young and very able man, who was filling in time at sea while waiting for a practice, he came bounding up the stairs to my room and together we extracted the man's history from him. It seemed that while he was serving with the British army in Germany after the war he had married a German girl whose parents were now living in America. He had brought his wife and their two children over to visit her parents and she had refused to return to England with him. Seeing that he was in a disturbed state, the doctor took him down to the hospital and gave him a sedative, and, about half an hour later, called me to say that the man seemed calmer, but he had decided to keep him under observation in the isolation hospital for a couple of days.

The weather was hot and sultry and just before 20.00 this man, who had slept most of the afternoon but had behaved normally and appeared to enjoy his evening meal, complained about the heat and asked if he could go out on deck for a breath of fresh air. His request seemed reasonable, so the sick berth attendant opened the door and went out on deck with him. Suddenly the man gave him a push which sent him flying, then rushed to the ship's side and jumped overboard, close to the stern. Picking himself up, the sick berth attendant grabbed a circular lifebuoy, with a self-igniting flare attached, and managed to fling it over the side so that it landed in the water quite close to the man, who had now evidently decided he did not want to die just yet, for he swam over and clung to it. At this moment I was just leaving my cabin to go down to dinner, but when I heard the jangle of the telegraphs reporting the man overboard I leapt up the single flight of stairs to the bridge, where I found the chief officer blowing the signal for 'Away seaboat's crew' on the ship's distinctive organ whistle, which on a still night like this could be heard all over the ship. This brought up not only the seaboat's crew, but also the bosun and every available man at the double. Then the doctor came dashing up to the bridge, and was sent with the seaboat's crew to go after him. By this time the commotion had completely emptied the dining rooms, and within a few minutes most of our 800 passengers were lining the ship's rails. The chief officer had already passed word to the engine room that this was an emergency, and we were very fortunate, because it was the change of the watch; so there were two watches of engine room staff down below and the senior second engineer managed to get steam on the astern turbines in double-quick time.

The sun had just set but there was still plenty of light in the afterglow and using an Aldis lamp we managed to contact an American destroyer six miles away who replied that she was coming to our assistance. In the meantime, as I watched the ship coming round in a mile-wide circle under full rudder and the seaboat was being slowly lowered to just above the water's edge, with much shaking and creaking as the rope falls were paid out round the stag horns and through the elderly blocks, my mind went back to Captain Guy Willoughby and that day off the North Cape during the war, and I wondered if I could possibly bring my ship round as close to the man in the water as he had done. Thanks to the chief officer's prompt and efficient action and to the splendid response we had from the engineers below, and helped by the favourable weather conditions, we may have got almost as close, but our big cumbersome boats with their heavy wooden blocks took a long time to unhook and to hook on again. Within a few minutes there was a tremendous cheer from passengers and crew alike as the boat with the doctor and his patient in it came slowly clear of the water and flash bulbs went off in all directions. We were then able to flash to the destroyer, still about a mile away, that our man had been recovered and no further assistance was required. By 20.30 I felt that the seaboat was sufficiently well secured to order the engine room telegraphs back to 'Full ahead' and bring the ship back to her course again. I felt extremely proud of my ship's company that night; the whole operation had taken less than half an hour, and after many painful experiences of boat drills in harbour, using our rather antiquated equipment, I would have been prepared to swear that it could not have been done in that time.

Our friend, apparently none the worse for his dip on a warm summer evening, was back in the ship's hospital, where he remained under double guard until we reached port and he was handed over to the duly authorized officer. He gave no further trouble and according to the doctor seemed quite rational, so I have often wondered if he thought his action might be reported in the press and serve to arouse his wife's sympathy.

The last three months of the Scythia's active life were spent under charter to the Canadian government, taking part in what they called 'brigade rotation'. This meant making two round trips between Quebec and Rotterdam, and a final trip from Halifax to Rotterdam and then back to Southampton. Carrying troops and their wives and families was different from our usual passenger service in many ways, and provided some unusual problems, one of which was how to assess in monetary terms the service that members of the catering department render to people travelling. In lieu of the tips they would normally get from passengers, on each voyage the Canadian government allocated a lump sum to the ship to be distributed as gratuities and we then had to try and divide up fairly. We never did manage to satisfy everybody. On one voyage, when the ship carried seven hundred women and children and only twenty-five men, we had a rough crossing, with a great many people seasick, and the main burden had fallen on the stewardesses; so I agreed with the chief steward's suggestion that they deserved the larger share of the gratuities. But a couple of hours after the crew bar opened that night, a very angry delegation arrived outside my cabin saying that the men of the Scythia would be the joke in all the pubs in Bootle once it was known that the women were paid more than they were. So we had to persuade the ladies, in the interests of social harmony, to be content with an equal share after all.

On the ship's final voyage from Halifax in December 1957 we had a very easy schedule, calling for an average speed of less than 12 knots, which, by the time we got half way, was down to 10 knots because a large anti-cyclone covering the Atlantic was giving quiet settled weather. We had managed to keep the ship looking well, though her active life was almost over, apart from our very prominent funnel. This had not been painted for more than six months and was streaky, so the bosun suggested that we might paint the funnel at sea. The chief officer approached me about this because the normal Cunard practice was to paint the funnel in port; however, because of the exceptionally fine weather I agreed that they could rig the stages and give it a coat the following day. This was done and it made a great difference to the ship's appearance, but apparently some of the sailors were not too happy about having to do the work. As they were finishing off the bottom fleets one of the soldiers asked: 'What the hell are you doing that for? The ship is going to be scrapped when she gets home, isn't she?' To which he got the reply 'I suppose it's the bloody captain! He wants to take her back the way he got her!'

The ship was up for sale, and by the middle of January had been sold for breaking up, so on the 18 January 1958, after thirty-seven years of faithful service in war and peace, the first ship of her class and the last to survive sailed from Southampton on her last sad voyage to Inverkeithing. We had all our regular officers, but the bulk of the crew was 'run crew', a scratch crew just engaged for the short trip round the coast. There was one very notable exception, the engine room storekeeper, who had joined the ship in the shipyard before her maiden voyage and had sailed with her on every voyage she made in peace and war for thirty-seven years (except for two voyages during the General Strike in 1926) and had asked to be allowed to stay with her until she reached the breaker's yard. After this he said he was going to retire, because he didn't feel he could get used to another ship.

Our voyage through a cold and wintry North Sea was uneventful and the ship behaved like the perfect lady that she was right up to the very end; even during the run up the long narrow channel to her final berth, alongside the half burned-down remains of her sister ship, the Franconia. I was asked what I would like as a souvenir, so I asked for the clock and barometer out of the captain's cabin.

Taking a last look at the ship from the train windows as we crossed the Forth Bridge on our way south, it was sad to see her sitting there looking so neat and trim among all those burned-down hulks, and to know that she was just waiting for someone to put a torch to her. Perhaps this is the logical end for ships: they begin in the furnace and end in the furnace.

CHAPTER ELEVEN

Alarms and excursions

In May 1958 I joined the then fairly new RMS Ivernia to start a spell of commanding ships on the Cunard Canadian service. It was to last nearly four years, apart from a break on the Liverpool-New York service in RMS Parthia. For sheer strain on the captain's nerves while navigating for so much of the time in fog, with so often the additional hazard of ice, the St Lawrence trade ranks among the toughest in the world. But for most Cunard captains it was just an unpleasant interlude between spells on the New York service or cruising, so I have always felt the greatest admiration, and sympathy, for captains in the Canadian Pacific or Manchester Liners, who spent most of their working lives on this trade and appeared to take it in their stride.

The Ivernia had been the second ship of the new class of 20,000-ton passenger/cargo liners which Cunard had just finished building. She was an attractive looking ship and she handled very well, but like her sisters she was a ship built without taking sufficient account of future demands for passenger comfort. She was not fully air-conditioned, she had very few tourist class cabins with facilities, and she was quite unsuitable for cruising. Yet with their accommodation for about 100 first class and 900 tourist passengers these ships were to enjoy a reasonable amount of prosperity for another five or six years, due to the continuing wave of immigration to Canada from Britain and the Continent. When people are moving their homes from one part of the world to another they still refuse to be impressed by the obvious advantages of air travel. If they intend to spend the rest of their lives in a place, they are not so interested in how quickly they can get there as in the amount of baggage they can take. So sea travel, with its unrestricted baggage allowance, still has many attractions.

As far as I was concerned, the great joy of serving in the Ivernia was that her home port was Southampton, and in those far-off days when ships did not turn round quite as quickly as they do today this meant that I had four clear days at home out of each three-week voyage.

Unfortunately, this was too good to last and in October 1958 I was sailing out of Liverpool once again, on the little Parthia in which I had done a relieving voyage three years before. The two smallest units in the Cunard passenger fleet, the Parthia and Media, had been designed as large cargo liners. They were being built for one of Cunard's associated companies, T & J Brocklebank, during that period after the war when the government were suggesting to various shipping companies that the tonnage of ships on order should be proportionate to the tonnage which they had lost through enemy action. After Cunard had taken them over on the stocks as a result of a book transaction, their design was altered and passenger accommodation for 250 passengers added, which gave them a rather dumpy appearance. Before they were fitted with stabilizers they also had had a most uncomfortable roll in a following sea, and another bad feature of their design was that all their cabins were fitted as three-berth rooms, which were never popular with the travelling public. So in spite of the fact that their full complement of passengers was officially 250, these ships seldom sailed with more than 200, even at the height of the season. But these 200 were all first class passengers and had the full run of the ship. Both were very friendly and happy ships, so during the sixteen years they ran for Cunard they built up a large following of loyal and devoted regular travellers, who looked upon them as the ideal way to cross the North Atlantic. Even during the winter crossings, when we could have as few as thirty passengers on the Parthia, our young and very enthusiastic purser, Ken Allen, managed to create such a family party atmosphere on board that by the end of the voyage everyone felt like old friends. Another feature of these ships which made them popular with their crews was that they shared with the Britannic that easy monthly round-voyage schedule whereby each ship spent a week in Liverpool followed by a week at sea, homeward bound, leaving a reasonable amount of time for the men to spend with their families.

Joining the Carinthia on 1 July 1959, although a promotion for me, also brought one back to the grim realities of the Canadian trade again, and this time on a ship whose home port was Liverpool. This meant that on top of all the difficulties of the St Lawrence each voyage began and ended with the hazards of getting in and out of Huskisson Dock through the Sandon Basin, which because of the size of these ships was seldom accomplished without putting another dent in the hull somewhere, and then making out the inevitable damage reports. Docking was followed by a long and often tortuous railway journey to Southampton. Then, after sometimes as little as thirty-six hours in my home, I had to repeat the journey in the opposite direction before starting off on another voyage.

The Carinthia was a younger sister of the Ivernia and, as each successive ship of a class usually incorporates improvements, she was a better ship in several ways. During the three years I was in command of her I became very attached to her.

However, although our passenger numbers continued to be good, during the summer of the following year, 1960, a definite feeling of unrest among our junior ratings became evident, which was being cleverly exploited by the militant Canadian seamen's union. Having by their excessive demands driven nearly all the Canadian flag foreign-going ships off the seas, these men now wanted to do the same for British flag ships. Going ashore in Montreal one frequently had to pass men carrying placards saying 'All officers are SCABS'. When we got back home, tensions were increased by the activity of the Seamen's Reform Movement, a Liverpool-based splinter-group exploiting the feeling that the NUS (still led by Sir Thomas Yates) were dragging their feet in their negotiations with the owners and that seamen were being allowed to fall behind in the scramble for higher wages.

The volcano did not finally erupt until 5 July 1960, although there had been preliminary rumblings on 22 June, while the Carinthia was making an overnight passage from Quebec to Montreal. At about 01.30 a band of young men who called themselves the ship's 'skiffle group' had been performing on the after mooring deck,

which is a crew recreation deck, but passengers in cabins further
forward on the same deck complained that the noise was excessive
and was preventing them from sleeping. So a junior catering officer
went along and told the men that they would have to quiet down,
but one of the group, to the evident amusement of his audience,
is alleged to have said: 'This is our deck, so you can go and get
stuffed!' This was reported to the senior officer of the watch, who
sent his junior officer to deal with the situation, and who also
arranged for the bosun's mate to take his gang along and wash
down the after mooring deck as a diversionary operation. The
arrival of an officer from the bridge evidently impressed all concerned that the matter was serious, and the group dispersed before
the wash-down gang arrived.

Next morning, five rather untidy individuals, members of the
skiffle group, were brought before me on the charge of having
used insulting language to an officer, which they all denied. I had
spent all night on the bridge coming up the river and was feeling
overtired, so I probably overreacted to this, for first I gave them all
a good dressing-down and told them that I would not have my
officers insulted when they were only carrying out their duty, and
that any officer when on duty was acting as the captain's personal
representative. I also said I should fine them all one day's pay and
on the ship's return to Liverpool they would be paid off and given
a bad discharge (a G for conduct, instead of the normal VG). The
following day the group complained that the punishment they had
been given was excessive, as they had not realized they were doing
wrong, and had dispersed when spoken to. I then agreed that,
provided they gave no more trouble on the homeward voyage and
I received a good report on their behaviour from the chief steward,
I would rescind the bad discharge; but, because I believed they had
been unnecessarily rude to the catering officer, the fines would
stand.

We were due to sail at 11.00 the following morning, but at 06.00
the fire gongs rang throughout the ship, for a fire in the cinema, our
largest public room. When the fire party reached it they found that
the heavy velvet curtains covering the screen had been soaked with
petrol and set alight, and that the flames had spread to the cinemascope screen before they could be put out by the sprinkler system.

There was some confusion in finding the correct control valve, and by the time the water had been turned off not only were the cinema carpets awash, but because the ship had a slight list four of the adjoining first class cabins were flooded. All the ship's seamen and a large number of catering ratings turned out to clear up the mess; but, while they were doing this, just before 06.30, the fire alarms sounded again for another fire, in Cabin A178 at the after end of the ship. Here again the sprinkler system had effectively put the fire out, but not before the bedding on one bed had been burnt and some smoke damage done.

This fire, like the one in the cinema, was obviously the work of an arsonist. Thanks to the efficiency of the sprinkler system, we had not needed to ask for any assistance from the local fire department, so nobody outside the ship except the company's officials—who had been informed by telephone—knew about the fires. They would have been very bad publicity and would have caused concern among the passengers joining the ship had they been reported by the local news media. With more than 900 passengers due to start embarkation in less than three hours' time, a hurried conference was held to see what could be done to ensure that as few as possible were aware of the situation. Our biggest problem was to try and get hold of a new cinemascope screen at such short notice. All hands set to and tackled the job with energy and enthusiasm; the velvet curtains were taken down, and the electricians dried the amplifiers and other equipment behind the screen, while another gang took up the water-sodden carpets from the cinema and adjoining cabins and stowed them in the hold. Fortunately there was linoleum underneath, so we could manage without them in the cinema, while various officers gave up the carpets from their rooms to replace those in the first class cabins. In Cabin A178 the joiners quickly replaced the charred woodwork, the seamen repainted it, the catering department supplied new soft furnishings, and the room was ready for occupation before embarkation commenced. The cinema had to be kept locked during embarkation, but after a number of phone calls our marine superintendent managed to locate a screen, which he brought down in his car at 10.30, together with yards of black hessian for masking it. After this, we all breathed a little easier. The joiner did a thoroughly professional job of fitting the screen and fixing the new black surround, so nobody seemed to miss the big curtains, and we were able to give our first cinema show at 16.30 that evening, the time shown on the programme of events, which had been printed the previous day. A very creditable performance by all concerned.

Together with my officers, I listened for any mention of fires by passengers because so often crew members like to pass bits of information on to them; but, so far as I know our secret was kept.

Naturally I was worried throughout the crossing in case there might be another outbreak of arson, but all went well and I withdrew the bad discharges against the five men. But feeling that they might be a bad influence, and could possibly have had something to do with the fires, when we got to Liverpool I asked that they be taken out of the ship.

When I returned to the ship on 4 July 1960, ready to start the next voyage, everything was normal on the surface, but I had a feeling that trouble was near. Preparations for sailing went ahead as usual, and on our sailing morning, 6 July, we managed to get from the Huskisson Dock into the Sandon Basin, but the wind was too strong to allow us to take her out through the Sandon locks into the river. Arrangements were made for our passengers to join the ship in Sandon Basin instead of at the Princes landing stage, but this had often happened before, and it was a fairly routine operation for passengers and baggage arriving on the special train from London to be brought down to the docks in chartered coaches.

Apparently a crew walk-off began as soon as the embarkation was completed, but had originally been planned to take place at the Princes landing stage, where it would have been much more in the public eye. I was told that the men were refusing to sail unless all the skiffle group were reinstated. Shortly after this the union delegate arrived in my cabin and told me that Mr P Furness, our general manager, had agreed that the five men could sign on the ship again provided the master assented. To avoid being the cause of a strike I agreed that the men could re-sign right away, but, as I still feared they might be a bad influence, they would be carefully watched, and dealt with if they gave any further trouble. When the union delegate went down on the dockside, where the men were all clustered round the foot of the gangway, and announced that I had agreed to take the five men back, he was greeted with jeers and catcalls, and demands for £10 more a month and a forty-hour week. Then, after agreeing by a show of hands to attend another meeting at 08.00 the next morning, they all dispersed.

All this had taken some time, but shortly after the men started to walk off it had become obvious that we were not going to be able to sail on that evening's tide, so the tugs had been dismissed and the sailing officially postponed until the next morning. In the meantime our passengers were being looked after by members of the female staff and a small group of volunteers, supplemented later by office personnel.

Then, surprisingly, T Laird, our assistant general manager, called a press conference in my cabin. This was such a departure from normal company practice, which was for happenings like this to be covered by a press release issued from the office of our publicity manager, that I was quite taken aback, and not sure what line the company would want me to take. However, without mentioning the sabotage attempt in Montreal, I simply told them the sequence of events, much as I have set it down here, and in their published reports they were remarkably kind to me, as they have been throughout my career at sea.

The walk-off was quite unofficial, and the union delegates would have nothing to do with their men's latest demands, as negotiations were at that time taking place in London between the NUS and the owners' representatives for a new wages and hours agreement. But at 08.00 the next morning Mr Laird and I decided to make a final effort to persuade the men to return and take the ship to sea. A large group had gathered near the ship's bows so I climbed up on the top of a bollard and tried to talk to them. As there was a BBC camera crew there most of my speech appeared on the Northern news that evening. As far as I can remember I said something like this:

Gentlemen, I have come down here this morning to talk to you not as your captain, but as a fellow member of a trades union, because I firmly believe that the men of the Merchant Navy have just as strong a case for an upward revision of their wages as the railwaymen. Also, I am convinced that we have a great deal of public sympathy for our cause. But I am equally sure that the British public is getting sick and tired of bad trade union discipline, and of groups of hotheads who do what you are proposing to do and take unofficial action against the advice of their union. Why don't you decide to come back on board and take the ship to sea? Before we get back home at the end of this voyage, a new agreement will probably have been worked out.

Although the attitude of the crowd was distinctly hostile and rude remarks were being shouted from the back of the crowd, I struggled on a little longer and then said: 'No employers are ever going to carry on with negotiations under duress, so by striking now you will probably hold up the talks which have already started.' But by now they were talking among themselves, so I climbed down to let Mr Laird have a try. They would not even give him a hearing, so we decided we were wasting our time and returned on board. By this time the number of volunteers, mostly bedroom stewards and other senior ratings, who had remained on board to take care of our passengers, was dwindling fast, so we were forced to cancel the voyage and let the passenger department find alternative ways for our passengers to reach their destination. After thirty-six hours everyone had left, and the ship was moved out of Sandon Basin and back to Huskisson Dock. All we could do was wait for the strike to end. As we had only a small fire party made up of members of the shore gang, it was decided that the captain and all officers must remain on board for security reasons. At the end of three weeks, after a second voyage had to be cancelled, I was due for leave, and found my home a delightful change from looking at the bomb-damaged buildings around Huskisson Dock.

At the end of three weeks I returned to find that the unofficial strike, which although it had spread to other ships in the port was still mainly confined to Merseyside, was showing signs of weakening. But it had been extremely bitter, and the stories of intimidation, especially of the treatment of the wives and families of men who had remained loyal to the company, were horrifying. However, both Cunard and the NUS felt that if an all-out effort could lead to the sailing of the Carinthia, the ship which had started the trouble, the strike would collapse. In a burst of activity, telephone calls were made all over the country, seamen were collected from places as far afield as Aberdeen and Plymouth, and a verbal pistol was held at the heads of some of the senior members of the kitchen staff of the Britannic, which had now returned from New York after being held up there for two months with engine trouble. Since that ship was on her way to the breakers, they could choose between sailing with us or being made redundant. Then a large number of young men, called 'commis' waiters, were collected from training establishments and other ships of the fleet, and it was hoped that these, together with a few loyal bedroom stewards, and the female staff, who, as in all other unofficial strikes, had remained loyal, would enable us to get by on the catering side. Down below, the boiler rooms would be manned with very junior engineer officers who had either been at home on leave or studying for their certificates.

It was now felt that we had an adequate crew to handle the ship, take care of the cooking, look after the cleaning of the cabins, and wait on the 100 first class passengers. But we could provide little or no service in the restaurant for our 800 passengers travelling in the tourist class. After all the passengers had embarked but before the ship sailed, at the request of the general manager, I asked as many tourist class passengers as possible to meet me in their lounge, where I made the following speech:

Ladies and Gentlemen, As many of you already know, the Carinthia will be sailing early tomorrow morning for Canada under very unusual circumstances, due to the unofficial seamen's strike. We have a sufficient crew to sail the ship and take you to Canada, a place which you might find it difficult to reach by any other means, because this is the peak of the holiday season and as far as I know all ships and planes crossing the North Atlantic are fully booked. Unfortunately our crew is not large enough to allow us to offer you the standard of service you would normally expect when you travel Cunard. I have therefore been asked by our general manager to apologize to you on his behalf and to offer you two alternatives: (a) If a large enough number of the younger members of your group are prepared to volunteer to act as waiters or waitresses during the crossing, they will be paid full National Maritime Board wages, plus any overtime they work, and with their assistance, we shall try to serve meals at the usual times in the normal way. Or (b) if we cannot get sufficient volunteers, all we can offer you is a kind of cafeteria messing. In this case we shall ask all heads of families to collect the food for their family from the kitchen, then take it to their table and serve it. But under this system the meals will have to be spread over a longer period to allow time for us to clear the tables and re-lay them.

I then thanked them for their attention and said: 'Our chief steward and his staff are waiting now to meet anyone who is willing to help, and to brief them on their duties.' As I left the room I got a rather half-hearted round of applause, but about seventy people offered to help which was much better than we expected and more than we really needed. But we had not reckoned on the weather we were going to meet on this crossing, which was so bad at times that we began to wonder if the clerk of the weather was on the side of the strikers.

As we left the River Mersey on 8 September the black cones were hoisted for southerly gales expected shortly, and the weather reports spoke of a rapidly deepening depression to the south of Iceland, moving east. However, at first things went remarkably well. Breakfast, which is always a lightly attended meal, was served while we were in smooth water, and lunch time found the ship still under the shelter of the Irish coast. So the chief steward reported that, although there had been a certain amount of confusion as our volunteers tried to find their way around, while getting in one another's way, they were all full of enthusiasm, and he was sure they would soon settle down. During that afternoon, as we steamed along the north coast of Ireland, the wind and sea were steadily rising, while our barometer fell like a stone. But it was not until we passed Inishtrahull at 17.00 that we felt the full impact of a Force 8 gale, with a tumbling sea superimposed on a heavy westerly swell. By any standards the ship became damned uncomfortable, and nothing we could do by altering course or speed seemed to make her any better, so when the time came to serve dinner the number of volunteers who could still stand on their feet had dwindled to less than twenty. For the same reason the number of passengers who were showing any interest in food had been reduced by an even greater percentage.

Because of the weather I did not go down to the restaurant myself that evening: I was quite happy with a cup of coffee and a sandwich on the bridge. But at 19.30 the chief steward came up to let me know the situation, and thought it was one that had to be seen to be believed. So I went down with him to the brightly lighted kitchens, where one young student had been given the job of scraping the uneaten food from the plates into a large bin called a rosey. He was hanging on as best he could, considering the ship's violent motion, and bravely carrying on with his job; but stopping every few minutes to retch over the vile looking mess. What utter chaos. So much greasy food had been spilt on the decks, it was almost impossible to stand without holding on to something. But by far our biggest problem was the almost continuous crash of breaking crockery or glasswear as our untrained helpers left piles of plates or trays of glasses balanced precariously, from which the ship's next lurch dislodged them. It was a scene I was very glad to leave behind, as I was not quite sure just how long I could have stayed down there without being seasick myself.

By the next morning the storm had passed and the ship was riding more comfortably, but during that one crossing we were to meet two other major storm centres, including the dying remnants of Hurricane Dora, before we reached Belle Isle. Reduced speed in the heavy seas had delayed us more than twenty-four hours. Most people gradually found their sea legs, and after the first couple of days the service steadily improved, though the breakages continued to be heavy and before the end of the voyage we were reduced to serving drinks in paper cups in tourist class.

To show our appreciation of the way these young volunteers had stuck to their jobs and adapted themselves to their strange tasks on a particularly uncomfortable voyage, we gave a special cocktail party for them the night before we reached Quebec. But the party went almost too well, and some of them got so much into the party spirit that they did not get down to the restaurant until very late, and the service was worse that night than it had been since we left the Irish coast!

On the homeward crossing our passenger numbers were low, and with our catering department bolstered by men transferred from other company ships, which also supplemented our supplies of crockery and glassware, life on board slowly came back to normal. By the time we docked in Liverpool the strike had collapsed, so our temporary crew signed off and many of the old hands returned. But the bitterness engendered by it among the men who had been out for nine weeks, and got nothing for it, was to linger on for months.

Towards the end of that year the Carinthia was chartered by the Canadian government for another brigade rotation, similar to the one I had done on the old Scythia three years before, and we sailed on 15 November 1960 on a voyage that was to keep us away from home until after Christmas. These trooping voyages were never as popular with the crew as our normal service: all the pent-up rancour left behind by the strike seemed to come to a head. Out of my total crew of 470, there were, apart from the officers, just twelve ratings who had remained loyal to the company and carried on working through the unofficial strike. To the more militant of the strikers they were all 'scabs', and during the coming weeks they were to suffer from a campaign of victimization which almost broke their nerve, and which neither I nor my officers could do anything to prevent.

One of the men concerned was a grill cook, a big powerful man who had been a boxer in his youth, but occasionally, when he was working at his grill, two junior kitchen ratings would come and stand a few feet away from him with their arms folded and say, 'We are just looking at a scab.' If he complained to one of the catering officers and the men were chased away, two more would come along, until the man's nerves were on edge. If any of the twelve went into the crew bar (always called the Pig and Whistle) they were soon made aware that they were not welcome. Men would edge over and flick cigarette ash into their beer, and say, 'Drink that, it's good enough for scabs.' Naturally they stopped using the bar, so the men developed another trick, which was to find out where these men slept; then late at night they would empty a bucket of water over one of them while he was in his bunk.

The first part of this voyage was a normal sailing to Montreal with passengers and cargo, but as soon as we had finished discharging we were sent down to Quebec, where we waited for five days for our first contingent of troops and their families to arrive. I was worried about this, because Quebec in late November can be a pretty desolate spot, and boredom could lead to violence. So I was not surprised on the morning of 29 November, the day we were due to sail, to get a report that there had been a fight in one of the stewards' gloryholes. But I wasn't prepared for the sight I saw when the doctor asked me to come to the ship's hospital and see one of our loyal ratings, a young Cypriot waiter, whose face had been badly battered with the heel of a shoe, and whose left eye was so seriously damaged that he might lose the sight of it. I asked him if he knew who had done it and through his swathe of bandages he whispered, 'Yes, sir, Cook, the kitchen porter.' I knew at once who he meant, and although Cook was not his name, it will serve for the purpose of this story to hide the identity of that tough, arrogant character, who as a kitchen porter was at the bottom end of the catering department, doing all the unskilled and unpleasant work in the galley, such as handling bulk stores and general cleaning.

I asked the chief steward and the chef to investigate the incident, and after interviewing Cook they reported that he was very cocky about the whole thing because there were no witnesses. There seemed no point in my seeing him in his present frame of mind, so after discussing the matter with our marine superintendent, I decided to telephone the Quebec City Police. I reported the incident and asked them to come and arrest Cook, as I felt he was the type who might crack under official investigation. With a scream of sirens a couple of police cars drew up alongside the gangway, two burly policemen came on board, and his astonished mates saw their insolent friend marched off to jail. This soon started rumblings on the mess decks, and after lunch the chief steward reported that he had heard that the whole of his department intended to walk ashore at 17.00 if Cook was not back on board by that time. As this was just the time the special train was due to bring our 700 passengers, most of whom were women and children, it could have been a difficult situation. But, at about 14.00 the police telephoned to say their prisoner had made a full confession, and they wanted to know if the injured man would proceed with the charge of inflicting bodily harm.

This presented a problem and could have landed the company in heavy expenses, because they would have been responsible for the cost of repatriating both men to England. So after finding out that the sick man wanted to stay on board and go home in the ship, I asked the police to bring Cook back on board. I would investigate the case and stand it over for legal action in England. By the time they brought him back, a lot of the fight had gone out of him, and when I charged him his defence was that the fight was fair and that he hadn't started it. The Cypriot's statement said that Cook had tripped him up as he was walking along the alleyway and dragged him into his cabin, where, with four or five other men watching, he had sat on his chest and smashed his face with the heel of shoe. This I submitted to the company's solicitors.

The injured man remained in hospital until the ship reached Rotterdam, when he was flown home to England for further treatment for his damaged eye. But I was advised by the solicitors that in a case like this legal proceedings can only be instituted by the injured party. As the Cypriot did not seem anxious to do this, and I did not want to keep Cook in the ship, there was nothing I could do but execute summary justice, and fine him one day's pay. I could also give him a DR for conduct (Decline to Report) in his seaman's discharge book, which would make it very difficult for him to get another job at sea. This did not seem like fair retribution to me, but the law is the law, even though it does not always result in justice being seen to be done.

We completed our trooping contract by carrying another load of Canadian troops and their dependents from Rotterdam to Halifax, Nova Scotia, where we arrived on 15 December, and then resumed normal Cunard operations, proceeding to New York to embark passengers and cargo, leaving there on 23 December and making another call at Halifax on our homeward journey before sailing for Liverpool in the early morning hours of Christmas day. Following our normal practice, the crew had been given their Christmas dinner in New York, and it had been a very convivial affair with the meal being served by the female staff and the officers, who acted as barkeepers and kept the men's glasses charged with beer. Indeed, it had all gone so well I was beginning to hope that the spirit in the ship was improving, and the old grudges were being forgotten.

On Christmas Day my senior officers and myself entertained all our forty-five first class passengers at a big cocktail party in the lounge, and this was followed by a gala dinner. After dinner I slipped along to wish our female staff a Merry Christmas, as they were being given a special dinner in the tourist class restaurant. I had just returned to the first class lounge, when I received an urgent message to say I was wanted on the bridge. The time was now 22.30 and it appears that shortly before this some of the wilder elements in the crew, who had been drinking heavily, had started a game called 'hunt the scabs'—what they intended to do when they caught them I never found out. But eleven of our loyal ratings had become so frightened that they had dashed into the ship's hospital and asked the doctor for protection. He had locked them in, then got in touch with the chief officer, T H Davies, who had stationed a master at arms outside the hospital. Thinking that the situation might be getting out of hand, and not being able to contact me, he had ordered all the crew bars closed.

By the time I arrived on the bridge Mr Davies was confronting a very angry delegation of crew members, who said they had been working late in the kitchens and dining rooms, and when they came off duty could not get a Christmas drink. I did not agree with what the chief officer had done, because nothing upsets a British seaman more than cutting off his beer. But he thought that to open the bars again would be a sign of weakness and would be letting him down. As I tried to work out some face-saving formula, a message came from the tourist class lounge to say that about a hundred crew members had walked in and taken up seats around the dance floor, announcing that they intended to sit there until the captain reopened their bars. The tourist passengers had been playing bingo, but the game had finished and they were waiting to start dancing when the incident happened. Fortunately our purser, M P Dawes, was in the room, and with great presence of mind he announced: 'Ladies and Gentlemen, it looks as though we have a little spot of bother on. Will you all come along to the smoke room and join me in a Christmas drink?' As I walked along the promenade deck preparing to meet the men, I wondered how Captain

Bligh, or some of our more despotic old-time Cunard captains, would have dealt with such a situation. But since I couldn't clap the men in irons, the only thing I could do was talk to them and hope that they would behave reasonably.

When I entered the room about forty or fifty men were sitting in chairs round the dance floor, with about the same number standing around just outside the doors waiting to see what was going to happen. So I said: 'You can all get out of those chairs. Taking over passenger accommodation and frightening passengers is almost an act of mutiny, and I will not discuss anything with you in here; but I am willing to listen to any grievances you may have on the deck outside.' They all stood up and shuffled out on deck after me as I left the room; then I managed to speak with one of their spokesmen, who told the same story that I had already heard, about men coming off duty and not being able to get a drink. Having carefully examined why this action had been taken, I told them that I would agree to the bars being opened up again for a period of two hours from 23.00 provided there was no more horse-play, and I would go round with the chief master at arms to see that all the bars were closed at 01.00. This seemed to satisfy them, and they dispersed quietly, but not before mental notes were made of the names of most of the men who had been actually sitting in the chairs.

Feeling that this was such a serious breach of Cunard discipline that the men ought to be made an example of by prosecution in a magistrate's court, I had fifty of the men up the following day and charged them with 'Disobedience of the master's orders, in occupying passenger accommodation without permission, and conduct likely to alarm passengers', then stood them all over, pending action in a civil court. I cabled full details of the case and the action I had taken to the company's solicitors in Liverpool, and asked for instructions. After taking counsel's advice, the company advised me that I should execute summary justice, which meant giving each man a DR for conduct and fining him one day's pay. Discussing this matter with the general manager following our arrival in Liverpool, I was told that the company wished to avoid the un-favourable publicity which would follow discussion of this affair in the press, and they felt that after listening to the men's story of poor sailors who couldn't get a drink on Christmas Day, the magistrates would either discharge them or bind them over as first offenders. At times I felt as if I didn't know which foot to stand on, or which way to face.

After we docked I stayed to put the ship into drydock on the last day of 1960, for her annual overhaul, which was expected to take about a month, and then I went home for a welcome spell of leave. But once the dock had been pumped dry and they had done enough work on vital things like the propellers, the rudder and the stabilizers to ensure that she was completely immobilized, the ship repair workers started a strike which was to last for five months and give me a lot of unexpected leave. Yet, not only was it leave at the most unpleasant time of the year, it somehow did not seem like leave that could be enjoyed, because, always hoping that a settlement might come, the company waited until about a week before each voyage was due to start before they cancelled it officially. With only one ship in the company affected, there was never any problem in finding space in other ships for the small number of passengers and the relatively small amount of cargo booked for the ship on those winter voyages. I heard later that this strike had involved the company in the minimum financial loss, as they normally did not expect to do better than break even on any voyage the ship made at this time of the year.

By April, I was ordered to do a voyage as relieving captain on one of my previous commands, the Ivernia. It was to be her first voyage of the season to Montreal, which, was always the most trying one from the captain's point of view; but this particular voyage was to prove difficult for other reasons as well.

When I came on deck at 08.00 on 25 April 1961 I was reminded very much of 1 January 1949 when we were stranded on board the Queen Mary, except that this time the winds were from a southeasterly direction and the forecasts did not sound quite so alarming. But as our sailing time of 12.00 drew near there were anxious conferences in my cabin with our pilot, Captain Bruce Bell, and our marine superintendent, because from where the ship was lying, up the River Itchen, she had to be towed stern-first for about a quarter of a mile down a fairly narrow channel to the swinging ground. However, with the two extra tugs that had been ordered because of the strong wind, Captain Bell and I were confident that we could handle the situation. We sailed on schedule, and as there was a marked lull in the wind at this time the first part of the operation went remarkably smoothly. Then, once the ship was steadied on the course to take her down Southampton Water towards Calshot, orders were given to let go first the after tugs and then the forward ones. Just as we were congratulating ourselves on our good fortune, but before we had sufficient way on the ship to have her fully under control, a violent squall hit us with blinding rain and wind speeds up to 50 miles an hour, striking the ship on the port side.

We soon noticed that although the ship was slowly picking up headway she was making a lot of leeway, and setting down towards the coastal minesweepers and other craft on our starboard side, which were moored close to the edge of the channel off Hythe pier. There were at this time two possible courses of action open to us: (a) we could have given a double ring 'Full ahead' on the engine-room telegraphs and called upon the engineers for maximum power, in the hope that the ship's tendency to run towards the wind's eye when going ahead would lift her clear of the mine-sweepers; or (b) we could check the ship's way by putting both engines full astern, and call back the tugs which were still only a few hundred yards away and get them to hold the ship until the squall passed.

Being wise after the fact, I now feel that had we had the courage to take the first course of action we might have kept out of trouble. But in an emergency, especially when the power of the elements is involved, one does what one thinks best at the time. So I fully agreed with Captain Bell in taking the second and more cautious action, because one always feels that the more slowly one's ship is moving at a time like this the less damage she is likely to do. But on a wet, windy day the natural reaction of any tugboat captain who thinks he has just completed a job successfully is to be mainly interested in getting back to his berth and probably a hot lunch, so it took a little time before the tugs realized our predicament. Then, after they had reversed course and got back to us, they found it a much more difficult job getting their lines aboard in a Force 9 gale and driving rain. So, although we had stopped the ship well clear of the minesweepers, it seemed an age before any of the tugs were made fast and able to help us. This meant that the ship was now entirely at the mercy of the wind, for we dared not use our engines while the tugs were making fast aft for fear of getting one of their ropes round our propellers.

By now the ship had drifted out of the channel and, as our bows got closer to the shallow water, the forward tugs were naturally not at all keen to venture in to put their lines on board. The two tugs that were eventually made fast aft got a good weight on their lines, but the wind was so strong that all they could do was to hold the stern into the wind while the bow landed gently on a mud, sand and shingle bank. Once the ship had grounded, three more tugs managed to get lines on board, and once they were fast we attempted to get her off by going full astern on both engines, with the tugs towing as hard as they dared. But after about ten minutes we had an anguished message from the chief engineer to say that his condensers were getting silted up by all the mud and sand stirred up by our propellers.

As we had gone ashore on a rapidly falling tide, about two hours after second high water, we were going to have to wait for about six hours for the ship to have any more water underneath her than she had at present. Yet neither Captain Bell nor I felt any undue concern, because we knew that the ship had only drifted gently on to a soft bank, with no feeling of impact at all; as the weather was moderating fast and the forecast was good, it was only a matter of tugs holding the ship where she was until the tide rose again and floated her off.

As we were in full view from Southampton Docks, our position was more embarrassing than dangerous, especially when on the BBC 13.00 news bulletin, which we put out over the loudspeakers on the promenade deck for the benefit of our passengers, who were all anxiously watching the proceedings, it was announced that the Cunard liner Ivernia had gone ashore in Southampton Water in a gale. After discussing the situation over VHF with the harbour-master and our marine superintendent, it was agreed that it would be unwise to make any further attempt to refloat the ship before 18.00. So after making a broadcast to the passengers over the ship's public-address system to put them in the picture, there was nothing we could do but sit there, with the tugs holding us in position, and wait.

Fortunately the weather continued to improve throughout the afternoon, and when we did refloat at 18.07, with our engines going full speed astern and all tugs making a maximum effort, the ship shot across the channel at such a rate that we had to ring full ahead on the telegraphs to stop her going ashore on the other side.

One thing that did impress me very much was the speed of the BBC reporting. At the start of the 18.00 news broadcast, which we again relayed to the passengers, they announced that we would attempt to refloat at the next high water. But in the summary of the news at 18.20, they announced that we had been successfully refloated. This was literally only about ten minutes after it had actually happened.

After refloating a diver examined our hull, and he reported no damage apart from the loss of a little paint. But our sailing was postponed until midnight to give the chief engineer time to clean the mud, sand and stones out of the condensers.

Perhaps the worst part of this stranding was on our return to Le Havre, after what had been a difficult voyage pushing our way through the pack ice in the Gulf of St Lawrence, and making the passage up and down the river before most of the winter buoys marking the channel had been replaced by the more easily visible summer buoys. As soon as we berthed in Le Havre the company's insurance manager, accompanied by four lawyers, came on board, and my officers and I spent most of the cross-Channel passage making detailed statements and giving the reasons for every engine movement that was made, without having any knowledge of the reasons given by Captain Bell in the official report he had already made.

Later Captain Bell and I travelled up to Liverpool to attend the company's inquiry into the stranding. They gave us a very sympathetic hearing, and at the end the only criticism of our handling of the ship was that, in view of the weather conditions, we would have been wiser to have kept the forward tugs fast until we were clear of the minesweepers.

By the time this inquiry was held the strike of ship repair workers was settled, and on 25 May the Carinthia was undocked and brought round to Huskisson Dock to load cargo for her first voyage of the year on 31 May 1961. By now, she had a largely new crew, and all the bitterness left by the strike of the previous year seemed to be quite forgotten.

Arriving in Liverpool from Canada via Greenock, we had anchored off Sandon Dock at about midnight, waiting to berth alongside the Princes stage at 06.00 the next morning. But when our pilot and I saw what the weather was like at 05.30, we decided it was impossible to move and went back to bed. Visibility was less than 300 feet, with absolutely still air and the surface of the river like a sheet of glass. At 08.00 it was still so thick that even the birds were walking, and nothing at all was moving on the river except the ferries, who have their own radar system. However, knowing that the ebb tide would continue until 10.30, I felt sure that with our radar, and provided we had that extra control at slow speeds that comes when stemming the tide, we could make the stage.

After discussing the situation with the pilot and our marine super-intendent on the VHF radio, we decided to have a go. I arranged that the marine superintendent would warn the ferries, and send one tug to meet us in mid-river and have another lying off the stage opposite our berth. When we picked up the first tug on our radar, we managed to talk him alongside by using our loud-hailers; and once he had made fast ahead we had even better control of the ship at slow speed, so we crept up until we sighted the other tug off the berth. Although we had gone slightly too far ahead, we dropped astern and slowly closed the stage, which we sighted about 300 feet away. As we finished mooring the staff photographer from the *Liverpool Echo* took a picture which gives some idea how thick the fog was. When a reporter came on board to interview me I tried to play down the incident in case the company might think I had been too venturesome, but the headlines in bold type across that evening's edition of the paper read: *'Carinthia's Two-Mile Fog Crawl Ends with Captain's Sunny Smile!'* I had slightly over-done the understatement.

It was 25 May 1962 when I finally left the Carinthia and the Canadian service with few regrets.

CHAPTER TWELVE

The Caronia and a return to luxury cruising

By 1962, as far as cruising was concerned, the golden years of the fifties were gone for ever, but the 'Green Goddess', as the Caronia was often called, was still managing to pay her way. In our head office in Liverpool there were graphs showing each ship's profits or losses. On the one for the Caronia the line first plunged heavily into the red after the bills for her annual overhaul had been paid, then during her world cruise climbed slowly back, levelled off a little during the spring cruise, but climbed very steeply during her North Cape cruise, only to sink slowly back towards the red during both the summer and autumn cruises. The reason for this was that the daily rate which people paid for their cabins on cruises was not governed by conference, as it was on the Atlantic service, but based solely on what the market would stand; and, as it turned out, people on the autumn cruise to the Mediterranean were only paying about half as much per day for the same cabin, food and service as they would have to have done on the highly popular North Cape cruise.

My first cruise this time was to the North Cape and, although this was probably the best cruise in her programme, it was never one on which the captain got a chance to relax, as there was so much intricate navigation through the fjords.

The North Cape cruise was followed by a delightful summer cruise to the Mediterranean, then a long autumn cruise through the Eastern Mediterranean and into the Black Sea. During this last cruise I spent four days in Cairo as the guest of American Express, the company who were organizing our shore excursions;

a most interesting and fascinating experience.

On this cruise we visited the two Russian Black Sea ports of Yalta and Odessa. Because of the shortage of English-speaking guides in the Crimea, twenty smartly dressed young ladies had been flown down from Moscow to meet the ship in Yalta. At the end of their duties there they boarded the ship and made the overnight voyage to Odessa with us. Our cruise director gave a special party to which he invited a group of young ship's officers, whom he thought they would enjoy dancing with. Both during this party and on one of the tours the following day I was able to have several long conversations with a couple of the girls, both of whom were eager to find out as much as possible about life in Britain and America, and asked endless questions. Having a daughter of just about their age, I was able to compare their salaries, the taxes they paid, and many items of their living costs, with hers. But all the time they were talking, especially when they were giving information to passengers, a propaganda line came through: in 1917 Russia had 95 per cent illiteracy, but now that was down to less than 5 per cent, and so on, plus endless statistics about home construction, education and other developments. Yet when we told them things about life at home and in America we were frequently met with an air of polite disbelief which seemed to say that they didn't believe our propaganda either!

All the time the ship was in Soviet waters, the crisis over the Cuban missile situation was getting steadily worse. We were in Odessa on the day President Kennedy issued orders to the US Navy to sink any Russian ships which refused to stop and be searched. Although a Russian submarine—probably on exercises—surfaced fairly close to the Caronia, there was no sign of hostility towards us or our American passengers at any time, but I did not breathe really freely again until we were out through the Bosphorus.

At the end of this autumn cruise we went to Liverpool for our annual overhaul, and again there was much labour unrest. One of the major repairs was the scaling and repainting of a large part of the port side of the hull. When the scaling had been completed and all but one small section had been given its priming coat of red lead, the painters decided that this was the psychological moment to go on strike for an increase of wages. They obviously thought that as the ship was already so well booked for the forth-coming world cruise Cunard would have no alternative but to give in to their demands. But the company refused to yield, and no further painting was done. When I came back from leave the ship looked a very peculiar sight, with the port side of the hull part rusty metal, part red lead, and the rest the distinctive Caronia green. The starboard side, which had not been touched, still looked fairly good, so I was told cheerfully that we would berth with the starboard side to the landing stage, so very few passengers would see the port side. Then, plenty of paint would be put on board so that the sailors could paint the hull at the ports of call during our outward voyage.

We sailed from Liverpool on 6 January 1963, via Barbados, Jamaica, Nassau and Port Everglades to New York, just as Europe was starting to feel the icy grip of the coldest winter she had known for many years. In addition to about sixty people who were going to make the world cruise with us, our passenger list included a large number of wealthy British people going out to spend the winter in the Caribbean sunshine, and it was heavily studded with titles. Out of the ten people sitting at my table six had titles, the highest number I can remember. Our schedule called for us to arrive at dawn and sail at dusk from all ports, and as at Bridge-town and Kingston we had to use our own launches to land and embark passengers, an operation which prevented us from using about 70 per cent of the ship's seamen for other work, it was prov-ing quite a struggle to get our multi-coloured hull painted. Even on our day in Nassau, when government tenders were used for the passengers, the weather was too rough for the men to work near the waterline.

So when we berthed in Port Everglades we still did not look much like a luxury cruise liner, and the bosun did not feel that his men would be able to finish the painting in the twelve hours we expected to be there. The weather forecasts were also indicating that when we reached New York we could expect temperatures well below freezing, making painting there impossible. The only solution seemed to be to persuade the company to allow us to extend our stay in Florida from twelve to twenty-four hours, which would mean arriving about six hours late in New York. When I called our general manager in New York and explained the situation he agreed to the change, which pleased many of our passengers as it gave them a chance to have a night out in Florida. The ship's seamen, by using floodlights after dark, had the ship completely painted by 03.00, and we steamed out of harbour at 06.00 looking as we should have done leaving Liverpool.

When we reached New York a stevedores' strike was just starting, and we were the last ship that the tugs docked before going out. We had had warning of this, so we had loaded most of our bulk stores in England and obtained our perishables in Port Everglades. But it still meant a lot of extra work for our crew, and when we sailed I had to take her out without tugs.

The 1963 world cruise was the only time that the Caronia went round the world from east to west. This had certain advantages: it enabled many of our American passengers to join the ship on the West Coast, so shortening the cruise for them by about ten days; it also meant that all the clock alterations we made during the cruise involved putting the clock back, which most people seem to prefer, since it gave them a little extra sleep. Naturally it had disadvantages as well, because instead of arriving in Japan at cherry blossom time, we were to reach Yokohama on 21 February, before the trees had bloomed. It also meant that during our long passages across the Pacific we would be bucking the prevailing winds. However, we were lucky with our weather on this part of the cruise, although we did meet some very long swells set up by storms to the north.

After leaving New York, we made a daylight transit of the Panama Canal followed by an overnight stop at Balboa; then, to break the long trip to Long Beach, we made a short call at Acapulco, where we arrived at 08.00 and sailed at 13.00. A small, frail, lady of eighty-two from Bridlington in Yorkshire, who was making her first long cruise entirely alone, decided to go ashore there. Although she had joined us in Liverpool, she was very quiet and few people seemed to have noticed her up to that time. By about 10.45 she had seen enough ashore and made her way down to the quayside but saw no sign of our cruise launches. Apparently a Mexican who owned a sailboat must have made her a deal, that he would take her back to the ship. For a while they made reasonable progress but towards the middle of the day the winds in Acapulco fall light, and the boat became becalmed some distance from the ship.

The last passenger launch was due to leave the shore at 12.30, so when the coxswain radioed us that he had no passengers on board, only cruise staff, I gave orders that the gangway should be hoisted and the anchor weighed, and instructed the launch to meet us near the harbour entrance. With as tight a schedule to keep as we had, minutes saved in this way can be important, and as soon as the staff captain informed me that the last launch was clear of the water I was able to proceed at full speed. The normal arrangement when passengers went ashore was that their cabins were locked by the bedroom steward; on their return they contacted him and he would then open their cabin for them and tick them off on his list as being on board. But because we were sailing right on lunchtime, some passengers had gone straight from the launch to the restaurant or one of the bars before returning to their rooms, so we had not had a 100 per cent check, and this lady's bedroom steward was wrongly informed that she was in the restaurant. However, he must have felt concerned, because when she had not come for her key by 14.00 or so a call for her or anyone who had seen her was put out on the public address system. When nobody came forward it soon became obvious that the lady was not on board, so a cable was sent to our agent, saying she appeared to have missed the ship. I understand that as soon as he received it he hurried down to the quay, where he found a very agitated lady surrounded by Mexicans who did not seem to understand what she was saying.

He collected her and drove her to a hotel, and that evening he and his wife escorted her to Mexico City. The following day she was put on a plane to Los Angeles, where a Cunard representative met her and gave her the red carpet treatment. Two days later, when the Caronia had berthed in Long Beach, she was brought to the ship and taken to the purser's cabin. A few minutes after this, I received a call from the purser to come and speak to her. As I entered the room she drew herself up to her full five feet, wagged an admonishing finger at me and said: 'Captain! You left me behind! My boat was quite close, and I waved and shouted, but you wouldn't stop. You just steamed away and left me with all those Mexicans!' Some passengers who were on the deck aft did say later that they had seen a small boat with somebody waving, but they assumed that it was just some local people giving us a Mexican farewell!

All I could do was to apologize and try to explain that we probably could not have seen her from the bridge; and anyhow we were not expecting our passengers to use local transport. She did seem a little mollified, and was even more comforted when the purser told her that Cunard would pay all the expenses involved in her unexpected shore excursion. So our shy little old lady, whom hardly anybody knew, became something of a ship's mascot for the rest of the cruise.

Apart from the heavy swells on our long beat to the westward, first to Honolulu and then on to Japan, the cruise was uneventful. But we had to cross the international date line, which meant that we lost a whole day in order to make up all those extra hours we had gained by retarding our clocks. Some clever planner in the office ashore had carefully arranged that the day we should lose would be a Sunday; we should go from 23.59 on Saturday to 00.01 on Monday. This meant that not only would the crew lose a day's leave in lieu of a Sunday spent at sea (as all work done on a Sunday counts as overtime) but also some members of the catering and engine departments, who had to work on Sundays, could lose at least eight and probably anything up to twelve to fourteen hours overtime, saving the company a considerable amount. At that time the Caronia had to my mind the finest crew that it has ever been my privilege to sail with; both men and women stayed in her year after year because they liked the ship, the life and the type of people she carried. Also, because they knew that they were going to be away from their homes for as much as six months at a time, the crew of that ship had set out to create a social life of their own on board, and the Caronia social and athletic club was by far the most active and best supported in the fleet. The standard of behaviour of her crew ashore was also one of the best I have ever seen, and, although they had their fun, they turned up to do their job, and very few people appeared before the staff captain as defaulters. Also, on this cruise the men had worked particularly hard to overcome the effects of the painters' strike in Liverpool and the stevedores strike in New York. As our American manager had made the cruise with us as far as Honolulu, I spoke to him about this, saying I did not think my crew were getting a fair deal. So we missed Saturday instead of Sunday, which may have reduced the company's margin of profit on the cruise a little, but I am sure the good effect it had on crew morale was more than worth it.

Another worrying time was during the ship's visit to Bali, which with its wonderful carvings and exotic dancers is always a highlight of any world cruise. While we were there Mount Agung, the huge volcano which dominates this beautiful and fertile island, was very active and from our anchorage we could see the flames and sparks shooting into the night sky as the white-hot streams of molten lava flowed down the mountainside. Each morning the sailors had to wash off the layer of fine dust that had settled on our decks and upperworks during the night, while our laundry and dry cleaning services had difficulty in coping with the rush when passengers who had been ashore needed a complete change of clothing on their return.

There had already been a number of deaths in Bali, mainly of priests who had refused to leave their temples in the path of the advancing lava but stayed to pray instead, hoping to propitiate the god of the mountain whom they thought was angry, and the whole island had a general air of foreboding. Standing on the bridge at night, watching the pyrotechnic display, I wondered where my duties would lie if there was a serious eruption: to try to get my ship away to a place of safety, or to stay and try to render what help I could. I was quite relieved when the time came for us to sail and I was able to watch the fiery tip of the mountain dip below the horizon.

A new stop was added on this cruise—Jessleton, a little town in North Borneo which had never been visited by a cruise liner before. This rather disconcerted a great many of our very regular travellers, who had been round the world so many times that they had developed a sort of snobbery about not going ashore as it was the fifth or more time that they had been to a place. When we got to Jessleton everybody had to go ashore. It was a port which had been largely destroyed by the Japanese during the war, and then rebuilt by the Australians, a neat little town on the edge of the jungle. I think our call was the biggest thing that had happened there for years and they went to a lot of trouble to make a success of our visit. The governor's wife organized an exhibition of native handicrafts in the school, and a display of native dancing was put on at the sports ground. It reminded one of an English village making an all-out effort for the village fête.

Next came Hong Kong. With its wonderful climate and its unlimited shopping opportunities, to most people it is the outstanding port on any world cruise. Without the weight restrictions imposed on travellers by air, it was fantastic the crates of stuff that arrived on board. When our baggage rooms were full we had to arrange to stow some of the crates on deck.

Going around the world the other way, which had brought us to Japan earlier in the year, also brought us into Bombay much later than the ship had been there on previous world cruises, so the crew and the handful of passengers who remained on board throughout our five-day stay found the weather hot and oppressive.

From India we went to Aden and then through the Red Sea to the Suez Canal. For part of the canal passage, in a large slow-moving northbound convoy, we had a strong beam wind, and the Caronia was never a very good ship to steer at slow speeds: with her huge funnel acting like a sail and trying to turn her into the wind, there were times when she required fifteen to twenty degrees of helm to keep her on course.

Coming home through the Mediterranean seemed rather an anticlimax to some of our sophisticated world travellers (they had seen it all before), but the call at Naples enabled us to land our European contingent, and we then called at Lisbon for fuel and water before starting our transatlantic voyage on 21 April.

When the ship was just south of the Newfoundland Banks we met a very bad storm. The weather had been getting steadily worse all morning and Washington's forecast spoke of a dangerous storm, with wind speeds over 60 knots and wave heights up to 40 feet. On my advice, the cruise director had cancelled a bridge tournament programmed for 14.30 in the observation lounge, but four male passengers were having a private bridge game in there just before 15.00 when the steward advised them to move away from the forward windows. On the bridge we had been steadily reducing speed as the height of the waves increased, but at 70 rpm she appeared to be riding fairly comfortably. Then, at 15.14, it suddenly felt as if the bows were going down and down into a bottomless pit, while the next oncoming greybeard towered menacingly over us. Before the bows really started to lift again several hundred tons of water crashed down on the foredeck, and rolled along it in a huge foaming wave which hit the crew's wooden swimming pool. This burst into a million pieces, and 90 per cent of it was never seen again; it must have gone straight over the side on the same wave. Several pieces of splintered timber were lifted about fifty feet by the spray and landed on the bridge, but some much heavier pieces crashed against the windows of the observation lounge and shattered three of them. Had it not been for the steward's presence of mind, there could have been some serious injuries. We then had to heave the ship to, stern to sea, while the carpenters replaced the broken windows with wood and the stewards swept up the splintered glass and removed the sodden curtains. It must have been just one rogue sea, because within an hour we were back on course doing 70 rpm and she never shipped anything but a little spray again.

Monday, 19 August 1963 saw me back in the Caronia once more, to do the summer and the long autumn cruises for the second year running. These were to be my last cruises in the Caronia and were to be as enjoyable as the others. The 'Green Goddess' was a beautiful ship, a symbol of luxury and leisure, and all her days were happy days; her ship's company were beyond reproach, and were proud to sail in her as she followed the sun.

CHAPTER THIRTEEN

Captaining the Queen Mary

From November 1963 to December 1965 I had no ship of my own, but acted instead as relieving captain for both of the Queens, as well as taking over for the occasional cruise in the Mauretania. The life of a relieving captain can be very pleasant because the trips are often very short and one served in almost a caretaker capacity. What really made this such a pleasant time was that between single voyages I got a lot of home leave. The idea of paying one of their captains for being at home doing nothing for long stretches at a time did not please the powers that be in Liverpool, so every now and then I would be sent to do a cruise on the Mauretania, which at this time was permanently cruising out of Southampton. On one cruise in January and February 1965, we sailed from Southampton, down to Las Palmas, then across the Atlantic—in the flying-fish latitudes—to Nassau. After a couple of weeks in the brilliant sunshine of the Caribbean we came back from St Thomas to Madeira, another fine-weather run, before coming north again and docking in Southampton on 21 February. We had fine weather and sunshine nearly every day and this seemed the ideal itinerary for people looking for relief from winter's gloom. With my aunt and uncle, who were among the passengers, we had a family reunion in Port Everglades with two of my first cousins from the Canadian and American branch of the family.

However, 1964-5 were extremely difficult years for Cunard. I was often reminded of a conversation I had had three years earlier with a shipping correspondent who was about to interview Sir John Brocklebank, shortly after he took over as chairman on the death of Colonel Dennis Bates. The correspondent knew a great deal about most of the large British shipping companies, so I asked him how he saw Cunard's future. He said 'I think Cunard still has a future, but things are in a hell of a mess and it could take at least five years to get rid of the dead hand of Colonel Bates. He boasted that he had never set foot in America, yet hoped to get 60 per cent of his business from there, and had only twice been on board the Queen Elizabeth, the largest unit in the fleet. His idea was that he and a couple of cronies could run a worldwide shipping company from his fifth floor office in Liverpool.'

In spite of all Sir John Brocklebank's efforts to find solutions to our problems, each balance sheet showed worse results than the one before, because so many of our problems had no easy solution. Jet aeroplanes were steadily taking more and more of our transatlantic passengers; we had a fleet of ageing ships, most of which were unsuitable for cruising; and with constant demands for higher wages there seemed to be no way of curbing our rapidly rising costs, yet to increase fares would only drive more people into the air.

Increasing concern to those of us on the sea staff was caused by the size of the Cunard shore organization, with more than 600 people employed in our Liverpool office alone. During 1965, the company's recently retired chief accountant was a passenger on one voyage, so I asked him to break down the figures in the latest balance sheet. I was amazed to find that out of the revenue earned by the fleet in that year nearly £6 million went to maintain the company's shore establishments, with another £2 million for advertising and promotion.

In spite of reductions in the size of the fleet, there never seemed to be any reduction in the size of the shore staff, and the gulf dividing the sea staff from the shore staff seemed to grow wider. During the early part of 1965 I was relieving captain for two voyages on the Queen Elizabeth when I was asked to attend a meeting on time and motion study, to see if this method could be used to improve efficiency and cut costs. The meeting, which was chaired by our assistant general manager, John Whitworth, was attended by department heads and senior petty officers, and we spent an interesting day listening to lectures and watching films. I felt that, although some of these new ideas might be tried in a new ship with new equipment, they could do little for us on board the Queen Elizabeth. When I was asked to open the discussion session at the end of the meeting, I said this; and then I added: 'In my opinion, there is only one way in which the efficiency of the Cunard Line can be improved: that is, by finding some way of breaking down the barriers that have built up over the years between the sea staff and the shore staff, between those of us who go to sea and do the job, and the people who sit in office chairs and try to tell us how it should be done, often without having any clear knowledge of the problems involved.' I then went on to say: 'I have noticed an increasing tendency on the part of the shore staff to look down their noses at the sea staff, as if they were a lesser breed without the law, and to think that if we had any real brains we would not be at sea, but would have been picked out and given shore jobs like themselves. Because,' I continued heatedly, 'we find increasingly that if we submit ideas for the better running of the ships they are either pigeon-holed or else damned with faint praise—obviously people ashore like to think they are the highly paid experts employed to run the company, so if an idea is a really good one they are the ones who will think of it!' Much of this was, I fear, not very well received at the time. But later, when Sir John Brocklebank called in business efficiency experts to look into the company's organization, one of the first things they said was that it was like investigating two entirely separate organizations.

My long spell of relieving duty was to end at the beginning of November 1965. I sailed in command of the Queen Mary for an Atlantic crossing, followed by two cruises to Nassau. On the first cruise the United States Navy League was holding its annual convention on board and sitting at my table I had four rear-admirals and two captains. When they all came to dinner wearing their dress uniforms the display of gold braid was quite dazzling. Our second cruise, which was over the Thanksgiving holiday, was well booked, and it was when we arrived in Nassau on the morning of Thursday, 25 November that film crews were taking the shots of the ship used in the Frank Sinatra film *Attack on a Queen*, in which some of our sailors were used as extras.

We arrived back in Southampton on 5 December and sailed again on 8 December for a normal Atlantic voyage. But at 06.00 the following morning as we were pushing our way down the English

Channel in the teeth of a westerly gale, we received an SOS message from the Greek ship Constantis to say that she was sinking in a position about 365 miles to the west of us. As we could not possibly reach this position until well after dark and the Greek ship was in an area where one normally expects to find a high concentration of shipping, I did not think that any action by the Queen Mary was likely to be required. Throughout the morning and afternoon signals were received from ships in contact with the casualty and at one point the crew attempted to abandon ship, only to have both of their lifeboats damaged by the heavy seas, with two crew members, the radio officer and the second engineer, thrown into the sea. These men did, however, manage to cling onto a raft and were later picked up by the SS Stove Vulcan, but unfortunately the radio officer died of exposure shortly after.

However by 17.00, when there was no sign of anyone being able to take the crew off, I felt that it was time for me to alter course towards the ship, whose position was about fifty miles to the south of our track, and see for myself what the situation was. After the course had been adjusted, a message was sent to the master of the Constantis telling him we hoped to be with him in a little over three hours. Notices were posted telling the passengers that we were going to the assistance of a ship in distress. This caused great excitement, and the passengers crowded the rails as we approached the Greek ship. Hardly anybody went down to dinner that night.

When we first sighted the Constantis, shortly after 20.00, there were four ships standing by her, with the Surrey Trader, which had been the first ship to establish contact, acting as the VHF control ship; the others being the Stove Vulcan, the Wolverine State and the Auctoritas, with a Shackleton aircraft of RAF Coastal Command circling overhead carrying inflatable lifeboats and other rescue gear. By 21.00 we were close enough to make her out in the light of our searchlights, and I was eventually able to close her to less than half a mile and got a good look at her condition. But the sight of the Queen Mary so close, looking like a small town with all her lights on, must have seemed their salvation to the Greek captain. At 21.49 he sent me a message saying that they were abandoning ship and needed our help. I advised him to remain on board because it was impossible for us to help him. This message was repeated because language difficulties were adding to the confusion. I stayed close to him for a couple of hours, had a good look, and was quite sure that the Constantis was in no immediate danger. She was well out of the water, and running comfortably before the westerly gale at about 5-6 knots. As our fuel reserves were low, and there was nothing which we could do that couldn't be done by the other ships in the area, I decided to continue the voyage. At 23.11 I sent a message to the Greek captain telling him that we were leaving. But I soon got another garbled message from him that indicated that they would feel forced to abandon ship if we left. I am sure that the psychological effect of having our 82,000 tons of brightly lit ship only half a mile away gave those Greek sailors a feeling of confidence until daylight came. So I sent another message saying that I would stay until first light, but telling him that any attempt to abandon ship would lead to almost certain death for many of his crew.

At 06.00 the following morning we learned that German salvage tugs were on their way and should be with the ship that afternoon. So, shortly after 08.00, we proceeded, but the delay had strained our fuel reserves to the limit. Normally we left Southampton with sufficient oil in our tanks to arrive in New York with enough oil for one day's steaming. But all that night we had been steaming back to the east at about six knots, over ground we had already covered, and we had to steam all that distance back again to get to where we had been. Then we had strong to gale force westerly winds against us all the way to New York, and the chief engineer and I watched our dwindling fuel stocks with apprehension. Eventually we reached the point where we had to reduce the speed to save fuel, making the ship thirty-six hours late arriving. Even then, we had only about 300 tons aboard, most of which was probably the sludge at the bottom of each tank which is generally looked upon as unpumpable. Our normal consumption was 1,200 tons a day.

We got back into Southampton at the end of this voyage on 21 December. Two days later we started out on a most unusual Christmas cruise, because the ship had been chartered by the Sunday newspaper *The News of the World*, and all of our passengers were to be the winners of a competition organized by the paper earlier in the year. To win a place in the cruise, *News of the World* readers had to place in the correct order the eight things that they thought they would enjoy most on the cruise, such as the good food, the lavish entertainment, etc., paying sixpence for each entry they sent in. The winners were entitled to a cruise for themselves, their wives and all their children under twenty-one. Unmarried winners could bring their parents, and in three cases where the winners were engaged and due to marry shortly, the paper paid all the wedding expenses so they could have their honeymoon on the cruise. The cruise was planned so that the people who were being brought from all parts of the United Kingdom at the *News of the World*'s expense would embark during the afternoon and evening of 23 December, spend Christmas Eve getting down into the fine weather for Christmas Day, then arrive in Las Palmas on Boxing Day morning. But, as on that strike-breaking voyage in the Carinthia, the people who planned the cruise had not arranged the weather.

Whenever I pick up a newspaper, after a glance at the head-lines, I almost instinctively turn to the little weather chart of the North Atlantic, but what I saw on the morning of 23 December almost spoiled my appetite for breakfast. A deepening depression north of the Azores was moving rapidly east into the Bay of Biscay, and I knew we should be joining it there the next day, with 1,200 passengers, more than 400 of them under twelve years of age. I knew, too, that 95 per cent of these passengers would have one thing in common: they would never before have been at sea in a bad storm.

The chairman of the newspaper and his wife, Sir William and Lady Carr, had invited a number of guests to join them on this cruise, including Cunard's deputy chairman and his wife, and a number of Cunard officials. At a cocktail party in Sir William's suite before we sailed I warned them about the weather prospects, so that they could arrange with the doctor to have their anti-seasickness shots before we left the berth.

As we pulled out of the Ocean Terminal at 23.00 that night the wind was just starting to freshen to Force 5-6, but before we got down to the Nab Tower it was getting near gale force and the sea was too rough to land our pilot, who always brought his little bag along, as he never minded being overcarried on the short cruises. Hoping to get through the bad weather as quickly as possible, we had started out at full speed, so by 08.00 on Christmas Eve morning we had passed Ushant and were heading across the Bay of Biscay in a Force 9 gale, with a rapidly rising sea that was making her lift uncomfortably. From the chief catering officer's report, less than 100 people availed themselves of the breakfast that was being served in two sittings in both restaurants. By 10.00 the wind was gusting up to storm Force 10, with a plunging barometer, and it was obviously time to start reducing our speed, although so far she was only shipping heavy spray.

Shortly after noon we were getting squalls of hurricane force, with the wind cutting the spray from the tops of the breaking seas and filling the air with flying spume that reduced the visibility to less than a mile. Then, at 13.38, she caught a heavy sea on the starboard shoulder which lifted the top off one of the big cowl ventilators on the forward end of the promenade deck. It must have weighed more than a ton, and crashed against the promenade deck windows, smashing two of them. These big windows are made of armoured glass more than $\frac{3}{4}$ in. thick and they are protected on the outside by massive steel shutters, which had been in place since the night before. But a sharp blow will shatter armoured glass, in spite of its great strength, into millions of tiny, razor-sharp fragments. Just at this moment one of our passengers was walking his three-year-old son around this deck, with the idea that the boy might feel better out in the fresh air. Suddenly he found himself showered with thousands of pieces of armoured glass.

Fortunately, he was able to protect his son, who only had two small cuts; but the poor father was bleeding from more than a dozen cuts around his face and hands. Of all his cuts none was more than an inch or so in length, and only one of them needed a stitch. He also needed treatment for shock, but I saw him walking around the next day.

We had to run the ship away before the wind and heave her to, stern to the wind and sea, which meant taking her across the main traffic stream while our sailors got out on the foredeck and secured the damage. Because of the reduced visibility we had to rely on radar, but the huge waves were producing such an excessive amount of sea clutter (radar echoes which are reflected back from wave tops) that ships we picked up on the radar at twelve to fifteen miles were disappearing in the sea clutter at six miles. Then, although we could estimate their positions roughly on the true motion plot, we were not sighting them visually until they were about a mile away. By mid-afternoon all was secured and we were able to bring the ship back to her course and slowly start to build up our speed again, for the storm centre had passed and the barometer was starting to rise. As often happens with fast-moving storms, once the weather began to moderate it did so quite quickly, and by 21.00, as we passed Cape Finisterre, we were back on full speed again. Life on board was rapidly returning to normal, and the bars and restaurants were full.

By Christmas morning the seas were smooth, with just a lazy swell, and although the weather was mainly cloudy it was warmer and people could get out on deck and enjoy the fresh air. It was quite astonishing how healthy everyone seemed to feel, so all the Christmas Day festivities went off well.

At 06.00 on Boxing Day morning, as we arrived at Las Palmas, the sun was just coming up out of the sea and it shone all day out of a clear blue sky. With the temperatures in the seventies it was a glorious day. Homeward bound the weather was kind to us, and as people were by now getting to know their way around the ship and to feel at home in her, and also getting to know one another, the tempo of the cruise started to build up, until the younger ones seemed to feel it was a waste of time to go to bed at night. By the time we docked in Southampton, everyone had had a wonderful holiday; and if they remembered the storm at all it was only to marvel at how large the waves had been.

This was to be my last voyage in the dear old Queen Mary, and she was a ship full of many happy memories since that first day I had joined her in 1938. With a wonderful reputation for being a happy ship, she seemed to arouse deep affection in all who sailed in her, and her crew were intensely loyal. I was never quite sure what to say when passengers asked me which of the two Queens I preferred, but I think it is fair to say that the Queen Mary had an air of graciousness, in her main lounge and her magnificent dining room, that will never be seen again; while the Queen Elizabeth had many features which were an improvement on her older sister, and with cleaner lines she was a more perfect model.

Looking at the company as a whole, these were days when momentous changes were taking place. Business efficiency experts were going through all departments. Often baffling, some of their changes made no sense to us at all. Then ill health forced Sir John Brocklebank to stand down and hand over the reins to Sir Basil Smallpeice. He made more changes and brought new blood into the higher echelons, to see if the young men could chart a course to keep us away from the dangerous rocks of bankruptcy. Our head office was moved to Southampton from Liverpool to allow easier contact with the passenger ships, and we now had a young, busy and bustling managing director, Phillip Bates, instead of a general manager. The size of the head office staff had been drastically cut to less than half; dozens of small branch offices were being closed. Many of these changes were good, but some came too late, and other changes seemed to me to bear little relation to the problems we were facing.

CHAPTER FOURTEEN

Troubled waters

My appointment as Commodore-Captain of the Cunard Line was announced on 1 January 1966, and a few days later I was invited to London to meet our new chairman, Sir Basil Smallpeice, for the first time. The meeting was to be in his Regent Street office, the other people present being the managing director Phillip Bates, the personnel director John Whitworth, and the company's nautical adviser Captain Angus Letty. After the usual courtesies had been exchanged the chairman made a short speech saying that he felt that the rank of commodore should not be based solely on seniority as it had in the past, but should be a reward for outstanding merit among the more senior captains. However, in my case they had not found the decision hard, as I should probably have been their choice on both counts.

Now, being wise after the fact, I realize that I ought to have made an equally brief reply, thanking them for the honour they had done me. The conversation would then have become general again and after a quarter of an hour we would have been offered glasses of sherry, then all gone our separate ways with no harm done.

But I had given a lot of thought to the statement which Sir Basil had made in his public announcement after accepting the chairmanship, when he said that he felt that the commodore, as the senior member of the seagoing staff, should be brought more into the policy-making side of the company. After thanking him for my appointment, I reminded him of this statement. Then I went on to say: 'I wonder if I could take this opportunity, sir, to put the point of view of many members of the sea staff, which you and these gentlemen may never have heard before?' He nodded, and

I launched into a long peroration. Naturally I cannot remember exactly what I said, but the main theme is still etched clearly in my mind. I started by saying that to me the Cunard Line was like a huge tree, with its roots in the ships and drawing its sustenance from their ability to earn money by carrying passengers and freight. I thought of the company's offices and shore establishments spreading out over Europe and North America as the branches of that tree. I then went on to talk about the Cunard Line's ten glorious years between 1947 and 1957, the year in which we had carried the largest number of transatlantic passengers in the company's history—but the year, too, in which the first jet aircraft had gone into regular service. During those years we had watched the branches grow, as shore establishments increased in size and new branch offices were opened or existing ones enlarged. This was quite all right so long as there was enough sustenance coming through the roots to support the branches, but as the number of jets had increased, the revenue from passengers had steadily declined. Surely, I suggested, if a tree were getting insufficient food and nourishment through its roots, one would have to be prepared to prune its branches ruthlessly to prevent it dying. This is what the sea staff felt was not being done in Cunard, I continued. The fleet was being reduced, but there didn't seem to us to be anything like the same reduction in the shore staff.

After telling him about my discussions with the retired chief accountant, I launched into the part of my theme that really made the hackles rise. 'I know it was before you came into the company, sir,' I said, 'but in 1962-3 I commanded the Caronia for nearly two years, on voyages that took us away from this country for as much as six months at a time. During most of this time we never saw a manager or a superintendent. As we approached each port, I would radio the company's agent to give him our ETA and let him know our requirements, and when we arrived the pilot and tugs would meet us, the mooring gangs would be waiting on the pier, the oil and water would be supplied, and our catering officer would order the stores he needed through the ship-chandler. After this process had been repeated at port after port all round the world, the ship returned at the end of the cruise in good heart, and both the passengers and crew were happy.

'Then we would get back to Southampton, where we would be met by four managers, four marine superintendents, five engineer superintendents, six catering superintendents, plus purchasing superintendents, furnishing superintendents, and the rest. Is it strange that we find ourselves wondering what all these people do, and how we managed so well without them? We watch the P&O Line bring their two biggest ships, the Canberra and the Oriana, into Southampton, and they are bigger than any ships the Cunard has except the Queens. Yet I understand that their agents make all the arrangements for the ship's reception and everything else is organized by two superintendents who come down from London. Yet these ships are ready to sail ten days later on another voyage that may take them round the world, looking just as smart as any Cunard ship.' The chairman by this time was looking at his watch, so I apologized for going on so long, and he said he had to leave as he was late for a luncheon appointment. John Whitworth also decided he ought to be somewhere else, leaving Phillip Bates to take Angus Letty and me to lunch at his club. After a couple of gins the tension relaxed a little. Phillip Bates said he was sure I was wrong about the way P&O ran their ships, while Angus Letty asked 'Just what the hell were you trying to do, Geoffrey, talk us all out of a job?'

If I had kept my big mouth shut my tour of duty as the commodore might have got away to a better start, for my relations with the managing director were never really cordial after that. Yet I still felt that I was justified in saying what I had for it needed to be said.

There was not much point in my going up to the Clyde to join my new command until the repairs were well advanced, so, as the Queen Elizabeth was due to come out of the Clyde drydock on Wednesday, 9 March, I travelled up to Glasgow two days before. When I went on board I naturally expected to find her almost ready for sea. She was looking extremely smart in her new coat of paint but on board the mess was incredible. The ship had now been on the Clyde for over four months and she was due to sail from Southampton in three weeks, yet of the 300 cabins that were being fitted with showers and toilets there was not a single one completed. The firm of builders was giving priority to another ship which was three months behind on her delivery date.

The structural part of our reconversion, which involved building a new lido deck and an outside swimming pool, had gone reasonably well, as had the work on a complete air-conditioning system for the ship. So on Tuesday, 8 March, when the chairman was having lunch with the officials of the Clyde drydock and then inspecting the ship, I found out that it was intended that he be shown only the new lido deck and those jobs which were nearing completion, whereas I thought that he should see the awful mess in the uncompleted cabins down on C and D decks. This led to an argument with the building firm's manager, Cunard's naval architect, and Cunard's technical director, who said it would not mean anything to Sir Basil to see all those uncompleted rooms, as all ships looked like that during a refit. But I insisted, knowing that we would either have to cancel a cruise and about three voyages, or sail the ship with many uncompleted rooms. I felt that if the chairman saw the situation for himself it would help him to understand this. Actually, when we sailed from Southampton on Tuesday, 29 March, for an Atlantic crossing followed by an Easter cruise to Bermuda, a big section of the ship on D deck was still completely empty: not even the framework of the cabins had been erected. We carried thirty workmen with us and they worked long hours to complete these rooms while the ship was at sea, but their progress was slow, and if the ship had not been held up in Southampton by the seamen's strike, those cabins would not have been ready for use in less than six months.

Another problem in Clydebank was the fantastic amount of pilfering that had been taking place, and before the ship could sail 700 new brass port nuts had to be supplied to replace those which had been taken ashore and sold. There was, it appears, a going rate, and one Cunard port nut equalled one glass of red biddy. The easiest thing to sell in the dockside pubs was copper piping, so the drill was that when a man saw a piece of pipe in an accessible position he first scratched the paint off to be sure it was copper and then hammered a nail into it to see if there was water in it. If not, he cut it up with a hacksaw into suitable lengths to fit down his trouser leg for going through the dock gates. This caused endless problems when we got back to sea again, because in many cases the panels had been replaced without anyone noticing that the pipes had been cut. Then, when the water was turned on at a certain section, we had floods which were very difficult to trace, because water could come out behind panelling a long way from the cut pipe.

Special arrangements had had to be made to fit the Queen Elizabeth into the Clyde drydock and, in spite of pumping out every drop of water that was not essential, and landing all the lifeboats, there were only about two days in each month when the tides were high enough to give her adequate clearance of the dock sill. So on 9 March, the first of those days, all eyes were on the weather, as the morning forecasts spoke of a deepening disturbance moving east to the south of Iceland. Our nautical adviser Captain Angus Letty, the Clyde pilot and I had all agreed that the maximum wind speed for undocking safely was 20 knots, but by 09.00 it was already gusting to 25 knots and a telephone call to the meteorological office at Renfrew airport brought us little comfort: they predicted gusts of 25-30 knots for that day, but Force 8 or 9 gales for the following morning, the last day that month on which we could undock. There was therefore nothing we could do but go, and hope that the force of the wind would hold the ship against the side of the dock and that we should be able to slide out on the fenders without losing more than some of our nice new paint off the side. The most difficult time came once we were clear of the dock and making the tugs fast before swinging her head down river; we had some difficult moments, but the Clyde pilot and the tugs did an excellent job. Then, escorted by six tugs, we made our stately progress down to Greenock, but in the wind that was blowing negotiating every bend became a major operation. The pilot thought that we had touched the bank a couple of times, but the tugs soon pulled her clear and there was no damage.

Down at the tail of the bank, our most difficult task was trying to hoist aboard eight new cruise launches and our other lifeboats—which had been overhauled ashore—in the gales which arrived the following day as predicted. The first day, after struggling for about four hours, the attempt had to be abandoned and the boats and their crews sent ashore for the night. The following day we had better luck and managed to get them all up, but it was a long, wet, cold and miserable job for the boats' crews.

We took a large contingent of workmen round the coast to Southampton with us and hundreds more came down by rail, but even working overtime, completion was an impossible task, although the thirty men who crossed with us did, with help from the ship's staff, manage to get most of C deck habitable before we sailed on our Bermuda cruise on 7 April. We had more than 1,200 passengers booked for this cruise, which pushed the ship to the absolute limit. Within two hours of sailing from New York we had twenty cabins flooded, because of the missing copper pipes. There was no alternative accommodation to offer, but the crew managed to dry everything up and provide new carpets and curtains, so within a couple of hours we had most people back in their rooms and nobody complained. We arrived at Bermuda on Saturday, 9 April and we were exceptionally fortunate in the weather during our two day stay.

After the cruise we went back on the North Atlantic service. Quickly settling down to the old routine, we could look forward to a bumper season because, in addition to now being fully air-conditioned and having more rooms with facilities in cabin and tourist classes, all our first class cabins had been extensively re-furbished. However, we had only made a couple of trips when the seamen's strike started to brew.

Arriving in Cherbourg on Monday, 16 May, we were the first big ship to be affected, and both the BBC and ITV had flown camera teams over to meet the ship and get our crew's reaction. I made every effort to avoid being interviewed; first, because I was not sure what line Cunard would want me to take, and second, because I did not want to say anything that might spoil my good relations with my crew with whom I hoped to sail again. In fact, while I was always anxious to see better conditions for people going to sea, I was against this particular strike because I thought that the seamen had been given a fair wage settlement the previous year. That settlement recognized that while a seaman should be compensated for the Sundays he spends away from home, it also took the realistic view that once a ship leaves port every day is the same, and that time off on Saturday and Sunday was wasted because there would be nothing to do during time off. But having got a 13 per cent wage increase on these terms, the seamen had now come back with a demand for a forty-hour week at sea. This made wonderful propaganda with which to play on the public's emotions, for the public could not see why poor sailors should have to work a longer week than anyone else. What they also did not realize was that the poor sailors were not interested in working only forty hours: they in fact wanted an extra sixteen hours overtime every week.

However, I think that most people now recognize that this long and bitter strike was the culmination of more than thirty years of bad industrial relations. Sailors had in the past never been very union-minded, because a man coming home at the end of a long voyage was more interested in getting home or into the nearest pub than giving up his valuable time to attend union meetings. Eventually, however, they came to think that the NUS had been in the shipowners' pockets for far too long, so new men who had now taken over the running of the union from Sir Thomas Yates tried to purge themselves of the stigma, but at a fantastic cost to the country.

When the Queen Elizabeth cleared Cherbourg, the BBC moved their cameras up on to the bridge, and I could avoid them no longer. I just said briefly that I thought this was a very sad day for the British Merchant Navy, and I felt very like Lord Grey at the start of the First World War. I knew that the lights would be going out in hundreds of ships during the next few days, and I was afraid that some of them might never come on again. The two Queens had been losing money for some time, so that a long strike, or a big increase in seamen's wages, could easily put the Queen Mary out of business, and it might do the same for the Queen Elizabeth, in spite of the fact that she had just been given a long and costly refit.

The Cunard Line was of course the hardest hit of the big shipping companies, because in less than two weeks the whole of its fleet was tied up, and as we were operating scheduled services, it took some weeks after the strike was finally settled to fit all the ships back into the right slots. I have seen various estimates as to just what the strike cost Cunard, some running as high as 4 million pounds, but it certainly took away any ability Sir Basil Smallpeice had to manoeuvre or make changes, and it was followed, in a little over a year, by a savage piece of legislation passed by the American Congress. This prevented any ships which did not comply fully with the latest Inter-governmental Maritime Consultative Organization (IMCO) regulations from carrying passengers from American ports, and was to prove the final blow to Cunard and the end of the Queen Elizabeth.

Back at Southampton, once we had docked and all the crew apart from the officers had left us, there was nothing to do but sit out the strike. During this period of enforced idleness, my wife and I decided that it was time to think about finding a smaller house in the country, in case the strike brought my career at sea to an end earlier than I expected. The result of many miles of motoring through Wiltshire and Dorset eventually turned up the seventeenth-century cottage in a quiet Wiltshire valley that is our home today.

On Saturday, 16 July I sailed again, on the Queen Elizabeth's first voyage after the strike had been finally settled, and we started to pick up the threads of the Atlantic season. It had been badly disrupted, because our foreign competitors, who had obliged our stranded passengers, had made a point of so far as possible securing their return business as well. On 21 September came her first long cruise, and it was to keep me out of the country until early December. The cruise had been designed to fill in that difficult period between the end of the Atlantic season and the start of winter cruising at Christmas, and it took the ship from New York down to Bermuda, then across the Atlantic in what was hoped would be fine-weather latitudes, to Ponta Delgada in the Azores and Lisbon. From there we went south via Gibraltar, Tangier and Madeira to Dakar, where we crossed the Atlantic again in the warm waters of the equatorial current to Barbados, then sailing north through the West Indies, via Curaçao and St Thomas to New York. Our call at Bermuda on 30 October was routine and everything went well until the second day after we left, when instead of the fine weather we had been hoping for so far south of our normal Atlantic route, we ran into easterly gales against which we had to battle all the way to Lisbon. It was most unusual weather for that area, where the Azores anticyclone normally maintains a moderate westerly airflow. The day we reached Ponta Delgada it was blowing a full Force 8 gale, with heavy seas, so all we could do was to close the breakwater while a small pilot launch battled its way out in heavy seas to deliver our mail. Because the Azores are mountain peaks rising almost vertically from the sea, we were able to take the ship round the island only about a mile from the shore and, particularly on the lee side where we got shelter from the gale, this enabled our passengers to see almost as much of some of the little villages as they would have done on an overland tour.

The weather when we arrived at Lisbon on Saturday, 5 November was also very stormy, although when we entered the harbour in the early morning the swell on the bar at the mouth of the River Tagus did not cause us any worry. However, the gale force winds made bringing the heavy barges and the floating crane to lift the gangways alongside very difficult, and after we had rigged a gangway on one side the weather forced us to abandon the attempt to rig one on the other. Nevertheless, we managed to get the ferry service started and the tours away. But that afternoon a vigorous cold front swept up the Tagus and gusts up to 60 miles an hour were recorded at Lisbon airport in a fierce rain squall. Two ferry-boats, both loaded with passengers, had to heave-to in mid-river because the seas were too rough to allow them to come alongside either the ship or the pier, while about four hundred of our passengers had to shelter in the ferry terminal not knowing whether they would be able to get back to the ship or not. Indeed, it looked so bad for a time that some passengers booked overnight accommodation in hotels, which they later expected the company to pay for. But by 18.00 the wind had dropped almost as quickly as it had sprung up, and the following day, although the weather was still cloudy with heavy showers, the wind had moderated to a fresh breeze.

We were due to weigh anchor at midnight that night so as to cross the bar at high water, which was at 02.00; but about two hours before we were due to sail the Portuguese pilot boarded and presented me with a most unusual problem. A deep depression passing to the south of Ireland the previous day had set up a heavy westerly swell on the bar, so he had been down to Cascais Bay that evening and made careful observations of the swells. He estimated that the average height from trough to crest was 12-15 feet, and the distance between the crests about 200 feet. Now the depth of water on the bar at low water is 36 feet, which means that according to the phase of the moon there would be between 45-48 feet at high water. Full of water and oil, as she would be on leaving, the Queen Elizabeth would have a deepest draught of 40 feet, and could in smooth water expect to have at least 5 feet of water under her keel. But what happens at the bottom of a 15-foot swell? Would her bows be left 10 feet in the sand? Our pilot reassured me that with our length of 1,031 feet we could get out safely, whereas with a shorter ship of the same draught, it would be dangerous. The reason for this is, we should be meeting the swells end-on, and our length would mean that the ship was always supported by at least four swells at any time, so the lift of her bows should not exceed 4 feet.

He had demonstrated all this very carefully with drawings, but as we moved slowly down the channel in the early hours of the morning, watching the minutes carefully so as to catch the top of the tide, I was far from happy about it. As we approached the bar we barely had steerage way on the ship, so that if the bows touched it would only be a bump on the soft sand; but although the echo-sounder showed less than 2 feet of water under the keel at times, nobody, not even the people in the engine room—who had been specially warned to listen for a bump—felt her touch the bottom. Eventually we were outside and breathing more freely, but the weather was far too rough to land the pilot so we had to carry him on to Gibraltar, where we arrived at about 09.00 the same day. Although the weather was still unpleasant, cloudy and rainy, we did manage to find a sheltered anchorage where the tenders could operate. After we had anchored I was handed a cable from our agent in Tangier, our next port, where we were due later that afternoon. This gave the weather forecast as northwesterly winds of 25-30 knots, with swells 16-18 feet high. I knew the anchorage at Tangier well from bitter experiences on both the Caronia and the Britannic, and if there was one place in the world I was not going to take the Queen Elizabeth in that sort of weather, it was Tangier. We decided to extend our stay at Gibraltar by twelve hours, but this did not please a lot of our passengers, who had now missed two out of the first five ports on their cruise, and who had been looking forward to the Tangier call as their only glimpse of the Arab world on this voyage.

The unpleasant weather was also giving rise to unfavourable comments. But when we arrived at our next port, Madeira, on Wednesday, 9 November and it was a bright sunny morning, I was able to put in my report to the company that the passengers were delighted to see the sun for the first time that month. So from there on down to Dakar, then cruising through the Cape Verde Islands to Barbados, it was sunshine all the way; in fact, it became too warm, and led to more problems. When the two Queens were built in the late thirties, air-conditioning was something out of science fiction, so when they came out with the public rooms air-conditioned, it was quite an innovation. So long as the ships remained in the cool waters of the North Atlantic this equipment had worked reasonably well for over a quarter of a century. During her reconversion, the Queen Elizabeth had been fully air-conditioned, but for reasons of economy the company decided to leave the old system to take care of the public rooms. Unfortunately, this old equipment depended for its efficiency on the cooling power of sea-water, and when we got into the equatorial current, with sea water temperatures of 87 degrees and over, it refused to function, and there was nothing our air-conditioning engineers could do to stop the temperature in the restaurants and the public rooms from climbing into the nineties. The heat in these rooms was all the more noticeable because the new plant was keeping the cabins at such a pleasant temperature, and eventually our cruise director had to move as much as possible of the evening's entertainment out on deck, under the stars, until we started to move north through the Caribbean and into cooler seas again.

On the ship's return to Southampton the experts were called in, and they managed to find a way to switch some of the surplus capacity of the modern plant to the public rooms, and we had no further problems on our later cruises; though perhaps this was because we managed to keep out of the equatorial current. The rest of the cruise went smoothly and was without incident. One's memory for discomfort is reasonably short, and just as our ten sunless days were soon buried under layers of sunburn and peeled noses, so, after a few days of cool weather, even the excessive heat was forgotten.

We arrived back from the Atlantic crossing after the cruise at the end of November and went into drydock. But the ship had already had all the refitting that the company could afford for that year, so very little was done and we sailed again on 16 December for New York to start our first season of winter cruising. It was during this time in Southampton that the Cunard Line held its first and last masters' conference. This was the brainchild of Sir Basil Small-peice, and about a dozen captains of the company's passenger and cargo ships spent three days meeting the chairman, two other directors and all the heads of the various departments in a social atmosphere, to discuss problems. This was an excellent idea and the first serious attempt to break down the barriers between shore staff and sea staff.

Yet it was at this conference that the way was being prepared to shorten my term of duty as commodore. The managing director, Phillip Bates, called me and said, 'I understand that you were told by Sir John Brocklebank that when the new ship came out, she would be the Commodore Ship and you would go there,' and I agreed that that was the case. He thereupon told me that the chairman had now decided that even when the new ship came out the commodore would remain in the Queen Elizabeth, because she would still be the largest unit of the fleet. The intention was to appoint Captain W E Warwick, then captain of the Caronia, to the new ship, because although she was not going to be ready for another two years they wanted him to act as the management representative during the construction period. Naturally I said that I was a little disappointed, because to me there is always an air of challenge about a new ship; but, as I was very proud of my present command and the ship's company, I should be happy to stay with them.

Unfortunately our first cruises from New York to the West Indies were not well booked, except the short cruises to Nassau over holiday periods. On one cruise in the middle of January the bookings were so poor that the company decided to cancel the cruise and send the ship on an unscheduled Atlantic crossing. This was a decision that I strongly disagreed with, because it meant running the ship at high speed, burning about 1,200 tons of fuel a day, to carry a total of about seventy passengers one way and about a hundred and thirty the other. In fact, we called it the 'ghost ship' voyage.

But it was when we arrived at New York at the end of this voyage that, because of a strike, I had to dock the ship in New York without tugs, an operation that had already been carried out several times before with both the Queens, since Commodore Sir Robert Irving's first unassisted docking of the Queen Mary in the early spring of 1939, when, as a junior officer, I had watched with amazement. But on all the previous occasions it had been done when the company still used Pier 90, which could take a Queen on either side, so it was possible to come up-river stemming the ebb tide, put the ship on the knuckle and then dock on the north side of the pier. By 1967 we had moved over to Pier 92, which had only been dredged to take a Queen on the south side, and this meant that I had to come up with the flood tide behind me a couple of hours before high water and turn the ship at rest above the berth, in order to approach the berth stemming the flood tide. Because the navigable part of the river at this point is less than three times the length of the ship, in strong winds a turn at rest in such a confined space could be extremely difficult, if not impossible to make. But this was the one day in my life when the weather was perfect.

My original intention was to drop the port anchor underfoot and use it to steady the bow as we let the ship drop down slowly on to the corner of the pier, where there was a special fender on which the hull could rest, while we waited for the young ebb tide to swing the stern round and let us move her into the slip. But after the port anchor had been dropped I found that instead of dragging through the mud, as I expected it to, the cable running underneath the hull was holding, and I was able to use this as a fulcrum on which to turn the ship with the engines. By this time a small boat had taken one of our lines ashore; and it was carried up the dock with a weight on it, to help steady the bow. Then, because the tide was almost slack and there was so little flood left, I was able to get the ship round almost into line with the slip. By now I had given up any idea of putting her on the knuckle, so we heaved the port anchor up and started to move into the slip. Once the bows were almost half way up the slip, the ship was not likely to be affected by the tide in the Hudson River, and all we had to do was keep her parallel with the dock until the stern lines were ashore; then, by heaving away at both ends together, we got her alongside.

When we had stopped in the Narrows for the immigration and other officials to board that day, I had seen the press men and TV cameras being brought on as well. They had then asked permission to set up their cameras on the bridge. 'You people are like a lot of ghouls,' I said. 'You've only come here in the hope that I'll hit the pier and give you some good pictures! This operation of docking the Queens without tugs has been done successfully so many times before, it cannot possibly be news.' However, I have always found that co-operation with the press pays handsome dividends, and this was to prove no exception; almost all the published accounts of that afternoon's work that I read were embarrassingly flattering.

After another short cruise to the West Indies, on Tuesday, 21 February we set off on a long cruise to the Mediterranean. As on our autumn cruise, the company had arranged for us to call at the two ports of Gibraltar and Tangier on the same day; but as we had passed Tangier on our way from Las Palmas and I saw the heavy swells rolling into the bay, I knew that any attempt to land passengers in that exposed anchorage could be disastrous. I informed the company that I intended to call at Palma, Majorca, instead, to which they did not take very kindly, for they always prefer to stick to the printed schedule. However, on this occasion I had been able to talk to most of the passengers in the main lounge the evening before, to explain why I was making the change and point out that because of the saving in distance they would be able to have a full day in Palma instead of half a day in Tangier, all of which was very well received.

After our call at Palma, which was favoured by perfect weather, we ran the full length of the Mediterranean, but at 01.14 on the morning of Saturday, 4 March I was hurriedly called by the officer of the watch, who said there was a man overboard, and I dashed up on the bridge to find that he had put the engines on 'Stand by' and was bringing the ship round to port. There was a good deal of confusion as to when the man had actually gone overboard, and although a lifebuoy had been thrown the light on it had not ignited.

Apparently the young man in question had been in a depressed state, and after drinking heavily had threatened to jump over the side; but the man who had dashed up to the bridge to give the alarm wasn't clear about what had happened.

It was a very nasty night with a wind of almost gale force from the WNW and a steep tumbling sea, conditions which would have made survival difficult for even a strong swimmer. We slowed the ship right down, posted lookouts along both sides and brought her back as close as possible to where we thought he had gone over, where we stopped to see if we could hear anyone shouting. For two hours we searched the area as well as we could, but with no certain focal point to start from and with the difficulty of turning in that wind it seemed hopeless. It was also difficult to believe that a man who was probably winded by falling 60 feet from the deck of a ship doing 20 knots could survive that long in such a rough sea. These decisions about when to leave someone who has fallen overboard are always the most difficult that any master has to make, because there are so many stories of people who have survived for long periods in almost incredible circumstances. I felt that I would have liked to wait for daylight, but that would have been six hours after he jumped, and even then it would have been like starting to look for a needle in a haystack. So shortly after 03.00 we resumed our course, after first making a broadcast asking all ships to keep a good lookout in that area, and increased speed to make up lost time.

But we need not have worried about trying to keep to our schedule, for when we reached our anchorage off Alexandria a Force 8 gale was blowing from the WNW, with 12-15 foot seas, and the waves pounding the breakwaters of the eastern harbour were sending columns of spray 30 feet into the air. One tug and a naval gunboat did venture out of the harbour, but they could not get anywhere near the ship. Our anchorage had no protection from the westerly gale, and even with two anchors down and using the engines to ease the weight on the cables the ship dragged for almost a mile, burnishing both anchors and cables by the polishing action of the sand. Shortly before noon I decided to weigh anchors and steam out to sea, to wait for an improvement in the weather.

The ship was scheduled to remain at anchor off Alexandria for four days, to allow the American Express Company to operate one of the most complex series of tours ever devised for a cruise ship. There were about fourteen different excursions due to start from this port, some lasting as long as seven days, after which the passengers would rejoin the ship at Beirut, down to one-day trips to Cairo, and they all involved reservations on trains, planes or coaches. The afternoon weather forecast brought us no comfort at all, predicting that a deep depression which had become stationary near Cyprus would probably start to fill but that there would be little change in the conditions off Alexandria for another seventy-two hours. I then called a conference with the department heads, the cruise director and the head of American Express and warned them that we could easily spend another four days here waiting for the weather to moderate, and then still perhaps have to abandon what was always the most interesting call on any Mediterranean cruise, making it necessary for American Express to hand back the many thousands of dollars they had collected for all the tours they had planned. Alternatively, we could make a 1,200-mile diversion to Athens, the only port in the Eastern Mediterranean where I felt that the ship could work in the present weather conditions, returning to Alexandria in four days' time, by which time we could hope that the weather might have moderated sufficiently to allow us to carry through our full published programme. Our scheduled calls were Alexandria, Beirut, Haifa, Rhodes, Athens, Messina; but this change would make it Athens, Alexandria, Beirut and Haifa. I estimated that by missing the half-day call at Rhodes the ship could be back on her published schedule by the time she got to Messina. However, this involved steaming an extra 1,200 miles at full speed, in order to fit in the two-day call at Athens and be back across in four days. This would add another £20,000 to our fuel bill and reduce the company's margin of profit, if any, by that amount; so I was going to have to get management approval.

By now it was 17.00 on a Saturday afternoon, but I managed to get hold of the duty manager in Southampton, and he contacted the managing director Phillip Bates at his home near Lymington; by 20.00 we had the official approval we needed. The next thing to do was to contact our agent in Athens, an elderly and rather excitable Greek gentleman, and tell him of our change of plan, and that we would need fuel and fresh water on our arrival at Piraeus at 09.00 the following morning, Sunday. The real burden, however, was to fall on American Express, who had to advance all the Athens tours and hotel reservations by ten days, and then to reschedule all the Alexandria, Beirut and Haifa ones four days later, and cancel those at Rhodes. Resignedly, they just settled down and kept two radio telephone circuits open all through the night.

I tried to explain the situation to the passengers in considerably less detail than I have here, and I found that frankness and preparing people for the worst that can happen paid off, because instead of complaints I got a most enthusiastic reception.

The next morning we were in the lee of the Greek mountains, with the weather quiet and sunny, though very cool. The hard work by American Express during the night produced results, as all the tours got away as planned. After another high-speed dash across the Mediterranean, we arrived back off Alexandria on the Wednesday morning to find that the wind had dropped to a gentle breeze and the weather was sunny and warm. Unfortunately, the storm had left behind a heavy swell which, although it went down slowly, was to remain with us for the whole of our four-day stay. This made landing and embarking passengers with the ship's launches difficult, especially on the first day.

A ship of the size of the Queen Elizabeth could provide a good lee in any weather, as long as some means can be devised to keep the wind and sea on one side. But while she is lying at anchor all the forces of nature combine to keep her lying head to wind and sea, and the waves running down the ship's side make life uncomfortable for boats coming alongside the landing platforms, even though ours were the largest and most substantial landing platforms that I had ever seen on any cruise ship. The Egyptian government had supplied a tug to help us to hold the ship across the wind to try to create a lee, but she wasn't nearly heavy enough to work in the open sea in a swell of that size. She plunged so heavily that she broke every rope that we could afford to lose; then, when we tried to use her pushing on the quarter, as we had done with the tug in Bermuda, she stove in her bow plates! However, she was of some help, and by using her, and twisting the ship with our engines, we managed to get everyone ashore who wanted to go (including one elderly lady in a wheelchair) and all the tours left on time.

It meant a lot of hard work for the ship's seamen, both the boat crews and the men on the landing platforms, who at times literally had to lift elderly or infirm people in and out of the launches. It was a very worrying time also, because there was always the risk of somebody being seriously injured, and it meant long weary hours on the bridge, ensuring that each boat as it came alongside had the best possible lee that we could give it. I was very relieved when we got through not only our four days there but the whole of the cruise without having a single passenger or crew member injured; but the launches took quite a bashing at times and they required a lot of minor repairs, both by the ship's staff during the cruise and after we got back to Southampton.

Once we got away from Alexandria, the remainder of the cruise went very well, and the only other port where we had problems with our boats was at Barcelona, where we had to anchor nearly a mile outside the breakwater, for although it was a beautiful day with no wind there was a heavy swell coming down from the Gulf of Lions. However, a couple of the harbour tugs towing on very long lines managed to hold us across the swell, though they had a very bumpy ride themselves.

Towards the end of this cruise I was beginning to feel the strain myself. In nearly seven months I had spent only seven days in my new home at Woodfalls, and after leaving Cannes I had caught a flu-type cold with laryngitis which left me speechless for a couple of days. But by the time we left Madeira, on our last leg across the Atlantic, I felt I was getting better and that I could now relax, as all our troubles were behind us. Almost, but not quite. Our first morning at sea I went up on the bridge at about 08.30 to talk to the officer of the watch and as I was leaving to return to my cabin, I fell on some detergent which had been spilled on the nylon cord matting. I concluded the performance lying on the deck with a dislocated right ankle, a fractured fibia and a cracked tibia, and in considerable pain. After I had been put under sedation I was taken down to the ship's hospital and given a general anaesthetic while they resolved the dislocation and put my broken bones in plaster. When I came round the doctor said: 'Well, Commodore, you're in a bit of a mess. But this could prove a blessing in disguise; you have been doing too much, so it was high time you slowed down a bit. This is going to keep you quiet for at least a couple of months.'

I had to hand over the command of the ship to my staff captain, George Smith, and go home as a passenger. By the time I arrived on Wednesday, 5 April, spring was well under way in our little Wiltshire valley, and during the next two months, while what must have been one of the most widely publicized broken legs for some time grew strong again, I gradually came to understand what my wife had seen in our new home, and to share her affection for it.

It was during this period of sick leave that Phillip Bates called at my home to brief me on the latest news, which was that because of the seamen's strike, with its heavy drain on the company's resources, and new restrictive legislation that the American Congress was now expected to pass, the Cunard board of directors had decided that the Queen Mary was to be retired and offered for sale at the end of 1967, and that the Queen Elizabeth would suffer the same fate one year later, just before the new ship was expected to go into service.

This was a very sad blow as far as the Queen Elizabeth was concerned, because she was only just feeling the full effect of her big refit, which had cost the company £1.75 million, and although her first season of winter cruising had not produced good financial results, it being a new role for her, I felt that she was only just getting into her stride. I thought that if the management would consult the ship's people about the selection of cruise ports where we *knew* that the ship could operate efficiently, she could do well, for I had received so many appreciative letters from passengers. I felt that it was a mistake, too, to announce the end of her useful life so long before it was to happen. It seemed to me that they could have put in that little word 'if' somewhere in their announcement; it would have done so much for my crew's morale, and it would have stopped all the passengers who came to my cabin for cocktails saying 'We feel so sad to think of your beautiful ship being scrapped, Commodore.'

At about this time I received a letter from a former passenger, Leonard Stevens, who was engaged in writing a book about a

Above RMS *Queen Elizabeth* docking in New York during a tug-boat strike on 1 February 1968. The port anchor has been dropped off the end of Pier 92, and a port bow-line run ashore. The ship is being turned with the engines to bring her parallel with the pier.

Below RMS *Queen Elizabeth* has now been turned almost parallel to the slip and the port anchor has been weighed, so she is ready to start moving in to her berth.

Above The ship is now about one-third of the way up the slip, with three bow-lines ashore.

Left Now it is only a matter of moving slowly into the berth as the ship is well over half-way into the slip, and no longer likely to be affected by the tide in the river.

Above I can breathe freely once again with the *Queen Elizabeth* safely in her berth and the seamen making her fast.

Right On the bridge of RMS *Queen Elizabeth* leaving Southampton on 24 September 1968. (*Photograph courtesy of Colin Walker*)

Above On the bridge of RMS *Queen Elizabeth* leaving Southampton on 24 September 1968. I am standing in the centre of the bridge with the Pilot Captain Jack Holt on my right, and the OOW Senior First Officer Gossett on my left. (*Photograph courtesy of Colin Walker*)

Below A press conference in the Verandah Grill of the *Queen Elizabeth* on 30 October 1968 with Mayor John Lindsay.

The RMS *Queen Elizabeth*'s final departure from the Port of New York on 30 October 1968, accompanied by a fleet of tugs and fireboats, with her paying off pennant streaming out in the stiff breeze on her port side.

Above The solid-silver rose bowl presented to me by the ships company of RMS *Queen Elizabeth* at their farewell dance on 2 November 1968.

Left On the bridge of RMS *Queen Elizabeth* during HM The Queen Mother's farewell visit to the ship on 6 November 1968. Sir Basil Smallpiece, the Cunard chairman, is standing by the wheel with Her Majesty and me.

Right Her Majesty Queen Elizabeth the Queen Mother, on the bridge of the RMS *Queen Elizabeth* during Her Majesty's farewell visit to the ship.

RMS *Queen Elizabeth* now the property of the Chinese shipping millionaire C Y Tung, and renamed SS *Seawise University* leaving Port Everglades, Florida, at the start of her voyage to Hong Kong on 10 February 1971.

The end of the world's largest passenger liner, RMS *Queen Elizabeth* on fire fore and aft in Hong Kong Harbour shortly before she sank on 8 January 1972.

complete round voyage he had made in the ship just after our big refit, which was to be published at the end of the year under the title *Elizabeth, the Passage of a Queen*, asking me as the commodore to write a foreword to his book. After I had written it I submitted it to the managing director for his approval, but he took his blue pencil and edited out large chunks of what I had written, because he said I had let my personal feelings show too strongly, and because my position as commodore might lead people to think that the views I was expressing reflected company policy. So the foreword that eventually appeared under my name bore little relation to the original. Now that it is all a matter of history and can affect no one, perhaps some of my readers might be interested to read the unexpurgated version given below:

FOREWORD

When I first heard the news that both of the great Queen liners were to be retired before the end of 1968, it came as a deep personal shock, because during the thirty years that have passed since I joined the Queen Mary as a junior officer early in 1938 these two remarkable ships seem to have somehow woven themselves into the tapestry of my life. When construction of the Queen Mary's replacement started on Clydebank, I realized that her days were numbered and this announcement has only brought forward the sad day of her final voyage by about a year. But I felt that the Queen Elizabeth, in which I was so proud to fly my flag as commodore, was still in great heart—having during her extensive overhaul on the Clyde in the winter of 1965-6 been fully air conditioned and fitted with lido decks and an outdoor swimming pool to enable her to operate as a cruise liner in those periods when the number of passengers crossing the North Atlantic by sea was insufficient to sustain a ship of her size. I was convinced that she still had several years of useful life ahead of her—both as a cruise ship and as a running mate for the new Cunarder in maintaining the two-ship weekly transatlantic express service that had been the dream of her creator, the late Sir Percy Bates. Unfortunately, the stern laws of economics—which we are told must be obeyed, if any commercial enterprise is to survive—leave no place for sentiment. Within the year, this magnificent ship has to follow her older sister into retirement, leaving many sad hearts among those who have sailed in her and grown to love her sea-kindly qualities and her atmosphere of solid comfort and luxury.

One of our oldest British traditions is summed up in those famous words 'The Queen is dead, Long live the Queen', and the Cunard Line's many friends will be glad to know that most of the Queen Elizabeth's crew, who have over the years built up her reputation for superb service, will, within a few weeks of her final voyage, transfer to take the new ship away on her maiden voyage. In her passing, this ship will hand on the torch to a younger, more modern, and hopefully more economical sister, who will, I am sure, carry the Cunard houseflag proudly both on the North Atlantic and on luxury cruises.

But to all those people who, like myself, have over the years developed a real affection for the Queens—who watched the Queen Mary capture the Blue Riband in those far off pre-war days—marvelled at their splendid wartime record, when each ship was bringing the equivalent of a division of troops at a time unescorted across the Atlantic—saw them in those years of great prosperity after the war, sailing voyage after voyage booked to capacity—and who have admired them lately in their gallant struggle against the economics of jet travel—one wonders if there can ever be anything to quite come up to these two wonderful ships. Surely the same thing must be said of them as was said of Winston Churchill: 'We shall never see their like again.' Their passing must mark the end of an era of a special kind of gracious living.

Fortunately, in this carefully observed and meticulously detailed account of an ocean crossing in the Queen Elizabeth, Professor Leonard Stevens has captured much of the atmosphere that will enable a 'Great Lady' to live on in our hearts long after she has crossed the North Atlantic for the last time.

Geoffrey Marr DSC, RD
Commodore

RMS Queen Elizabeth
New York
15 August 1967

By the middle of June the orthopaedic surgeon pronounced my leg strong enough to stand the rigours of sea life again, and on 29 June I rejoined my ship in Southampton. But because sick leave does not count against one's ordinary leave entitlement, with the year more than half over I still had a lot of leave due to me. I therefore remember the summer of 1967 as the time I was doing two voyages and then having a voyage off, and thus seeing more of my home than I had for a long time. These were far from happy days for the company, and it soon became known that the Caronia, a ship only nineteen years old, would be another victim of the new American legislation, and because the company could not afford the quarter of a million pounds it was going to cost to bring her into line with the 1966 IMCO regulations, she would be sold, a fate from which this once beautiful, luxurious and popular ship (whose reputation with discerning world travellers stood so high that she is still the standard by which they judge all other cruise ships) has not so far recovered, for her fortunes today are indeed low.

In November came the night of the long knives, when I had to assemble my ship's company and read to them the chairman's message telling them that, in addition to the two Queens, which they already knew about, the Caronia, Sylvania and Carinthia were all to be withdrawn from service and put up for sale. In effect— Cunard was for sale. Thus, 1957's greatest passenger fleet on the North Atlantic was within ten short years to be reduced to three ships. But it was what this meant in terms of human lives that was important, because within the space of a couple of months 2,700 men and women, many of them with a lifetime of service, were to lose their means of livelihood. It was certainly a grim time and, as the ships came into their home port, those on whom the axe was to fall were called in and told that it was a case of being given redundancy pay or taking early retirement.

However one looks at it, the choice was bitter, and it seemed a poor reward to those who had in many cases devoted the whole of their working lives to the service of the once great Cunard Line. Quite a number of the younger men managed to find other more or less suitable posts, but the situation left behind a trail of hopes betrayed and lives shadowed and bewildered by the unexpected turn of events: particularly among older men and women who were not old enough for ordinary retirement. It is a sad tale, but one that is too often retold in the business climate of today.

CHAPTER FIFTEEN

The last voyage

With the Queen Mary away on her last
cruise to her new home in Long Beach, California, and the
Caronia sold away to Greece for the refit that Cunard could not
afford, for her final season the Queen Elizabeth had both the New
York cruise market and the North Atlantic to herself as far as
Cunard passengers were concerned, and business became better than
it had been for some years.

I felt that it was a tactical mistake for the company to be so
definite about the ship's withdrawal so long before the actual date.
It made me feel that she was like a cheap store that has huge notices
outside which say Final Closing Down Sale more or less permanently displayed. However, it must be admitted that some of our
passengers both on the cruises we made that winter and on our
Atlantic voyages made a special effort to travel in the ship for
nostalgic reasons. Whether for such reasons or not, our numbers
during that last series of cruises from New York were a great improvement on the previous year, and we only sailed on one cruise
with less than 1,000 passengers. The company had at last agreed to
send the ship only to ports where the facilities were suitable for a
vessel of her size. This meant that all the cruises we made were
highly successful, and I had some enthusiastic reports from passengers. But where the management did not take the ship's staff's
advice was in fitting in a series of North Atlantic winter voyages
between the cruises. As these were properly scheduled voyages they
were nothing like as bad as our 'ghost ship' voyage of the winter
before, but with total passenger lists of under 700 in all classes,
they all lost money, for not only did we run up extremely heavy
fuel bills as we tried to maintain our 28½ knot schedule through

the winter gales, but the racking and straining of the ship in heavy weather, plus the effects of the wind, rain and smoke, made it so difficult to keep our paintwork looking like a cruise ship's should —immaculate.

It was on one of our last cruises that Sir Basil Smallpeice, our chairman, joined the ship in Barbados, and did the last five days of the cruise to New York with us. Apart from the very formal meeting in his Regent Street office, when I had said my piece about how I saw the company's future, and a few brief encounters during the masters' conference, this was the first opportunity that I had ever had to spend any length of time with the chairman and get to know him a little better. Boldly I made the most of the opportunities presented to put forward more of my views regarding the Queen Elizabeth. This time, having already been told by the managing director that once my ship came out of service I should be taking retirement, I felt I had nothing to lose, and found myself saying, 'You know, sir, I am in a rather unique position in that, knowing I am now leaving the company, I can probably talk to you more freely and frankly than any other of your senior employees.' Although he probably thought that I had too much to say, I went on that I felt that the board was making a mistake in retiring the Queen Elizabeth so soon after investing millions in her major overhaul, because I was confident that if only they could find the extra money to bring her into line with the new regulations she could pay her way and provide a reasonable return on their investment. I pointed out how popular this season's cruises had been, and that he could see for himself how well our present cruise was going. We could hold our own with the new ship, I told him, by doing the shorter West Indies cruises from New York, plus one West Indies cruise from England each year, like the one I had done in 1965 in the Mauretania. This would leave the new ship to take the Caronia's place in doing the more glamorous longer cruises, including even a shortened world cruise. We could then do the Atlantic voyages at the beginning and end of the season, when the numbers are not so good, and they would be able to maintain the Cunard tradition of a weekly service with two ships all through the peak season.

I must say that he listened politely to this and to many other suggestions I made about other aspects of the company's business, but I believed that the 1967 decisions had to stand, because once the board had made a decision, it would be unlikely to reverse it, if for *no other reason* than that it might lose face. The most I got out of these discussions was an admission that some mistakes had been made by the 'new boys', and with this I had to be content; but I couldn't help reflecting that, working under the same difficulties of the seamen's strike, rising costs, and so on, other shipping companies appeared to be doing well. Surely it could not be by accident?

Once we got back on our regular Atlantic run for the summer season, our passenger numbers steadily improved, and by May earnings started to overtake expenses. Since she had not had an expensive refit that year the ship started to contribute a small but steadily increasing profit to the company's accounts.

There was little of note to report about our final season, except how pleasant it was to meet so many old friends again, and to hear so many glowing tributes paid to the ship and her crew, although even on our final voyage we seemed a little under the shadow of the tremendous amount of publicity given to the very popular Queen Mary the year before. This popularity was hard to understand in some ways, as in the USA people seem to give both ships equal note because of the war service they shared in ferrying American troops.

However, when we left New York for the last time, on Wednesday, 30 October, there was no doubt about the warmth of the traditional send-off they gave us on a bright, clear autumn day. Mayor John Lindsay came on board and made a very fine speech, detailing the close connection the two ships had always had with the city. He then presented a plaque from the American government, as a citation for the ship's war service, and a bronze medallion from the city of New York in recognition of the close links between the ship and the city. As we left the pier the ship had known so well, and during our royal progress downriver to the south of Manhattan island, the tugs and fireboats, together with all the ships in the harbour, saluted us. Indeed, some of the tugboats had their decks crowded with sightseers and stayed with us right to the

Narrows, only pulling away when we started to increase speed after passing under Verrazano Bridge.

My most treasured memento of that day, however, and one of my proudest possessions, is the following letter I received from the one-time Ambassador to the Court of St James, L W Douglas— a man held in great affection by his British colleagues and friends— whose daughter Sharon was making her honeymoon voyage with us. He wrote:

My dear Commodore Marr:

On the eve of the Queen Elizabeth's last voyage to her native shores it is fitting that the people of the western world should be reminded of the indispensable role that she and her older sister, the Queen Mary, played in the last great world-wide convulsion.

For almost three years these two Sovereigns of the Seas silently sped across the waters of the North Atlantic, carrying with them more than two million fighting men from this continent to join the soldiers of the English-speaking world who had fought so gallantly, and were to continue to engage so successfully, the evil forces that Hitler had unleashed on the world.

In the darkness of the night, each of the great ships would quietly slip into the sheltering harbours of the Clyde or New York and, within less than seventy-two hours, in the greyness of the dawn, or the blackness of midnight, unheralded and un-sung, would vanish into the vast spaces of the Atlantic, to run the gauntlet of the hostile German wolf-packs awaiting them. Unescorted during the last few miles of each voyage, their speed, under the skilful command of their officers, enabled them success-fully to elude the vigilant enemy who would have sent them to the bottom of the ocean.

Each ship made two round trips a month. During every summer month, when the North Atlantic was less boisterous, together they carried almost 70,000 soldiers to fight for freedom in England and in Europe; during each of the winter months, when the seas were apt to be more turbulent, they lifted almost 62,000 men in uniform to the white cliffs of southern England.

There is in history a chain of events that, as the first link is welded, leads on to others. So it is in the case of these noble ships. Had it not been for Sir Percy Bates's determination to cause the Queens to be constructed and slip down their ways into the Clyde; had they not been available to move more than two million American troops across the North Atlantic; had these troops not been assembled in Britain for the cross-Channel *Operation Overlord* in June 1944, there would have been no invasion of Normandy, and the 'buzz-bomb' launching pads on the European continent would not have been captured in time to save London from being reduced to a pile of rubble.

The two great Queens thus soldered the chain which was to frustrate Hitler's ambition to obliterate the basic freedoms of the civilized world.

And so—as you guide the last of the two matchless Queens on her final voyage, will you bid her an affectionate and reverent *Ave atque vale* from those in this troubled world who owe so much to their uninterrupted and glorious contribution to the cause of free men, everywhere.

They have merited a high place on the roster of the world's immortals. One generation succeeds another. Soon another Queen will replace the one we now salute. She will carry on the unfinished task of binding the Old World closer to the New.

Yours very sincerely,

L W Douglas

The last event of that voyage was a poignant occasion. At the end of the entertainment I made a speech thanking all the artists who had taken part, and also thanking our passengers for the part they had played in making it such a memorable final Atlantic crossing. Then all the cabaret artists, the staff, and as many of the passengers as could do so, crowded on to the dance floor and linked arms for a fervent, final rendering of 'Auld Lang Syne' which brought a lump to my throat and tears to the eyes of many people, who knew that it was the end of an era. It was hard to bear.

It was during our stay in Southampton, before starting our farewell cruise to Las Palmas, that Her Majesty Queen Elizabeth, the Queen Mother, made a special journey from London on 6 November, to say a royal farewell to the ship she had launched just a little over thirty years before. It was a cool, but bright clear day and although the ship had been looking rather grimy when we docked, after a stormy Atlantic crossing during which we had a couple of our forced draught fans out of commission, the shore gang had managed to wash the funnels and the white paintwork on the starboard side, the one you could see from the dock, and all hands had worked with a will, polishing everything inside the ship that could be polished. Also, Cunard and British Rail had gone to town in lining both R deck square where her Majesty would board the ship, and inside the terminal, where she was to be received by civic dignitaries, with banks of flowering plants. She really did look a ship that we could be proud of when the Queen Mother stepped on board shortly before noon, to be greeted by the staff captain W J Law and myself. By strange coincidence, we had been the two men most closely associated with her during the Atlantic crossing that she made in 1954, when I had been staff captain of the Queen Mary, with Captain Law holding the same position on the Queen Elizabeth.

After she had talked for a while to the crew members, drawn up as a guard of honour on R deck square, the chairman, Captain Law and I escorted her to the promenade deck where, in the Midships Bar, she was introduced to all of the ship's senior officers and to representatives of the directors and managers. Then cocktails were served before we went up to the Verandah Grill for lunch, during which Sir Basil Smallpeice sat on her left and I sat on her right. With Her Majesty's wonderful capacity for making everyone feel completely at ease, lunch was a very pleasant affair, and she asked many searching questions about what would happen to the ship when she arrived in Florida at the beginning of December, and expressed the hope that the end of her life would be in line with the same proud tradition that she had maintained in both war and peace. I kept my forebodings to myself.

At the end of the lunch, Sir Basil made a short speech thanking Her Majesty for the honour she had done both to the ship and to the Cunard Line by giving up a whole day to make this visit—and asked her to accept a set of the numbered glass goblets which had been specially designed to commemorate our final voyage. Her Majesty made a short reply, mentioning how closely she had followed the career of the ship that bore her name.

She then made a tour of the main public rooms and the bridge, which at her own request had been specially arranged to give her the opportunity to meet as many as possible of the men and women of all departments who had long periods of service either with the ship or with the Cunard Line.

The following day was also rather an emotional one for me, because the ship's company were holding their farewell dance at a ballroom in Southampton. It really was a splendid occasion, and the hall was packed to the doors by people connected with the QE, and I met many old shipmates there. During the evening Staff Captain W J Law presented me with a beautiful silver bowl which bears the inscription: 'To Commodore G T Marr, DSC, RD. From the ship's company of RMS Queen Elizabeth on her final voyage. In appreciation of his unfailing thoughtfulness and his many timely arrivals.'

On 8 November we sailed on our last cruise, which rather strangely was the first cruise that the ship had ever made from a British port, an eight-day farewell cruise to Las Palmas and Gibraltar, with a full passenger list including eight members of the Marr family who had made a special effort to be with me on this voyage. We were fortunate to have good weather out and home, everything went well, and all our passengers seemed to enjoy themselves. The only incident of note occurred as we were leaving Gibraltar, when the Navy and the RAF combined to give us a spectacular send-off. When we sailed we were escorted to sea by all the Royal Navy ships in the port, led by the flag officer in charge, flying his flag in HMS Cambrian; as we gradually built up our speed, the naval ships came alongside in turn, saluted us, then peeled away and returned to harbour, while the jet fighters of the RAF roared overhead, banking in tight turns to avoid crossing into Spanish air space. It was a wonderful farewell. The dreadful thought behind it was that it was farewell.

Back in Southampton on Friday, 15 November, the ship 'paid off' on the night of arrival and her crew all left the ship and went their various ways, apart from the 193 who were going to take her out to Florida. So the last official function held on board, the officers' farewell dance on the evening of 18 November, had to be catered for by an outside firm. This was attended by the mayor of Southampton, and I think by almost every officer who had ever sailed in the ship and was able to get there. The demand for tickets far exceeded the supply and, although dancing was taking place in two rooms at the same time, all the public rooms were so crowded that there was hardly room to move. The bars were doing great business, and I understand that it developed into quite a lively party later on. But my wife, our daughter and I took our leave just before midnight, because we hadn't the heart to stay any longer and the following day I had to be up early, to go to the American embassy in Grosvenor Square and get my visa for my air trip to Florida.

This visit which the chief engineer, John Grant, and I made to Port Everglades was interesting, and I think useful, as we were able to see for ourselves the preparations that had been made for the ship's reception, make suggestions as to how they could be improved and, most important, get a good idea of the problems that we should have to deal with. They were many. The trip unfortunately took up more than half of the precious few days we might have had at home before we set out for what was to be a very long tour of duty, under strange circumstances, doing a job we had never done before and not knowing what the future held, or what a strange conglomeration it was to prove to be.

Compared with all the glamour of the Queen Mary's departure from Southampton the previous year, with a full load of cruise passengers, flags flying, bands playing and aircraft flying overhead in salute, the Queen Elizabeth almost folded her tents like the Arabs and silently stole away. It compared ill with the farewells in New York and Gibraltar, a British understatement with a vengeance, as though the British world of ships and shiplovers looked the other way until she had gone. The morning of 28 November was cloudy and dull, with patchy fog, as my wife and daughter drove me across the New Forest at 06.00, and although there was enough visibility for us to sail, it was only barely daylight as a skeleton crew of less than half our normal complement of seamen were struggling to take in the ropes and make fast the tugs. Indeed, it was this shortage of manpower that allowed the ship to come so far off the quay that the gangway had to be let down hurriedly a few minutes before our scheduled sailing time of 08.00, so that my wife and daughter, together with a number of shore officials, had to be landed by tug after the ship had completed her swing in the upper swinging ground.

The few ships in harbour on that dull damp morning did salute us as we passed, and before the tugs finally left they all gave us three long blasts on their whistles; but in answering them an electrical fault developed which put our whistles out of action until the following day. Only the Royal Navy gave the ship the send-off she really deserved when, as we were passing the Nab Tower just before 11.00, HMS Hampshire, one of the large guided missile destroyers which look almost like small cruisers, steamed close alongside with her crew manning the rails and 'cheered ship' for us. It was a very welcome tribute, and I was disturbed that I could not acknowledge it with three blasts on our powerful and distinctive whistles. I could only express my thanks and apologies in a brief radio telephone conversation with her captain. Then, as we were making our way down-Channel at about 18.00 that evening, the Carmania, returning from a Mediterranean cruise, came close alongside with all her lights on and saluted us. We also had a signal from the new Queen Elizabeth II, doing her trials off the Isle of Arran, wishing us success in our new role, which made some of us smile wryly.

As we settled down to make the best of our ghost ship voyage none of us felt very cheerful: it had been a dismal departure for a ship that had given such long and valuable service. Indeed, as my wife said in one of her letters, it was almost a shameful departure, and many people felt that day that the Queen Elizabeth was being quietly swept under the carpet. However, as we got down to the warm sunshine again and gradually managed to get the ship spruced up, our spirits rose a little and we started to wonder what Florida might have in store for us.

CHAPTER SIXTEEN

Queen for sale

Our arrival date in Florida was supposed to be Saturday, 7 December 1968, but two days before this I had received a radio telephone call from James Nall of the Investment Company of Florida, whom the Cunard Line had engaged to act as our local administrator, telling me that the dredging operations would not be completed in time for us to berth on the Saturday morning. He suggested that, as we were already so close, we should use the Saturday to show the flag, by approaching the coast in the vicinity of Boca Raton and then steaming slowly south along the fifty-fathom contour as far as Key Biscayne. He then hoped that everything would be in order for us to dock at about 09.00 on the Sunday morning. This I agreed to do.

The weather on that Saturday morning as we approached the coast was as near perfect as anything even Florida can produce. The winds were light and, although the seas were a little choppy around 11.00 as the first of the larger yachts met us off Boca Raton, they moderated to almost a calm as we moved south during the day, and all day long the sun shone out of a clear blue sky and the temperature remained in the seventies. There was obviously a genuine interest on the part of the local press and radio, and everyone who had a boat over twenty feet long, and some a good deal smaller, seemed to be out that day. Several of the bigger yachts stayed with us for a few hours, but the smaller ones came out in droves from every inlet as we passed; then as they headed for the shore, another relay streaked out to join us. Through our binoculars we could see thousands of people and hundreds of cars lining the beaches, and there must have been almost as many more looking out from the seaward windows of the high-rise apartment buildings that line the coast. Slowing down to about 6 knots, it took us until about 16.00 to reach Key Biscayne; then we turned and came slowly back, looking, I was told, even more majestic, as the setting sun lit up our black and white hull and the large red and black funnels. About 19.00 we were back off the entrance to Port Everglades and then we continued north as far as Palm Beach, with our floodlights and all our overside lights on. At about midnight we moved out to sea and came slowly south to wait for 06.00 on the Sunday morning, when I had arranged to talk to the chief pilot on VHF.

At a conference held during my visit to Florida a couple of weeks before, it had been decided that it would not be wise to attempt to dock with a wind speed of over 20 knots. So the news that the pilot gave me was not too cheerful: a weak cold front which had been moving steadily south all night was expected to pass Port Everglades at about 09.00, the time that we were due to enter harbour, bringing with it winds gusting up to 20 knots. The wind speed at this time was only about 10 knots so, hoping that the weathermen might be taking a rather gloomy view, I said to the pilot: 'I have found that there are times in life when one just has to take a chance, and I think that this is one of those times; so we will meet you at the sea buoy at 07.30.' Actually the front came through a little ahead of time, and the 10-15 knot NNW breeze behind the front gave us conditions for our docking operation as good as we could ever have hoped for. Stopping the engines as we approached the outer buoys of the entrance channel, the ship slid quietly through the cut, steering easily. By using all four engines in plenty of time, she pulled up on entering the turning basin without our having to call on the engine room for maximum power astern, and she then turned easily into the moderate NNW breeze.

Once we had the wind right ahead it was exerting the minimum pressure on our three and a half acres of exposed side and it was easy for the six tugs to hold her in position and line her up with the Intercoastal Waterway and hold her steady while we backed into our berth. Although we met with some difficulty, and the operation took about an hour, neither the pilot or I had any real worries now: with three good ropes out at each end and six tugs to hold her, she could not do more than scratch the paint. At 11.25 we were able to ring 'Finished with engines' for what we all thought was the last time, and leave it to the seamen fore and aft to put out all the extra ropes and wires necessary to hold a ship of her great size.

Shortly after we docked I received a cable from our nautical adviser in Southampton, which read: 'For Commodore Marr, in Queen Elizabeth on arrival. Acts 27 Verse 39 (signed) Storey.' It reads: 'And when it was day, they knew not the land: but they discovered a certain creek with a shore, into which they were minded, if it were possible, to thrust in the ship.' This is a very apt quotation. The long, tangled and sometimes sordid story of all the wheeling and dealing that went on in connection with the first sale of the Queen Elizabeth, the decision to bring her to Port Everglades, and later her sale to Queen Ltd is not for me to tell, for the simple reason that I seldom had more than a vague idea of what was going on. Although I did meet many of the principal people concerned from time to time, and always found them acceptable and courteous, the financial side was a closed book to me. For those people who may be interested, and it's a remarkable story, the whole matter has been investigated in great detail by an American author, Greg Walter, who published his carefully documented findings in an article in the *Philadelphia Magazine* dated June 1968, entitled 'What is a nice Queen like you doing in a place like this?' He followed it with another article in *Life* magazine, in August 1970, called 'Final Insult to a Queen'. It is all there.

All that my crew and I knew was that we had signed a most unusual type of agreement to 'stand by' the ship for nine months, by which time it was hoped that she would have been moved to a permanent berth, and be ready to change over to shore power. But in the meantime we had to keep the after engine room and the necessary boilers in working order and to be prepared to take her to sea on short notice. The ship was, we were told, now owned by a new company registered in the state of Delaware, called the Elizabeth (Cunard) Corporation, of which Cunard owned 85 per cent of the stock. We also understood that when the ship was moved Cunard hoped to have a financial interest in the proposed development of the large tract of land down the Intercoastal Waterway. I therefore felt, that apart from looking after my crew and getting ready for the tourists who were shortly to be shown round the bridge and public rooms in conducted tours at a charge of $2.50 per head, my main task was on the public relations side, to do what I could to improve Anglo-American relations and to give talks about the ship and her historical background so that people would get to know more about her. Somehow I found myself launched into a circuit. I spoke at Rotary Clubs, Kiwanis, Chambers of Commerce, Shrine Clubs, Power Squadrons, and other meetings, until eventually I began to have the feeling that I was getting over-exposed, for every now and then someone would come up to me and say: 'This is the second time I've heard you, I was at such and such a Club three weeks ago when you spoke there.'

It was all so different from my usual life on board, or indeed anywhere, that I often felt I didn't know what on earth was going to be the end of it. However, the people who were handling the publicity side evidently thought it was doing some good, because later on they asked me to go to Tampa, Jacksonville, and Orlando, in Florida, as well as Atlanta, Georgia, and Cleveland and Cincinnati, Ohio, for radio interviews or guest appearances on TV talks shows: all of which gave me a wonderful opportunity to see parts of America which were quite new to me and which I should otherwise never have had any chance to visit. Thanks to all this publicity I re-established contacts with many people who had travelled with me on board the Queens over the years, and also with old friends from the Caronia where, because of the longer cruises, conditions were more conducive to getting to know people. So I received many invitations to parties and social functions.

Apart from looking after the interests of the British crew and seeing that the ship was kept clean and tidy for the visitors, who since the middle of February had been averaging about 2,000 per day, my main job during this period seemed to be showing VIPs around the ship or entertaining them in my quarters, with particular attention to those who might be interested in joining the project. I used to say I felt more like a used-ship salesman than a ship's captain. But these were very unsettling days, for both my ship's company and myself, and also for their families, who were 4,000 miles away and knew even less about the situation than we did.

During our early days in Florida we had fairly frequent visits from our deputy chairman, who appeared to be master-minding the project. The president of the company's American interests used to come down from New York, together with Allan Dumont, who was conducting a feasibility study on the project; but it was extremely difficult to get any idea of what was going on, for they didn't seem to know either. However, our deputy chairman, Phillip Shirley, did eventually agree that it would be a good idea to let the married members of the British crew have their wives and any children under eighteen fly out for a holiday so that they could see what Florida was like, in case there might be a chance for a permanent job there later on.

This was something entirely different from anything we had done before, and there were so many borderline cases that one almost required the judgment of Solomon to decide which children qualified for this trip and which did not. Then there were the domestic arrangements on board to make, because our very small catering staff could not be expected to cope with looking after more than a hundred extra people, unless the wives helped to keep the cabins clean and we changed over to a cafeteria type of messing.

But on the whole things worked out very well, thanks to the fantastic amount of work put in by various American ladies who, together with British people living in Florida, organized outings and provided entertainment for the 104 women and children who flew out on a charter flight in early March and went home again in the Carmania on 11 April, after what most of them agreed had been the holiday of their lives. Then, as the months wore on, we found we were seeing less and less of any of our top executives. My crew were getting increasingly apprehensive, because more than half of our nine months had gone and we could get no definite news about the ship's future.

On 11 April I flew home to England for a short vacation, and a welcome seventeen days at home just as spring was arriving brought me up to date with family affairs and my wife's latest additions to our cottage; but I could have enjoyed it all much more had there not been this apprehensive feeling about the ship, because we could not this time depend on no news being good news. On Monday, 28 April, the day before I was to return, I had a long interview with Phillip Shirley in his London office, and although he did not have any special news I could see that things were not working out the way he had hoped, whatever that may have been. He seemed worried about the ship's future, because the company had spent a lot of money getting her out to Florida and the income we were earning from the tours was not even covering our day-to-day expenses. On my return to Florida I held a meeting of the ship's company and tried to explain the situation to them as best I could. They seemed to accept it: what else could be done? So we settled down to await the expiration of our contracts on 9 September, when the company would have to fly us home.

Rumours of all kinds continued to circulate, and the numbers of people from all parts of the world who expressed an interest in buying the ship increased. Indeed, on Saturday, 31 May I entertained the men who came to look at her on behalf of C Y Tung, the man who eventually bought her. By the end of June the Cunard Line issued a statement to the effect that, if she had not been sold by the end of July, she would leave Port Everglades and return to England. So our chief engineer started an intensive programme of testing the boilers we should need to use and putting steam on and warming through the after engines to check the condenser vacuum. Then two radio engineers flew over from England to repair the radar and reactivate the radio station, and on 5 July I made a trip over to Freeport to look into the facilities for supplying bunkers and fresh water if the draught limitations prevented us from taking on sufficient supplies in Port Everglades for the Atlantic crossing. Then suddenly everything was changed. A fresh customer appeared on the horizon, in the form of another Philadelphia group, called Utilities Leasing, and Phillip Shirley reappeared, all smiles and good humour. All preparations for leaving were dropped and crew members were advised that all those who were not required by the new company would be flying home at the beginning of August, a whole month before their contracts expired. More mixed feelings—I just wanted to heave up the anchor and sail home.

However, there were long sessions of hard bargaining in London before a final agreement was hammered out, and we on board gradually began to think that something might emerge. Life for us began once more to take on a sense of purpose; we now had a definite date to look forward to. Then those men were interviewed who had said they would like to stay and work for Queen Ltd. I was not among this happy band, so, like the bulk of the ship's company, I started packing and saying goodbye to the friends I had made during the eight months in the Sunshine State.

On Monday, 4 August, the coaches drew up alongside the ship at about 18.00 and about 120 of us said farewell to the ship which to so many of us had been a second home for so long, and to those of our shipmates who were staying behind, about twenty in all. With the half-dozen or so new American wives of our crew members, we climbed on board for the drive to Miami International Airport. The Pan-American Boeing 707 which had been chartered for the flight had been specially renamed 'Clipper Queen Elizabeth', while the Gulf Stream Pipe Band came down in force and good 'blow' to play us away—and, with the many friends who came to say goodbye, we had a really rousing send-off. Back home it was only a matter of visits to the Southampton office to clear up a few details, then an invitation from the chairman to lunch with the directors in London after the monthly board meeting, and at the end of the day I was officially 'on leave' until my retirement from Cunard on 31 December 1969. So here it was—the end of the line, and time to begin another life ashore.

However, before the month was out I was to have another nasty fall in the garden, and what is more it took place just two days before my wife and I were planning to go on a motoring holiday. I climbed a tree, lost my footing and fell a considerable distance— ending with a leg badly broken below the knee. It was a fragile tree and I hadn't secured the ladder, so it was my own fault. The attentions of the doctors seemed to sort things out surgically, but for two months I had to remain in Odstock Hospital, flat on my back with my leg in traction, reflecting on my foolishness in climbing a brittle tree. On top of it all, the plums I was gathering were no good anyway—it would have been better to have forgotten them! At home, after Odstock, frustration was the order of the day. My poor family grew to appreciate the odd 'good day' when I felt I was really making some progress. However, at long last I found myself with two good legs and looking at life with a bright eye, wondering what it had in store for me now. Meantime I plodded about the garden and tried to accustom myself to being a landlubber.

CHAPTER SEVENTEEN

New roles for old

During the spring and summer of 1970 my broken leg continued to mend and I gradually settled down to the routine of taking care of our large garden and trying to keep two three-acre paddocks clear of weeds. This was to prove a full-time job, for unfortunately we had during the previous November lost the services of our elderly gardener, who had over the previous four years helped my wife restore an old garden along the front of the house and create a new garden at the back of a meadow. Through the kindness of my friends in Florida, who continued to send me a steady stream of clippings from the local newspapers, I still followed with very great interest what was happening to my old ship. So while I knew that she had been bought by a C Y Tung at the bankruptcy sale, it still came as a surprise to receive a telephone call from the nautical adviser to Cunard International Technical Services in London, Captain F J Storey, RD, RNR, to say that Mr Tung had been in touch with him to ask if I would be prepared to act as technical adviser during the voyage from Port Everglades to Hong Kong. I replied with alacrity that I was very interested in the project, and within half an hour spoke to Mr Tung in person. He said he was delighted to hear that I was prepared to help and told me he was going to contact R E Philip, who had been chief engineer of the ship during 1966-8, to ask if he would be willing to act in a similar capacity on the engineering side. We made an arrangement to meet in London on the following day.

Our first meeting with Mr Tung was at a party he was giving at Shell House to show a film he had made himself about one of his newest 225,000 ton tankers, the SS Energy Evolution. This was followed by a cocktail party for about 100 guests, after which Mr Philip and I had dinner at a Chinese restaurant with Mr Tung and half a dozen senior members of the staff of his London office. This gave us our first chance to have a private talk with the man who was to play such an important role in our lives for the next nine months. My first impression of 'CY', as his friends call him, was of a solidly built man of average height, whose features quickly relaxed into a warm and friendly smile. He bubbled over with enthusiasm and good humour. But what made the greatest impression on me was the wonderfully easy, friendly relationship that he appeared to have with all the members of his staff. While being very much the father figure, he was a benign and easily approachable person, with whom even the more junior men appeared to be able to discuss things much more freely than I had ever felt able to do with our senior executives in Cunard.

It was also a great pleasure for me to be able to hear at first hand his ambitious plans for the ship's future, which were later outlined in a statement issued to the British press on 12 October:

The world-famous passenger liner Queen Elizabeth has now been renamed Seawise University. Lying in Port Everglades, Florida, she is now undergoing a check-up and the necessary repairs are being done to make her fit for sea again. When she leaves Port Everglades she will follow her old wartime track round the Cape of Good Hope to Singapore and Hong Kong, where extensive refitting will be carried out. While preserving her original beauty and elegance, the major work of her conversion will be to make her suitable for the floating campus project now being formulated, and when she sails again it will be with students, faculty members and cruising passengers.

The ship's new owners recognize the challenge imposed in operating, by today's standards, such an uneconomic ship in an unviable trade. It is to meet this challenge and keep the 'Old Queen' afloat that every possible effort is now being exerted. The Queen Elizabeth is the largest passenger liner ever built and it is extremely unlikely, in this modern jet age, that another ship of her size and capacity will ever be constructed. It is felt that for sentimental and historical reasons—her profile, the shipbuilding know-how of Clydebank (which built nearly 10 million rivets into her hull), her various refinements and her past glories —that the presence of this magnificent ship in Eastern waters will arouse much interest and general appreciation.

It is also hoped that when she cruises around the world she will help in promoting mutual understanding and an exchange of culture between East and West.

It was for this aim that the Seawise University was named and dedicated, despite the burdens both technical and financial already foreseen.

It is recalled that it cost the American government almost 4 million dollars a year to keep the first atomic merchant ship, the Savannah, at sea; and she has now had to be laid up.

'To keep a ship of this enormous size ploughing the oceans is not a simple or light task,' said the Duke of Westminster, chairman of the Maritime Trust of London, in a letter to Mr C Y Tung praising him for his efforts to save this fine ship, and the ship's new owner has received much support and encouragement from interested members of the public.

Because of the deep personal affection I had always had for the two Queens, this announcement made a great impression on me, as I stressed on a BBC news broadcast and during two interviews on Southern ITA and Harlech TV. I also quoted part of a magazine article written by the American author Noel Mostert, which he called 'Farewell to the Great Ships':

> The two Queens undoubtedly will always remain the greatest ships ever built, no matter how large those super super tankers grow (and they are talking now about 500,000-tonners, which will be a third again as long as a Queen). Nothing like them will ever be seen again, because no tanker, no matter what its size, can ever have the visual impact of these two magnificent ships. Especially when seen at speed, flinging the ocean aside in huge combers, 'oceanic palaces' of staggering dimensions.

Part of the reason that I felt so elated was that, as I am sure my readers have already suspected, I felt strongly that the ship that I had been so proud to command had been given a raw deal.

After her costly refit on the Clyde in 1966, which was supposed to give her another ten-year lease of life, the Cunard Line's economic difficulties had forced her into retirement in under two years, just as she was starting to build up her reputation on the North American winter cruise market. Then, because Cunard had sold her to the highest bidders without making a very close investigation into their financial or personal backgrounds, she had become a pawn in some rather shady Florida politics, which seemed to me a sad end for a ship with such an unblemished record in both war and peace.

Now, it seemed that the Queen Elizabeth was to be given a new lease of life and a chance to do a worthwhile job; and it was wonderful to think of her being restored to her natural element once more, with the great engines that are her heart throbbing as they drive her across the ocean, instead of just lying rotting away in a Florida creek at the mercy of men whose only real interest was trying to use her as a means of making a fast buck.

After a meeting in Southampton with the London manager of the C Y Tung organization to discuss details, a contract was drawn up which R E Philip and I signed in London on 2 October. This was followed by a party in London to which we brought our wives to meet Mr Tung before he left for America. Following this, several weeks were to elapse before Mr Philip was asked to fly to Port Everglades, taking with him an ex-repair manager from Thornycrofts, the Southampton shipbuilders responsible for the major overhauls on the Queens for so many years. I followed on 17 November.

Arriving on the direct flight from London to Miami, I only got a distant view of the ship as I was being driven to my hotel in Fort Lauderdale in the late afternoon. But Mr Philip, who together with the Chinese captain, Commodore William Hsuan, had met me at the airport, was able to brief me about the conditions I was likely to find on board. Even so, when I went down to the ship at 08.30 the following morning I got quite a surprise. Outwardly she did not look too bad; just a little rustier and dirtier than when the British crew had left her fifteen months before, but still a most imposing sight, towering above the quay and dwarfing every other ship in the port. However, stepping off the gangway onto C deck alleyway, I couldn't believe the scene of utter desolation that met the eye, because dirt and rubble which had been brought up from the engine and boiler rooms that were being repaired was piled in the butcher's shop and in every available corner, ready to be dumped overboard once the ship got away to sea. Also, because all efforts were being concentrated on making the engines work and getting the hull seaworthy, there were no hands to spare for even ordinary cleaning. The effect of this accumulation of dust and dirt was made even worse by the fact that the ship was shut down, with only the odd dim light here and there, supplied by an emergency generator on the after mooring deck. So, as one crept around like a mole with the aid of an electric torch, everything looked drab, dirty and depressing.

Officially the target sailing date at this time was still supposed to be early in December, but after a few hours on board I felt quite sure that the ship could never be ready to leave before the end of January. While visiting some of my old friends in the port commissioner's office next morning, I voiced my opinion to a reporter from the *Fort Lauderdale News*. When it then appeared in print, it caused a little consternation among the Chinese on board; but in fact my guess turned out to be reasonably accurate, because the main engines were tried on 3 February and, given favourable conditions, we could have sailed any day after that.

Although saddened by the physical condition of the ship, the two and a half months that were to elapse before we actually sailed were to prove an extremely pleasant interlude for me. My duties as an adviser were not arduous and, having spent eight months standing by the ship after her arrival in Florida in December 1968, I already knew that many of my old friends from cruising days in the Caronia, and my many years in the Queens, now either lived in Florida or had winter homes there. Also, on the ship's first arrival there had been a great deal of publicity, and I had been given a fair amount of exposure on the various news media by the firm handling the public relations. This had led to the round of public-speaking engagements so I was probably a lot better known in South Florida than I am in England. It was very flattering to return and still find how many people remembered me, all of which tended to make Florida seem like a second home.

As the weeks sped by I found myself with an ever-increasing round of social engagements, including a five-day Christmas vacation spent with friends in Boca Raton.

But while I was avoiding the dark cold days of the English winter, and enjoying the warm Florida sunshine and the even greater warmth of Florida hospitality, the man upon whom the mantle of my former responsibilities had fallen, Commodore William Hsuan, the Chinese captain of the Seawise University (the ship's new name was, by the way, a play on C Y Tung's initials), was having a multitude of problems.

Each day, when I came down to the ship from my comfortable hotel to discuss the situation with Commodore Hsuan, I became more and more conscious of how little there was that I could do to help him, because the situation he faced was so different in every way from what it had been when I had commanded the ship. I had always had a highly trained and efficient crew, with more than 130 years of Cunard tradition behind them. Indeed, apart from the French Line and the United States Lines, Cunard was about the only company with the knowledge and experience of operating such large and complicated ships. But Commodore Hsuan had a crew drawn from many other vessels of Mr Tung's huge fleet, many of whom, while not inexperienced, had never previously set foot on board a ship like this and all of whom were going to require considerable training in order to accustom themselves to the size and complexity of the world's largest passenger liner. Also, there was a strong feeling, even among the most senior members of the engineering staff, that because of the bad state of the ship's boilers after two years of neglect, the easiest way to get the ship to Hong Kong would be to tow her there. In spite of the repeated assertions of the Port Everglades harbour commissioners, and the chief pilot, that it was impossible to move a ship of her great size out of Port Everglades without at least two of the ship's main engines (because although at least six tugs would be needed to manoeuvre the ship and control her direction of movement, the energy necessary to move 83,000 tons ahead and astern, in such a confined space, must come from her own propellers), the idea persisted until a few days before we sailed that, if certain problems could not be solved, suitable tugs to tow the ship out without main power might be found.

What was to prove one of the most difficult problems to solve, however, was how to get rid of the 4,000 or so tons of water, much of it slightly contaminated with oil, which had accumulated inside the ship over the past two years. Most of this was there as a result of the decision by Queen Ltd, after the ship had broken adrift from her moorings during a gale in the spring of 1970, to flood all the ship's fuel oil tanks and the lower parts of Nos 1 and 2 holds with water in order to sit her on the bottom of the harbour. The ship was fitted with two oily water separators specifically designed to deal with a situation like this, and they had been in constant use throughout the ship's thirty years of Cunard service. These, like so many other things on board, were in need of repair; but although Mr Philip, starting shortly after he joined the ship and strongly supported by me, sent repeated written requests to Commodore Hsuan pointing out the dangerous loss of stability, due to the 'free surface' effect of large quantities of loose water in the bottom of the ship, no attempt was made to deal with this oily water problem. The Chinese engineers insisted that there were many other items of higher priority, and even expressed doubts that this particular type of separator was capable of dealing with oil of the high viscosity that we had in our bilges.

One way in which they tried to deal with the matter was to charter a small coastal tanker, the San Martin, to take some of the contaminated water out to sea and dump it on the other side of the Gulf Stream; but this failed because there are regulations against the dumping of any oil at sea. As our sailing date drew closer, it became absolutely imperative to get enough of the contaminated water out to reduce the ship's maximum draught below the 38 feet 3 inches which the US Coastguard insisted she must have in order to sail. So, as a last desperate measure, it was decided to pump it out between the ship and the dockside into an area contained between two oil booms, one at the bow and one at the stern, using the ship's Chinese seamen to clean the oil from the surface of the water by soaking it up with large quantities of straw. This was a disgustingly dirty job which these men tackled with great fortitude day after day, placing the oil-soaked straw in large metal containers which were picked up by dump trucks. Unfortunately, they were not always picked up promptly enough and some of the oil drained out of the straw on to the dockside and, two days before the ship sailed, a torrential rainstorm washed a quantity of this oil back into the Intercoastal Waterway, leading to a number of complaints against the ship.

Another very big problem that Commodore Hsuan had was trying to maintain the morale of his Chinese crew, who were in a strange country a very long way from home. They had to live under appalling conditions during the long period that the ship was without main power, when there were few essential services and the only cooking facilities were charcoal braziers fashioned out of old oil drums; all of which may seem incredible. Because of all these hardships, and the language barrier when they went ashore, most of the crew did not like being in America; yet, in any case involving a serious breach of ship's discipline, the only punishment the commodore could inflict was to send the man home. This did remove a potential troublemaker from the ship and prevent him from upsetting other crew members, but from the company's point of view it was a most expensive way of dealing with the problem, because by the time his relief had been flown from Hong Kong they were faced with a double air fare of at least $1,200. Another problem that caused the commodore a good deal of worry was dealing with the large number of shipyard workers who had been flown over from the company's shipyards in Hong Kong to help with repair work on the engines and boilers, because besides the language barrier, these men were all shore employees, unused to shipboard life, and not subject to ordinary ship's discipline.

Thus each day Commodore Hsuan sat in his office on board and tried to find answers to these problems and, in many cases, apart from lending a sympathetic ear, I found that the only way I could really help him was with his correspondence, the bulk of which had to be written in English. Whenever he had written the draft of a letter, he would hand it to me and say 'Commodore Marr, would you please change my Chinese English into your English English?' While Commodore Hsuan had an excellent grasp of conversational English, many of his officers, particularly on the engineering side, were not so well endowed. This made things particularly difficult for Mr Philip and the dozen or so of the English engineer officers with previous experience in the ship who had been retained to act as advisers, because the dreadful language barrier so often prevented even quite senior officers from fully understanding and appreciating the advice they were being offered.

However, in spite of all these fantastic difficulties, progress was being made, and it was a great moment for everyone when, on the last day of the old year, the first two repaired boilers were flashed up and there was once again a plume of smoke rising from the after funnel—an outward and visible sign of returning life. Then two of the ship's main generators were restarted, and there was sufficient power to restore the essential services and to once again have lights on all over the ship. This also allowed the two huge red and black smokestacks, for so long a feature of the night sky of Port Everglades, to be floodlit at night, and we felt that we were on the way.

By now experts had overhauled all the ship's navigational and radio equipment and either made it work or, as in the case of the radio station, replaced it with new equipment, while all the safety equipment and watertight doors were checked and tested to the satisfaction of the Lloyds surveyors. During the time all this was being done, skin divers were working steadily, removing two years' marine growth, including weed up to two feet long, from the hull and propellers. As our sailing date drew nearer the anchors and cables which had been landed ashore, and buried in the coral to provide additional moorings, were picked up by crane and returned to their proper places, and those lifeboats which had been removed were replaced in their davits. On Wednesday, 3 February we held engine trials, and for the first time in more than two years the huge turbines in the after engine room revolved under steam pressure. The ship became a living thing, with a heart that was beating again, if only slowly.

We were now officially ready to sail, but we still had to overcome the biggest problem of all: the weather. It had been fully agreed by all parties concerned that, with her greatly reduced power to weight ratio, it would be courting disaster to attempt to move the vessel, with her vast expanse of exposed side, in a windspeed of more than 15-20 knots. Also, there were only certain days in each month when ideal tidal conditions coincided with daylight, and for us these had to be days on which no large passenger vessels were scheduled to arrive or sail from Port Everglades or Miami Port, because we should need all of the six tugs available in the area.

However, at this particular moment, I was feeling rather removed from such problems, because on the day of the engine trials I went down with one of the worst attacks of flu I had had for many years, and the doctor put me into Broward General Hospital. Fortunately, by the time the weather showed signs of being suitable to move the ship my temperature had come down and, although the doctor still felt I was not sufficiently recovered, I did manage to persuade him that if I could stand up I must get out of hospital and down to the ship. After coming so far and waiting for so long, I felt it would be an awful anticlimax if I chickened out at the last minute.

After a vigorous cold front had swept across Florida on Tuesday, 9 February, the weather experts at last held out definite hopes that the following morning might provide just the conditions that we had been waiting for. So throughout that day there was a hurried tightening up of all sorts of loose ends and Mr Philip and I said goodbye to the Marina Motor Inn, where we had been very well looked after for almost three months, and moved all our gear on board the ship. Personally, I was feeling so weak and physically exhausted from flu that, if it had not been for the good offices of my ex-steward Harry Patterson, now living in Florida, who came and collected me from the hospital, packed up my belongings in the hotel and settled me in my cabin on the ship, I do not think I could have made the move.

The morning of Wednesday, 10 February 1971 was one of those brilliantly clear but bitterly cold mornings which usually follow the passage of a winter cold front in Florida, when the northerly wind comes straight from the frozen heartland of America with ice on it's breath. It was also a night with a full moon, so, although day had not broken at 06.00, there was enough light to start the preparations for the first voyage of the once-proud Queen Elizabeth under her new name, Seawise University, as the chief pilot of Port Everglades and the captain of the United States Coastguard boarded and our six tugs came alongside.

The strong to gale force winds of the past few days had now moderated to a crisp 15-18 knot breeze from the NNW, but with the early-morning temperature down in the high thirties the breeze felt as though it were going through my flu-weakened body like a knife, in spite of the fact that I was wearing all the clothes I could find. Yet professionally I could not but agree with Commodore Hsuan and the others that we might wait for weeks and still not find a more suitable morning for undocking the world's largest passenger liner. Indeed, apart from the wind being just a little bit stronger, the weather conditions were almost identical to those we had had for docking the ship on 8 December 1968 and, as then, the NNW wind was right ahead of the ship during the most difficult part of the operation, the direction from which it would exert least pressure on her huge hull. Unfortunately, this bit of good news was cancelled out by bad news from the engine room; that one of our six operational boilers had developed leaky tubes during the night and had been shut down. One stroke against us.

At the start of the operation things went extremely well. Helped by the breeze and the flood tide, the pilot, by his skilful use of all six tugs pushing on the starboard side, was able to bring the ship round the corner from our berth and then move her out into the swinging basin, without once having to call on the ship's seamen to heave on any of the four lines that were being carried along the dock by the line handlers. During this period the ship's engines were only required to give short bursts of either slow ahead or slow astern, and they responded well to these orders up to about 30 rpm.

But as the tugs started to turn the vessel in the swinging basin, bringing her slowly beam-on to the wind, the effect of the pressure which the fresh breeze was exerting on her three and a half acres of exposed side became more apparent, and the four tugs pushing on the starboard bow had to snort and push very hard to get the ship far enough up to windward for the pilot to start his final run through the 300-foot-wide entrance channel that led to the open sea. This was the most dangerous part of the whole operation; and the moment of truth as far as the engines were concerned was when, after lying idle for more than two years, 'Full ahead' was rung on the telegraphs to the after engine room for the first time. Knowing how vitally important it was that the ship should pick up her way as quickly as possible, I telephoned Mr Philip, on duty in the after engine room, and said: 'We are committed to the channel now. See that they give her everything they can!' The watchers ashore must have seen the dense clouds of black smoke that billowed from our after funnel as the engineers on duty in Nos 3 and 4 boiler rooms brought up the fires to generate the steam necessary to get 83,000 tons moving at about 5 knots. The ship appeared to be slowly and steadily picking speed; then, just as she was approaching the Point of Americas high-rise apartments, disaster struck: a tube burst in another boiler, releasing a quantity of water into the furnace and superimposing a cloud of brilliant white steam on the black smoke—a remarkable sight. Down below in the boiler room, emergency procedures had to be adopted to shut this boiler down as quickly as possible, and so the engine revolutions began to drop back quickly.

Fortunately, the ship had already built up sufficient way to carry her clear of the dredged channel, with a maximum effort on the part of the tugs to keep her on course in spite of the pressure of the beam wind. But had this boiler gone ten or even five minutes earlier, it could have been a very different story: without sufficient headway the tugs would have been powerless to prevent the ship grounding in the approach channel and perhaps breaking her back as the tide fell, thus becoming the cork that would have most effectively bottled up the harbour of Port Everglades for many weeks.

Just before the boiler went, Commodore Hsuan had decided to thank the many hundreds of people who had braved the bitter winds and turned out to wish us well at the start of our long journey, by giving them three blasts on the ship's deep-throated whistles, which had been such a feature on her first arrival at Port Everglades. But our steam pressure was already so low that the first blast just tailed away to a rather pathetic whimper. It was a good idea—but we should have known better. As the ship left the shelter of the harbour and made her way very slowly to the sea buoy, she began to feel the full force of the fresh to strong NNW breeze which, because it was blowing directly opposite to the flow of the Gulf Stream, was producing a very choppy sea. When the time came to discharge the pilot, the ship's lack of power prevented her manoeuvring to create a lee. Realizing that getting away from the ship was going to be a very uncomfortable operation, the pilot had ordered his small pilot cutter back into harbour, and arranged to land in the Port Everglades tug Tarus, which stayed with us out to the buoy. But in the sea that was running it took the tug some time to get into a suitable position for him and his five companions to jump safely down on to her heaving deck. One of the five men with him was the Port Everglades harbour commissioner, W Phil McConaghey, who had obtained special permission from the Coastguard to make the trip. As he had been the man who had had more uncomplimentary things to say about the ship than anyone else in Florida, one can only assume that he had come along to see the last of the ship he had worked to get rid of. His last few minutes on board her must have been extremely anxious ones as he stood in the shell door and watched the gyrations of the wildly plunging tug on to whose deck he had to jump; and a lot of people would have thought it no more than poetic justice had he missed his footing and the Old Lady dunked him into the sea as a farewell gesture. However, he made it safely.

In spite of all the difficulties, everybody was safely clear by 10.00 and the ship could be brought slowly round to the course for the Providence channel and her departure taken. Down below in the engine room and boiler rooms, things were settling down, and the ship's speed on her four remaining boilers gradually built up to between 7 and 8 knots. On deck the sailors were busy closing the shell doors and securing the ship for sea as Commodore Hsuan and I, on the bridge, looked back over the events of the morning and congratulated ourselves that, taking all things into consideration, the maiden voyage of the SS Seawise University had started as well as could reasonably be expected. At least we were out of Port Everglades, so the big drain on Mr Tung's supply of American dollars would stop, and we should no longer have the pollution control officers breathing down our necks day and night.

The cold but very clear weather was ideal for navigation as the ship made her way slowly past Great Isaac light and out into the Atlantic. The following morning, Thursday 11 February, we were making a steady 10 knots down the outside of the southerly islands of the Bahama chain as we passed Eleuthera and Cat Island. But down below in the boiler rooms things were going far from well, as the ship's limited supply of reserve feed water was found to be disappearing at an alarming rate. By that afternoon, the chief engineer informed the commodore that he would have to shut the engines in, to try to conserve water; but the ship was still moving and the early hours of the following day, Friday, saw us passing San Salvador or Watling Island, and then heading through the Mira-por-Vos channel into the Caribbean. It was while we were still in this channel, at about 10.30, that the chief engineer came up to the bridge to tell the commodore that his boiler feed water situation was now so desperate that he had been forced to close down No 4 boiler room completely. The story of our operable boilers was beginning to sound like the old nursery rhyme 'Now there were three', and these were only capable of keeping the engines turning over slowly and operating the auxiliaries. Then at 13.15 the engine room rang the bridge to say that further troubles had developed and they would have to stop the engines.

Commodore Hsuan immediately organized a conference in his office, at which all the Europeans were present, to discuss the feed water problem and all possible ways of making and saving water with Chief Engineer W C Cheng and his senior Chinese engineers. At the end of this meeting, Mr Philip, with all the British engineers, volunteered to go down below and restart the main engines, using their own methods to make boiler feed water. This was agreed and by 15.25 the vessel was under way once more, and slowly worked up to a speed of more than 7 knots. Throughout that night the situation appeared to be steadily improving as the ship moved down into the Windward Passage, where she was to spend the next three days. Indeed I was feeling particularly cheerful when I went up on the bridge just before 08.00 the following morning. The weather was warm and sunny and the heavy cloud of mental depression that so often follows a bad dose of flu seemed to be lifting; Cape Maysi lighthouse on the western end of Cuba was in sight, and the officer of the watch had reported that the speed on three boilers had now built up to over 9 knots. But the best news was when the engineers reported that they had finally managed to get the low-pressure flash evaporator (the ship's main source of distilled water for boiler feed) working, and were now making more water than the boilers were using. A cheerful report, but our cheer was short-lived. At about 09.35 our most serious problem yet developed, as the fire alarms throughout the ship rang, for a fire in No 3 boiler room, the only one still operating. Fortunately, all personnel in the boiler room had managed to get out safely. The boiler room was then isolated, the fuel supply to the boilers cut off and firefighting procedures put into operation. But, of course, as the steam pressure dropped rapidly the main engines and the auxiliaries had to be shut down.

From the bridge the situation looked extremely alarming, with clouds of dense black smoke billowing up through engine room skylights and ventilators. However, after about thirty minutes, several engineer officers wearing breathing apparatus managed to get back into the boiler room and attack the fire with foam extinguishers, and by 10.30 the chief engineer was able to report to the bridge that the fire was under control. But he also reported that the damage to B3 boiler was so bad that this boiler must be considered incapable of further use until major repairs could be made. All our spirits slumped again.

As soon as it was possible to get the key personnel together, Commodore Hsuan held yet another conference. All the senior Chinese engineers strongly supported Mr Cheng, the chief engineer, in his view that the ship was now no longer capable of proceeding under her own power, and would have to be towed to a port of refuge for major boiler repairs to be carried out. On the other hand, while admitting that the situation had become extremely grave (the only boiler now capable of supplying steam for auxiliary purposes was A3, which was being blown down when the fire started, so that no one could be sure just how much water it still contained), Mr Philip and all the British engineers still wished to attempt to run the turbo generators with the three boilers thought to be undamaged; then, if the boiler feed water situation could be controlled, to use them to supply some motive power. When the question of asking for tugs was put to the meeting by Commodore Hsuan, it was unanimously agreed that the services of at least one ocean tug were essential. So a message was sent to the owners in New York, informing them of the situation and asking that a tug be dispatched immediately.

Following this conference the engineers went down below again, and sufficient steam was raised to restart the main generators by 17.00 that afternoon; but there was still serious disagreement between the Chinese and the European engineers as to what could and could not be done. I only heard about this indirectly and, not being an engineer myself, I am not qualified to pass an opinion on technical matters; all I do know is that after they had run through the night apart from the odd breakdown, the ship's main generators were finally shut down at noon the following day, Sunday, 14 February. Mr Philip and a group of British engineers then asked me to accompany them to Commodore Hsuan's cabin, as a witness to the fact that they disagreed strongly with Chief Engineer Cheng's decision to shut down all the boilers and rely exclusively on the small diesel emergency generator on the after deck to supply the power for a limited number of essential services. Also without technical knowledge, Commodore Hsuan had no alternative but to uphold the decision of his chief engineer, who was the official Chinese technical expert, holding the ultimate responsibility; whereas Mr Philip, in spite of all his years of experience in the ship, was, like all the other Europeans on board, merely an adviser, an anomalous position and a very frustrating one. She was now a Chinese ship.

During all this time our huge ship was drifting helplessly at the mercy of the winds and currents between Cuba and Haiti. But fortunately the weather remained quiet, and the wind appeared to counteract the current, because at no time during the three days we were drifting did the ship come dangerously close to land. Due to the fact that we had only limited supplies of diesel fuel for our generator, and no idea how long it would be before we reached port, it was deemed prudent to run it for only a few hours each day; so it was stopped at 21.00 each evening, leaving the ship completely blacked out except for a dim white oil light at the bow and stern, and two dim red 'not under command' lights on the foremast. This was the condition we were in when the brilliantly illuminated Norwegian cruise liner Starward closed us just before midnight that Sunday night. Our ship must have looked a very sad and desolate sight to the hundreds of passengers crowding her decks. After steaming in close up and down both sides of the ship, with her searchlights playing on us and the flashbulbs from dozens of cameras making bright pinpoints of light, she asked us through her loud-hailers if there was anything she could do for us. We replied, 'No, thank you' and she veered away, increased to full speed and resumed her course to Port au Prince—leaving many of us old Cunard hands feeling very dashed, and wondering what the hell we were doing there.

The following morning, Monday, 15 February, I was again asked to accompany a delegation of British engineers to the commodore's cabin, this time to make a final plea to be allowed to try a new plan which they had worked out for raising steam on the undamaged boilers. But by now Commodore Hsuan had some solid news to please the Chinese crew. The salvage tug Rescue had already left Kingston, Jamaica, and would be with us the following morning, while the Dutch salvage tug Jacob van Heemskerk from San Juan, Puerto Rico, expected to reach us about twenty-four hours later. So it was decided to take no further action with regard to raising steam, and we just sat there and waited.

Tuesday, 16 February turned out to be a lovely sunny day, with winds and calm seas, and after three days of utter frustration while we had been drifting, our spirits got an ironic lift as we watched the squat sturdy form of the tug Rescue come over the horizon. As she got closer we could see the creamy bow wave that gave some indication of her power. About 10.15 she ranged alongside and passed her tow line on board. This meant that we once again had motive power. We were no longer completely at the mercy of the elements; we were actually going somewhere, even if not very fast. Unfortunately, the Rescue's 3,500 horsepower was only sufficient to handle the 83,000 ton bulk of this ship effectively while the winds remained light and the seas smooth. When the wind speed increased to over 15 knots just before midnight, the effect of the wind pressure on the huge area of her hull was to make the ship sail round and try to seek the wind's eye, in spite of our efforts to try and give what help we could with the steering gear, because the small amount of headway the Rescue was able to give us proved insufficient to make our rudder angle effective. At this point we were being towed towards Kingston, Jamaica, which was our nearest port of refuge. But as the wind speed continued to increase we found that, even with the tug towing broad out on the port bow, the ship was making a crab-like course to the westward which seemed likely to take her uncomfortably close to the dangerous Formigas shoal. It became, therefore, increasingly clear that it was vitally necessary for us to have a second tug as soon as possible, if our vessel was to be kept under proper control.

By the following morning, Wednesday, 17 February, or exactly one week after our hectic departure from Port Everglades, the arrival of a cold front through the Windward Passage had caused a considerable deterioration in our weather, with the wind gusting up to about 25-30 knots in the fairly frequent rain squalls. We therefore felt very relieved when we sighted the salvage tug Jacob van Heemskerk at lunchtime and, after some delay while he checked by radio with his New York office that the towing agreement had actually been signed, he came alongside to pick up our big insurance wire. Due to the rough weather, this was not an easy operation, and many of the tug's crew got very wet before she took up her towing position on our port bow at about 16.00. Both tugs were approximately the same horsepower, but by now the wind was so strong that it was about as much as the pair of them could do to control the ship properly. To make sure of clearing the Formigas shoal, they had to tow her right round through the wind and then away to the south towards Nevassa Island. However, this eventually proved to be the direction in which we wanted to go, because that evening we received a signal from New York instructing us to proceed to Curaçao instead of Kingston, and make our repairs there. Due to the cloudy weather we had not been able to get an accurate navigational fix for more than twenty-four hours, and it had been difficult to estimate the course that the tugs had been making over the ground. So we were very thankful to sight the light on Nevassa Island between the rain squalls just before midnight. Then by 04.20 we had rounded the island, and the tugs brought us on to the direct course for Curaçao, more than 500 miles away.

Because of adverse currents and the strength of the trade winds, this was to prove a long, hard tow, and during the next six days our two little seahorses, nearly a quarter of a mile ahead of us at the end of their long towlines, were to take quite a beating as they bounced over eight- to ten-foot-high seas.

Our destination was later changed to the island of Aruba, which offered better and safer anchorages; but having been able to maintain an average speed of only a little over 3 knots under tow, we did not reach there until the morning of Wednesday, 24 February, exactly two weeks after leaving Port Everglades on a section of our voyage which we had estimated would only take just over four days.

The anchorage which the harbourmaster at Oranjestad had suggested for the ship was exactly one mile from the old Shell Oil Company pier at Manchebo Point, and about three miles from the entrance to Oranjestad harbour; but, probably due to the difficulty of handling a ship under tow, the pilot had let go our anchor about three cables outside this, on the edge of a fairly steep shelf. By the time the error was discovered the tugs had left us, and having no power it was not possible to correct it. The ship did, however, ride there quietly for four days, while we anxiously awaited the arrival of a group of senior officials from The Island Navigation Company of Hong Kong, led by their general manager, Y S Kung, and including their senior engineer, W S Pau. With Ray Crowther of London Salvage, they would examine the extent of the damage and be responsible for the vital decisions about what repairs were to be done and by whom.

Unfortunately, our troubles were not yet over. On the last day of February, which was a Sunday, the trade winds had freshened considerably, and at 19.00 it was noticed that the ship had dragged her anchor off the edge of the shelf and was drifting into deep water. Having no power, there was nothing we could do except contact the shore by VHF and try to obtain the services of the ocean tug based at Willemstad. Around Aruba at this time of the year both winds and currents are strong, but they were combining to take us away from the land and by 23.30 they had carried us over an offshore sandbank, where the ship re-anchored herself in about fifty fathoms of water four miles to the west of her original anchorage. She lay there quietly, and was in no danger; but she was exposed to the full force of the trade winds so there was no shelter for the launch, which provided our sole communication with the shore, to come alongside. This meant that when she attempted to come alongside on her last trip from Oranjestad that night, though one or two people made the hazardous leap on to the bottom of the gangway, she had to take the bulk of her passengers back ashore again. This gave some of the British engineers, who had their wives with them, an unexpected four-day vacation in Aruba, because it was impossible to resume the launch service until 08.00 on Thursday, 4 March.

In the meantime negotiations had been taking place ashore for the Dutch salvage tug Schelde, based in Willemstad, to come to our assistance, but her captain appeared to be playing hard to get. When he did finally close the ship at about 03.00 on the Monday morning, his first question when he contacted us on VHF was: 'Is your captain prepared to sign Lloyds' open form?' I then explained to him most carefully that the ship was in no danger; she was just riding quietly to her anchor. But we should definitely require his assistance at first light, to move the ship back to a sheltered anchorage to enable us to continue our boiler repairs. The Dutch captain's reply to this was to the effect that his company only did business on the basis of Lloyds' open form, and if our captain was not prepared to sign this it left him no alternative but to return to Willemstad, which he proceeded to do.

The only thing that we could do at this juncture was to inform our agents, SEL Maduro (Aruba) Ltd by VHF of what had happened. Later that morning they must have worked something out, because just after lunch the Schelde came alongside again, and without a word of explanation, and no mention of Lloyds' open form, informed us that he would put his tow line up on our starboard bow. Our port anchor was aweigh at 13.52; the Schelde then commenced towing us—we naturally assumed, back towards our anchorage. But on checking the position by cross bearings we found that in two hours he had only towed us about two miles to the north, just clear of the sandbank on which we had been anchored but into water too deep for us to let go our anchor again. I began to wonder if I was having a nightmare. He then called us up on VHF and announced that he had developed engine trouble, and that we were to slip his tow line. We did this at 15.50 and, having cast us adrift in deep water, the Schelde steamed away inshore and anchored, presumably to make engine repairs. While we once again started to drift westward under the influence of strong trade winds and the equatorial current, thoughts of a long-running English radio programme 'Desert Island Discs' crossed my mind. At intervals of approximately two hours the Schelde would call us on VHF with encouraging messages to the effect that his engine problems did not appear to be serious and he hoped to be back with us in about an hour. But all this time we continued our steady drift to the west, and the lights of Oranjestad had almost dipped below the horizon when he called us at 23.45 and said, 'I am afraid I have bad news for you. My engineers are unable to fix the engines. I shall have to go into Oranjestad for shore assistance.' However, the currents had once again carried us over an off-lying sandbank; at 00.30 on Tuesday, 2 March we were able to walk back seven shackles on the port anchor and the ship brought up in fifty fathoms of water, approximately sixteen miles from land. I can only say it was not in accordance with the book.

Later that morning two of C Y Tung's senior officials from New York visited the Schelde in Oranjestad to inquire into her mysterious breakdown; but when the engineer superintendent, G F Tang, asked to be taken down to the engine room, everything was suddenly all right again. Then the Dutch captain told Marine Superintendent T K Yip that he felt that his tug lacked sufficient power to handle the Seawise University alone, so another tug was ordered from Maracaibo to assist in towing us back to Aruba.

Meanwhile, on board the ship we waited all day, wondering what was happening, because we were again short of diesel fuel for the emergency generator, which was maintaining the essential services on board, and we knew that the Schelde could supply this for us. After more false alarms, the Dutch captain eventually decided at 20.00 that evening that he was ready to leave harbour, but this time Captain Yip decided to put up with the discomfort and ride out on the tug, to guard against any more mysterious breakdowns or other monkeyshines. The Schelde was back with us at 21.30, but as there was still no sign of Los Cocos, the tug from Venezuela, it was decided to do nothing that night.

The next day, Wednesday, 3 March, at 09.00 the Schelde made

fast astern and started passing us the diesel fuel, which at this time was the ship's life blood. While this was being done, the Los Cocos hove in sight. Everyone was taken aback by her size; she looked so small compared to the Schelde that as we watched her bouncing about in the choppy sea Commodore Hsuan remarked, 'They have only sent us a mini tug.' To which I replied, 'Yes, and she doesn't look as though she could pull the skin off a rice pudding.' If you can imagine an elephant being led by a huge Saint Bernard dog on one side, and a little Yorkshire terrier on the other, you will have a general picture of what it looked like when both tugs had made fast ahead and started towing. But I still doubt if you could grasp the language problem that we had, with Chinese, Dutch and Spanish all trying to communicate in their own particular kind of English. It was absolutely fantastic. In an effort to sort things out I found myself acting as communications officer, because, due to the distortions one gets on VHF, passing messages is never easy, even when everyone is speaking the same language.

By 14.30 that afternoon both tugs were fast and had weights on their lines, so at 14.45 we were able to weigh the port anchor again and start the slow tow back to our anchorage off Aruba, which we reached at 08.00 the following morning, Thursday, 4 March, having been drifting and dragging around for four days. But this time, on the orders of the harbourmaster, the pilot took us to a much more secure anchorage about one mile south of the Noordpundt Light, and we moored with two anchors down. From the point of view of getting on with the repairs, our new anchorage was not so convenient as the other, for it was a six-mile launch trip to Oranjestad, from where everything we needed had to come. But I felt confident that this was such a safe anchorage, with two 16 ton anchors well bedded in coral sand, that the ship would be able to ride out anything, even a hurricane. Everyone could at last settle down and concentrate on the overdue boiler repairs.

CHAPTER EIGHTEEN

The travelling university

After our interesting experiences with the tugs Schelde and Los Cocos of happy memory, the repair work on the boilers continued in a desultory manner and without any real sense of purpose, pending the arrival of yet another adviser, W S Pau. As the senior engineer in the Tung organization, he was the only Chinese with the technical knowledge and the authority to make the vital decisions about her future. Following his appearance about four days after we had reached our new anchorage, a series of long technical discussions took place with the chief engineer W C Cheng, the advisory chief engineer R E Philip, Ray Crowther of the London Salvage Association, and one of the top troubleshooters from the firm which had designed our boilers. It is fair to say that we had almost everybody there, but in the end it proved worth it, because the decision was reached that, regardless of expense, a thorough repair job must be done on all six of the ship's steaming boilers, with particular attention to A3 and B3, the boilers on which she depended for auxiliary steam. This meant flying down more than 600 new boiler tubes from New York to replace those found to be defective, while other spares were air-freighted out from England. However, to do all this required a great deal of time. In the first place, only a limited number of boilermakers were available; and then, in spite of the fact that the ship was completely shut down and all her boilers were cold because of the tropical heat and high humidity, working conditions were still far from pleasant for men working in such a very confined space as the inside of a boiler. Eventually the ship had to spend nearly eleven weeks (seventy-four days) at her anchorage.

Speaking for myself and the bulk of the ship's company—who were not actively involved in the boiler repairs—I do not think it would have been possible to find a pleasanter climate in which to break down than the sun-kissed island of Aruba, lying just off the coast of Venezuela in the Netherlands Antilles. The sun shines on the island every day and almost the only rain that falls is the odd shower brought in by the trade winds, which blow steadily for about 85 per cent of the time and provide nature's own very special brand of air-conditioning, seldom letting the thermometer fall below 78° or rise above 85°. Yet the sun and the wind between them have burned the island so brown that from its own resources it would probably be able to support only a few dozen people and a few herds of goats. The only reason for its high population density, and its people enjoying one of the highest standards of living in the West Indies, lies in one word: *oil*. When the rich Venezuelan oilfields were discovered in the Gulf of Maracaibo, the gulf was found to be too shallow for ocean-going ships. So the Mosquito fleet of small, shallow-draught tankers was built, to bring the oil to the deep water harbours and refineries which had been built on the lee side of Aruba and its larger neighbour island, Curaçao. Modern dredging methods have now made it possible to build deep-water harbours in the gulf, so the Mosquito fleet has gone, and although the refineries remain (indeed, the Esso plant at St Nicholas has grown to be one of the largest in the world), these are becoming more and more automated, and therefore employing fewer and fewer people.

Yet providence, like the sun, continues to shine on these fortunate islands, sending them a new kind of gold to replace the black sticky kind: tourist gold, brought in by jet planes and cruise liners. The Dutch have proved good administrators and the natives friendly hosts, so, with international finance building huge modern hotels, these islands seem to have everything that the winter visitor is looking for—which is mainly enough guaranteed sunshine every day in which to bake oneself to a suitable shade of red or brown, in one long weekend, to impress the folks back home in those colder northern latitudes. Besides the trade winds and pleasant temperatures, they also have sparkling white beaches of coral sand as fine as granulated sugar, safe bathing in crystal clear water filled with brilliant tropical fish, unlimited opportunities to gamble in well-run casinos attached to the principal hotels—and all this only three hours' flying time from New York. The bulk of the population seems to be made up of a mixture of Spanish, Dutch and South American Indian, who have freely intermarried. The local dialect (called *Papiamento* and spoken only in the Netherlands Antilles) is strongly based on Spanish, the official language is Dutch, and most people seem to speak a little English.

While we were there the only fault we could find with the weather was that at that time of the year the trade winds blew strongly enough to set up a choppy sea, making the six-mile launch trip from the ship to Oranjestad like a rather wet ride on a roller-coaster, which either began or ended with a precarious leap on or off the small platform at the foot of the ship's accommodation ladder. As a result of this, the strongly built local launch Elvira, which throughout our stay maintained a splendid service in all weathers, finished up with a lot of dents in her hull, and the platform at the foot of our ladder took such a pounding that after leaving Aruba it had to be written off as unfit for further use. As I had suffered with two broken legs in as many years, one of which I was only just getting back into shape, I could see little point in risking one of them again by leaping either on or off a wildly plunging launch unless I had some definite and worthwhile reason to go ashore. So after spending two months mainly confined to the ship, I was beginning to get rather bored with having few definite duties, as well as with the constant trade winds and sunshine. When Mr Philip and myself were offered the opportunity to fly home to England for a two-week vacation over the Easter holidays, we both leapt at what seemed to us a heaven-sent break in the monotony. It was now more than four months since we had seen our homes and families, months spent in what was in effect an alien world, full of uncertainties and strange situations. Also, we now knew that at least another three months must elapse before the ship could reach Hong Kong, so this break would make those months seem like another voyage. During the few days that elapsed after official leave had been granted, we were in high spirits; and then the bright morning came when we skipped away home, via Curaçao, Miami and London.

Coming down through the overcast into a gloomy Heathrow Airport on the morning of Tuesday, 1 April, I thought that London seemed not only cold and damp but, in the bone-chilling drizzle, drab and uninviting. The news broadcasts on the BBC Overseas Service, which had provided one of our principal links with home during the postal workers' strike, had said that it had been a very mild winter, so one found oneself gazing hopefully through the steamed-up windows of the airport bus, looking for signs of spring. But spring still seemed to be waiting in the wings, apart from faint touches of green on the willows and the occasional patch of bright yellow from forsythia bushes or clumps of daffodils in the suburban gardens we passed. However, it was wonderful to be home in one's own familiar surroundings again, hearing only British voices and feeling absurdly pleased with everything; so we hardly noticed the difference in the temperature.

About two days after we arrived there was a call from C Y Tung in London saying that he wanted to see Mr Philip and me. Unfortunately, by this time Mr Philip had picked up flu, so the meeting had to be postponed until Tuesday, 6 April, the day before Mr Tung was leaving for New York. As the staff of British Rail had chosen that day to work to rule as a protest about something, one could not be sure how the trains would run; but both Mr and Mrs Philip, and my wife and I, managed to reach Mr Tung's London home within half an hour of the appointed time. Outwardly, his home looks exactly like any of its neighbours in that quiet street in the heart of Mayfair; but once the solid front door closes, the overwhelming impression is of being magically transported to the Orient. The rich Chinese carpets, the beautifully carved screens, elegant furniture and other appointments, give the house a wonderful atmosphere. As before, the warmth of our welcome made us feel very much at home, and I think most people would be struck by C Y Tung's genuine friendliness. His warm smile and his ebullient, welcoming manner are very relaxing. Yet behind all this, the keenness of his mind is shown by his searching and knowledgeable questions, which covered every aspect of the difficulties the ship had encountered, both during her time in

Florida and during her adventurous voyage. He certainly knows what he is doing.

Twelve of us sat down to dinner at a huge round table, Mrs Philip and my wife being the only ladies present. The other guests were CY's elder brother and six of the top men in his organization in London and Hong Kong. During the time it took to serve the dozen or so courses of a superbly cooked Chinese meal, the conversation ranged widely over the many problems which still remained to be solved before CY's dream could become a reality, but it was a gay and friendly gathering, in some ways more like a family reunion.

The dull weather which had greeted our arrival, with cold easterly winds and heavily overcast skies, was to continue for ten days over southern England. But on Easter Saturday the clouds finally rolled away and four days of quiet weather with really warm spring sunshine effected an almost magical transformation in the countryside scene. Each succeeding day seemed to produce a richer shade of green to contrast with the willows, while the early flowering trees of the prunus family covered their bare branches with pink and cream blossoms, which stood out against the solid yellow of the forsythia. But it was not until the last afternoon of the holiday, when with my wife and daughter I visited the magnificent gardens on the Rothschild estate at Exbury in Hampshire, with its huge banks of rhododendrons, camellias and magnolias, that I felt spring had really arrived. This impression was strengthened the following day as Mr Philip and I drove back to London Airport past field after field of cattle their heads down, feasting on the rich grass, a sight which was to make the wind-burned hills of Aruba look even browner on our return.

Fortunately, by the time we got back to the ship the repairs were making good progress, and following a personal visit which C Y Tung had made to the ship while we were at home, there seemed to be an entirely new spirit on board. Not only had all the oil from the engine room and boiler rooms been disposed of, but a very thorough cleaning job had been done to remove all traces of oil from the bilges and the sides of the boilers. All the engine and boiler rooms in use had been cleaned up and painted out, so that down below she not only looked but really was a very different ship from the one which had staggered out of Port Everglades in such a shocking condition. She was indeed beginning to look so much more like she used to do in her Cunard days that for the first time one could really feel she was being given a new lease of life. The crew had worked really hard, and with a sense of purpose, which up to now many of them had lacked.

But the most important changes were on the personnel side. Older and more experienced firemen had been flown from Hong Kong to replace the younger men who had been so frightened by the boiler room fire. On the advice of Ray Crowther, it was also officially agreed by G F Tang, Mr Cheng and Mr Philip that a European engineer, with previous experience of the ship, would be in charge of each boiler room the whole time until the vessel reached Hong Kong. Of course, the language problem still remained as baffling as ever, but now at least there were more smiles all round.

As the two boilers in No 4 boiler room were tested and then flashed up, allowing the ship's main turbo-generators to be re-started during the last week in April, everyone's spirit began to rise. For while the diesel generator on the after deck had done yeoman service in enabling life on board to continue, its power was limited; as in Florida, going back on to main power allowed all essential services to be restored, which meant lights all over the ship, sanitary water, unlimited cooking facilities, etc. In a way, it was like the signs of returning life in spring after a long, hard winter.

It was not until Sunday, 9 May that all the tests were finally completed, and we put the engines on stand by and started to weigh the two anchors which had held us securely for so long. Even this was to prove a false start, because while we were using the engines to turn the ship on the starboard anchor—which had been shortened to three shackles—the chief engineer reported a burst in the main feed pipe, so the sailing had to be postponed for twenty-four hours to enable repairs to be carried out. The following day, things went very much better, and after the anchor was weighed at 16.16 we once again had the thrill of feeling the great ship moving under her own power, exactly three months to the day since leaving Port Everglades. It was a beautiful evening, and all hands were on deck to watch the ship steam slowly past the town of Oranje-stad, our port of refuge, from which we had received both hospital-ity and help with our repairs. We saluted it with three blasts on our powerful whistles, and this time they worked.

The short passage to the neighbour island of Curaçao was made at greatly reduced speed, to allow us to berth alongside in Caracas Bay the next morning (11 May). We were to spend forty-eight hours there, taking on 7,700 tons of fuel oil and 4,000 tons of fresh water to fill our tanks to capacity, and collecting scattered remnants of our mail, the mail arrangements in Aruba having been shocking. We left Curaçao at 09.30 on Thursday, 13 May, bound for Trinidad; because so far we had still not been able to get a proper check on the ship's daily consumption of fuel or water, or make an accurate estimate of her probable speed, with her two locked propellers, it had therefore been deemed prudent to call at Port of Spain to top off the ship's fuel and water supplies before starting the long, 3,306 mile sea passage to Rio de Janeiro. But, as we still had only five of our six boilers working, and the full force of the equatorial current and the trade winds against us, our average speed for the two-day passage was only 8.5 knots. This made us feel rather depressed for, although we were delighted to be under way again, unless we could do better than this we looked like being a very slow boat to China.

We anchored off Port of Spain at 14.14 on Saturday, 15 May and it took only a few hours to top off our fuel and water tanks; but because the chief engineer was concerned about one of his turbine bearings, which had been overheating, it was decided that the ship would remain at the anchorage until Monday morning to allow him time to open it up for examination. At 07.30 on Monday, 17 May we sailed on our first long ocean passage and as the ship passed out through the spectacular Boca Navios, with all six boilers now on the line, the engines slowly built up to what was to be their top speed, about 97 rpm. Everybody began to feel more cheer-ful, because for the first time in more than two years the engines had a definite pulse to them, the beat of which could be felt throughout the ship. Our collective spirits seemed to rise or fall with the speed or progress the ship was making: we were her barometer. Mr Cheng, however, was determined to pursue a policy of safety first, and not to put any undue pressure on his newly repaired boilers before we reached Hong Kong. So he allowed only five fires to be used on each boiler instead of the normal seven, and even these were only allowed to use the very small ·28 burner tips, while the pressure developed by each boiler was restricted to 325 lbs per square inch, or 100 lbs below their normal operating pressure. This was to give us a top speed of slightly over 11 knots in good weather, on a fuel consumption of about 300 tons per day. At this rate the ship would have been able to make the 5,300 mile trip direct to Capetown with an adequate margin, which would have saved us several days by avoiding a call at Rio. Unfortunately, during those first, vital days of a voyage when such a decision has to be made, the ship was still bucking the full force of the equatorial current, which kept her daily average speeds below 10 knots. As the chief engineer's daily fuel oil consumption figures were still not conclusive, Commodore Hsuan decided to play for safety and alter course for Rio. Then, as so often happens, once the decision had been taken and the course adjusted, both the speed and the fuel consumption figures started to improve. However, as the ship started to move south out of the tropics, life on board became pleasanter for everyone, as both the temperature and the humidity fell.

The Seawise University slid quietly into the sheltered waters of Rio de Janeiro's magnificent harbour before breakfast on the morning of Sunday, 30 May. As this was her first peacetime visit she attracted considerable attention, and passengers on the passing ferry boats could be seen crowding the rails to look at her. The local press, who were no doubt looking forward to her return the following year in her new role as a luxury cruise liner and sailing university, also gave her a friendly reception.

Our ship's company was given a very welcome run ashore in this beautiful city, which I had not visited before but which I found both gracious and splendid. We were ready to sail again, with full fuel tanks, by 16.00 the following day. It was a lovely sunny afternoon and the ship must have provided the people watching from the shore with the opportunity to take some excellent pictures as she passed close alongside the famous Sugar Loaf and then through the deep water channel which took her about a mile off the world-renowned beach, with its wide sweep of white sand bounded by luxury hotels.

The 3,343 mile run across the South Atlantic was made in almost perfect weather, with sunshine every day. Although we didn't sight another ship on this rather lonely ocean, about half way across we picked up an escort of two albatrosses, and these huge, graceful white birds, whose number later increased to half a dozen, stayed with us until we were within sight of the African coast. They made a beautiful picture, riding the wind with scarcely any perceptible movement of their wings, and beguiled many a quiet half-hour. Towards the end of the crossing the westerly winds began to increase gradually in force, and we picked up those long heavy swells coming up from the Roaring Forties known as the Cape rollers. But with both the wind and the swell behind her the ship rode very comfortably, and was not delayed. In fact, our average speed for this crossing was to be our best for the whole voyage: we made 11·26 knots on a fuel consumption of less than 300 tons per day. These figures helped to remove finally one of the biggest worries about the next leg of our journey, because away back in those dark days when both the ship's speed and probable fuel consumption were unknown factors, it had proved extremely difficult to arrange a suitable refuelling port for her on the long haul from Capetown to Singapore. We knew now that, with all our fuel tanks filled to capacity, we could set out confidently on the 5,750 mile non-stop trip, and arrive with about three days' fuel in hand.

The change to the much cooler weather of the South African winter came as a shock to many people who, like myself, had not brought much warm clothing. However, after such a very long spell in the tropics, it came as a pleasant change to get up in the morning and think about clothes as something necessary to keep you warm, rather than just to satisfy the conventions.

As it had been at Rio, our arrival at Capetown was made in the early hours of a Sunday morning, but as the date was 13 June and I have had a lifelong aversion to doing things on the 13th, I had been a little worried about this. My gloomy forebodings were not justified, however, because although Table Mountain had its cloth on—meaning that its head was hidden in the clouds—and there was an unpleasant drizzle, there was absolutely no wind, and with a skilful pilot assisted by four heavy and powerful tugs the ship glided quietly and easily into her berth, making fast at 08.40.

Being the largest passenger vessel ever to enter Duncan Harbour, our arrival received a lot of publicity in the local press as well as on the radio. The press conference arranged by the owner's representative in Africa for 11.00 the next day, to publicize the ship in her new role, was well attended and the ship was given excellent coverage, with friendly comment and some very good pictures. But perhaps the best evidence of public interest was the large gallery of spectators which lined the quay by the Union Castle berth to watch the ship pass out between the breakwaters when she sailed at 16.00 that afternoon.

The weather on our sailing day was to prove much less kind to us than it had been when we arrived, and heavy squally showers, which had been blowing up all day, had caused the harbourmaster and pilots some concern. But although the wind had been gusting up to 20 knots while we were making the tugs fast and singling up our moorings, just as we let go the last line there was a lull which lasted till we cleared the harbour, and the pilot who brought us out found it necessary to use only three of the four tugs at his disposal for the tricky operation of swinging the ship into line with the entrance channel before starting the run out between the breakwaters—which reminded me a little of leaving Port Everglades. Indeed he was quite enthusiastic about the way the ship handled at low speeds in shallow water, in spite of the drag of her two locked propellers, giving me the impression that the ship would be a welcome visitor at Capetown on future calls. This pleased me greatly, because I wanted her to do well and be as popular as she used to be.

After we had rounded the Cape of Good Hope and were heading east, we found even larger, longer versions of the Cape rollers waiting for us, with strong cold winds bringing up wintry showers from the south polar regions. So, standing on our vast, empty promenade deck watching the ship rolling easily in the big quarter swell, it did not require a lot of imagination to picture the Old Lady as being back on her old stamping ground, the North

Atlantic, where so much of her life had been spent in weather like this. With all of her tanks full of oil and water, she rode the 'greybeards' very well, and it was only when we passed the big tankers going the other way and shipping huge seas that we realized just how comfortable we were. We did sound very like a ghost ship as, with every roll, dozens of cupboard and locker doors which had been left open in unoccupied cabins banged monotonously.

Our biggest difficulty at this stage of the voyage was not the weather, which was mainly behind us and helping us along, but the fact that we were now heading into the full strength of the well known Agulhas Current, which runs nearly as strongly round the southern tip of Africa as the Gulf Stream does along the coast of Florida; so for several days our speed was to prove very disappointing. Also, it soon became obvious that our chief engineer, Mr Cheng, was determined to keep his hand even more firmly on the throttle during this long leg. This meant that our average speed on this section of the voyage was going to be about a knot less than it had been on the South Atlantic, which proved very irksome to Mr Philip and the British engineers, who knew the ship's capabilities, and who, now that the boilers had been thoroughly tested, itched to have a go. All the Europeans silently fumed.

Fortunately our spell of really wintry weather was to be short-lived and before we had been a week at sea the sun once again had a warmth that you could feel; so on the day we sighted the mountains of Madagascar in the distance, Monday, 21 June, in spite of the fact that it was the shortest day of the year in the southern hemisphere, it felt like spring again. Two days later we had another break from the monotony of sea and sky as we passed fairly close to the spectacular French island of Reunion, with its 10,000 ft mountain peaks rising almost straight from the sea. But, alas, a glance astern that morning showed that our faithful escort of albatrosses, who had picked us up again the day after we left Capetown, had now deserted us, and we felt very sad to lose them, so beautiful and so graceful. In the evening of the same day we passed the gentler British island of Mauritius, at about the same distance off. Nightfall had converted it into a low black shape which in the sparklingly clear air had the appearance of being studded with thousands of diamonds, with every now and then an even more brilliant gleam, as cars with their headlights on moved along the island's roads.

Shortly after passing these two islands we started to pick up the south-east trade winds, which gradually merged into the hot and very humid weather with overcast skies and frequent torrential rainstorms of the south-east monsoon, and before another week had passed we found ourselves thinking nostalgically of the nice, cool weather round South Africa. But as far as this voyage was concerned, cool weather was to be very much a thing of the past, and when we did see the sun again it was in the sweltering heat of the equatorial calms, and from there to and including Hong Kong it was to be very hot all the way.

When we entered the Straits of Malacca on Sunday, 4 July we felt we were really in Eastern waters at last, and because our speed had by now been cut right back to about 8 knots, to make arrival in Singapore fall on Wednesday, 7 July, cargo vessels using this busy seaway were overtaking us every few minutes as we made our stately progress past One Fathom Bank lighthouse. It was at this point that we were escorted for about an hour by two Shackleton aircraft of the RAF, who flew low round the ship and took some most impressive pictures which filled the front pages of the Singapore newspapers when we arrived next day.

In spite of our speed reductions, we still arrived in Singapore too early and had to anchor in the Jurong anchorage at 05.00 to await suitable tidal conditions for going alongside. Then at 11.00, just as we were weighing anchor to proceed in to our berth, six fighter aircraft of the RAF flew low over the ship in tight formation, followed a few minutes later by six Royal Navy helicopters who circled the ship twice, both services apparently anxious to salute the Grand Old Lady who for so long had been the pride of Britain's merchant fleet. Under the skilled guidance of Singapore's chief pilot, we safely negotiated the Jurong channel with, in places, less than two feet of water under our keel, and assisted by four tugs, berthed alongside the Mobil oil company's Jurong wharf at 12.30. Because our berth was fourteen miles from the city centre, and also because they preferred to wait until she could be seen in all the splendour of her new paint after her refit, the company had decided that this time there would be no official reception or press conference. But local interest in the ship and her history was so great that a party of about twenty press, radio and TV people boarded her at about 16.00, after Commodore Hsuan and most of his senior officers had gone ashore. So, probably for the last time, I found myself doing the honours and showing them round my old ship. I must say, I did so with mixed feelings and once more I said to myself, 'What is she doing here? What am I doing here? Why couldn't she have stayed in Britain?'

With the ship's air-conditioning plant only operating in the main public rooms, I am afraid my main impression of Singapore on this visit was of overpowering equatorial heat and, having been there three times before, I could not even raise sufficient energy to make the long taxi ride into the city. Yet I must have been one of the only people on board who did not do so, because for our Chinese crew this was the first time that they had been back among their own people for many long weary months, and they must have felt like I did when home on leave. The pilot boarded the ship again the following morning, and we left our berth at 10.05. After an enjoyable cruise through the many islands that dot Singapore harbour, we landed him just south of St John's Island at noon and started the last leg of our long journey. But our passage through the South China Sea was to bring no relief from the heat and humidity, because for part of the time we were on the fringe of tropical storm Kim, and although the wind speed never exceeded Force 7 on the Beaufort scale, there was torrential rain and excessively high humidity. In making their arrangements for the ship's reception, the company had accepted Commodore Hsuan's view that there was an element of doubt about the ship being able to arrive off Hong Kong in time to enter harbour at first light on Wednesday, 14 July and had arranged her reception for the following day. On a comparatively short run, this reduced the average speed required to less than 9 knots, but the navigational hazards of the South China Sea made it imprudent to steam as slowly as this in the vicinity of a tropical storm until the ship was clear of the channel between the Paracel Islands and Macclesfield reef, so the last part of our journey had to be made at a crawl, and we still arrived nearly twenty-four hours too soon. Standing on the bridge watching the ship floundering along at about 4 knots, barely enough to make her steer properly, one could not help casting one's mind back to the days when she had maintained an average speed of 28.5 knots across the Atlantic, in fair weather or foul, and we had regularly brought her alongside the Ocean Terminal in Southampton, or Pier 92 in New York, within minutes of her scheduled time, like the Royal Scot coming into Euston Station.

Eventually, having spent a whole day cruising around just outside the entrance to Hong Kong harbour—rather like a nervous prima donna waiting apprehensively in the wings before making her big entrance—we started our slow and stately trip through the multitude of islands which make up Hong Kong's beautiful harbour at 04.42 on the morning of Thursday, 15 July, threading our way through many hundreds of brilliantly lighted fishing junks. Then, as the rising sun showed up the rich green of the dense foliage covering the islands, we were met by an escort of two army helicopters, followed by two of the marine department's large patrol craft, which stationed themselves one on each bow to clear a pathway for us through the hundreds of small craft we were to meet later, and see that nobody impeded our progress by getting across our bows. After the pilot boarded and as we got closer to the city, the size of our escort, both of small craft and helicopters, steadily increased, with the Hong Kong fire boat putting up a much finer display of water fountains than I had ever seen in New York. As we passed Green Island four powerful tugs joined to escort us to our anchorage. But the ship continued to handle so well under her own power that their services were not required, and the pilot put the anchor down on the exact spot at 09.30. Hong Kong had, we felt, really put itself out to give us a welcome fit for a Queen and, for the three days that I remained in the colony, news items about the ship occupied the front pages of the local papers. A delightful ultimate touch came when one of the RAF pilots brought his big helicopter down right between our funnels and landed on the sports deck, and I was just able to have a few words with him before he lightheartedly took off again. It was a happy landing and everyone seemed delighted to see the ship safely here at last, but in spite of her new name nearly everyone seemed to think of her as the Queen Elizabeth, and one got the feeling it was as this that she was being welcomed. However, plans to refit her as the Seawise University were actively under way, and before I left the ship for the last time that afternoon I had seen the plans which one of Lloyds' senior ship surveyors from London, was going through with the shipyard representatives and the man who was in charge of the reconversion. The alterations required to bring the ship into line with the 1966 IMCO convention on safety of life at sea were going to cost millions of pounds.

For the three following days Mr Philip and myself were given the red carpet treatment as house guests at C Y Tung's palatial villa between Deepwater Bay and Repulse Bay, with its magnificent terraced gardens of nearly two acres. They had been carved out of the hillside, with the terraces running down to a swimming pool and private bathing beaches, and contained a collection of tropical flowering trees and plants almost impossible to describe. One of the company's senior executives, K H Tang, devoted himself almost entirely to seeing that we were royally entertained, and to ensuring that we saw as much as possible of both Hong Kong island and the New Territories in the time at our disposal, while still leaving us ample time for what everybody wants to do in Hong Kong—shopping. With dinner parties and Oriental entertainment organized by the general manager Y S Kung and senior company officials on two evenings, time passed remarkably quickly, and in no time at all it was time to board the BOAC plane for the long flight home on the Sunday evening.

This was to prove a most interesting flight, because when dinner had been served shortly after takeoff I received an invitation from the captain of the aircraft to visit the flight deck. At this time the plane was flying south along the coast of Vietnam and, just as he was pointing out to me the lights of the big American base at Danang close to the DMZ, two parachute flares were fired into the sky and drifted down with their brilliant but rather eerie light. It made the war seem very close, but the captain said: 'I don't think that means there is any real activity down there; they just seem to do it from time to time, to make the Viet Cong keep their heads down.'

Flying to the westward, in the same direction that the sun moves around the earth, our relative time changes were slow, and our flight across Burma and the Bay of Bengal to Calcutta, then across

India to Karachi and on over the Near East, was all made in darkness. But it was full daylight when we landed in Rome to change our aircrew and, after breakfast had been served and we had had an opportunity to wash and shave, I received another invitation to the flight deck from our new captain. This time the plane was flying over the Alps on a glorious summer morning with not a cloud in the sky and unlimited visibility. It was an absolutely breathtaking spectacle, as our course took us right over the top of Mont Blanc, and it was hard to believe that this peaceful looking, wide, white world spread out below us, with the blue of Lake Geneva in the distance, was part of the same planet as the angry-looking skies over Vietnam the previous evening. After flying over the fields of France, we came winging in across the Channel to find cloudless skies over Heathrow, and we landed fifteen minutes ahead of schedule, the perfect English summer day seeming a very marked contrast to my previous arrival there on 1 April. During the journey down to my home in Wiltshire, through the lush green of the English countryside now in the full flush of summer, I found myself reflecting that another chapter of my life had now closed.

Looking back and trying to sum up this unique and historic voyage, one's mind flies back to Florida and those first few months of Chinese ownership, when most members of the new crew were quite definitely nervous of the ship's size and complexity; while we British felt quite at home, having had to deal so many times with her problems, which all ships produce at times. We were prepared to tackle anything and help in any way we could; but we were of completely different races and outlook, and for most of us the language barrier constituted an almost impossible hurdle—we could scarcely communicate. During the voyage some of the Europeans did make an effort to learn Chinese, but few of them progressed far beyond the schoolboy's *'la plume de ma tante'* stage. On the other side most of the Chinese officers had to have a basic knowledge of English in order to do their job, but it was limited and of little use in a friendly way, not being at all colloquial or idiomatic. In mixed conversation there could be no jokes, especially not within an atmosphere of watchful regard; so however correct and amiable a meeting might appear to be, without trust and real confidence on both sides, it was bound to be frustrating in terms of communication.

Then, in those early days there were so many almost insuperable problems, like those with the boilers and the oily bilge water, that were the direct result of gross neglect during the Queen Elizabeth's two years 'up the creek'. But the owner's representatives and the ship's officers had their own ideas on how these problems could or should be solved, and all too often advice offered in good faith by us was either received with a thinly disguised hostility, or rejected outright. For both Mr Philip and myself this was particularly frustrating at times, for in the past we had had complete responsibility for the running of the ship, and we just itched for the chance to take over and get on with the job of getting her to Hong Kong, instead of just floundering about. But we had to keep reminding ourselves that she was their ship now, and we were only advisers.

After all her early vicissitudes, both in leaving Port Everglades and on the voyage (and I still find it hard to believe it all happened to the Queen Elizabeth), and the subsequent slow improvement in personal relationships during the deliberate crawl across the oceans to her ultimate destination, I am now conscious of, and appreciate, what a long way we all came together, and how trust and confidence grew as we all slowly got to know one another over the miles and months.

Much was done on the long ocean stretches towards creating a friendly and companionable atmosphere among the officers by a series of parties, started by Y S Kung when he gave a Crossing the Line party to celebrate the ship's crossing of the Equator between Trinidad and Rio. The European engineers and their wives then organized birthday parties for three members of the group who had birthdays during the trip. Then both Commodore Hsuan and Chief Engineer Cheng gave parties, to which Mr Philip and I responded with what we thought was to be a farewell party just before reaching Singapore; but the shipyard officials and technicians who joined the ship in Singapore to prepare for the refit oranized another and bigger farewell party two days before we reached Hong Kong. Most of these parties were held in the Midships Bar, the scene of many a gay evening in other days as many of our passengers will remember. It still looked very much as it used to do, but its great asset to us was that it could be air-conditioned for the occasion. Having a few European engineers' wives on board for the voyage helped to make these parties quite gay affairs, and I am convinced that the ladies did a lot towards warming the atmosphere. They also helped to break down the barriers of suspicion, and once this is achieved it is quite amazing how much communication you can have even with a limited vocabulary. Well, 'limited' is scarcely the word for my efforts with the Chinese language: I was a dead loss—as the Americans say, 'I couldn't get to first base'—but I do enjoy Chinese food. To sum the situation up, I felt that by the time we reached Singapore we were no longer so much Occidentals or Orientals as shipmates, any of whom I would be very happy to meet again.

Trying, at this time, to look into the future and make a reasonable assessment of the ship's chances of success, based on my personal experiences over the past nine months, was something I found extremely difficult to do. Technically, I had every confidence that with Mr Tung's money and determination and the skilled craftsmen available to him, the ship could be put back into first-class condition and brought into line with the new safety regulations. It was going to cost a fabulous amount of money, but provided the hull and engines were basically sound it was just a matter of ripping out everything that needed replacing, and it would still be a lot cheaper than building a new ship of even a quarter the size at today's prices.

But when it came to running her, I was not nearly so confident. I have always held that any ship, no matter how large or expensively fitted out, is just another piece of hardware until you get the right crew for her; and it has to be a crew who like the ship, and who are prepared to stay with her and help to build up her reputation with the travelling public for excellent service and safety. And what is even more important, with the travel agents, upon whom every shipping company has to depend if it is going to survive. It was going to be a fantastically difficult task for Mr Tung's organization to find, and in a few short months to train, nearly 1,000 men and women to operate a ship as complex as this, and to give that very high standard of service which the wealthy American cruise passengers, upon whom he would have to depend for the bulk of his revenue, demand. Having been not very favourably impressed with the standard of discipline I had seen on board, I found it hard to believe that he could, because a well-run ship requires a lot of organization, and my experience of the Chinese generally was that they were hard workers but poor organizers.

Still, I was very anxious that he should succeed, because I felt that the old seafaring nations of the western world were one by one abandoning their attempts to operate these large passenger liners. In the face of operating costs which continue to rise at a fantastic rate, they consider them uneconomical. So one is left hoping that perhaps an Eastern nation, with no unions and much lower wage bills, will be able to give them a new lease of life, thus conferring a benefit on all those people who, like myself, prefer a more relaxing mode of transport to rushing around in jet aircraft; those who would like to travel in a more civilized way.

CHAPTER NINETEEN

A tragic end for the Queen of the Seas

As the result of the tragic loss by fire on 9 January 1972 of the Queen Elizabeth, the bright hopes of her sailing the seas once more were confounded for ever, and nothing to equal her will ever be seen again.

I had been kept well posted by members of the Tung organization, and in letters from CY himself, about the excellent progress of her refit, and I had been delighted to hear that her four engines and all twelve boilers had been put back into full working order. I had also read with great interest the announcements in the American press and travel magazines of her first seventy-five-day luxury Pacific cruise, due to start from Long Beach, California, on 24 April 1972.

It was therefore with shock and horror that I first heard the news on an early-morning telephone call from the BBC that she was on fire fore and aft, blazing furiously, and expected to become a total loss. I just could not bring myself to believe that a ship with such a good fire-safety record (and as a result of her reconversion should have been more fireproof than she had ever been before) could burn so quickly and so completely, unless fires had been deliberately started in several parts of the ship at the same time. My expression of these opinions in press and TV interviews caused a certain amount of consternation, and I even received a telephone call from a leading Hong Kong newspaper asking me to clarify what I based these opinions on. All I could say was that I felt I knew the ship very well, and as I had already suffered at the hands of an arsonist on board the Carinthia in Montreal, one does not forget the significant details.

Fire destroys all evidence so completely, I very much doubt—no matter how many 'official inquiries' are held—whether anyone will ever know for certain just who, or what, caused the tragic end of this gracious lady. Speaking, I am sure, for all those who sailed or served in her, we mourn her passing. She was held in great affection by so many, in all parts of the world.

In her splendid voyaging in both war and peace, she earned a Viking's funeral. If there is a Valhalla for ships—she will be there.

We who knew her in fair weather and foul, we salute her.

Perhaps I should end this book with an attempt to sum up my personal voyage through life so far, which has taken me across the oceans of the world for almost fifty years. I have had a very good life, one which has been satisfying in a professional sense. Learning from watching other and better sailors doing their job in the days when standards of behaviour and excellence were higher than they are today, I have attempted to follow their flag and to pass on their standards.

I have been extremely fortunate in that the years of my responsibility at sea coincided with those years during which the two great Queens dominated a flourishing Cunard economy, as they carried the famous personalities of the world to and fro across the North Atlantic. This gave me a unique opportunity to meet a large cross-section of influential and interesting people in the relaxed social atmosphere of either a five-day Atlantic crossing or a luxury cruise, as a result of which I made many friends both at home and abroad, with whom I still maintain contact. World cruises and shorter ones have also enabled me to visit all quarters of the globe, and to see places most people only read about, in a great deal of comfort.

But beyond all this, the main attraction of a sea career has been the challenge of navigating the North Atlantic, an ocean which, with its winter storms and summer fogs, gets some of the worst weather in the world, and of doing this for most of the time without the benefit of the highly sophisticated navigational aids found in some of the newer vessels today. It may have been a bit 'By guess, or by God' at times, but over the years we managed to maintain a tight schedule with very little reserve speed; and yet, in spite of all the hazards, to bring in the two Queens right on time, in voyage after voyage, to everyone's comfort and satisfaction.

During my years in command, I think there can have been few men more fortunate than I was in the crews I sailed with. They were my charge, my ship family, and anything I was able to do for them was repaid one hundredfold by the loyalty they showed me. So my happiest memories of my years at sea will always be of the good personal relationship I was able to establish with so many of my shipmates.

So much for the Merchant Navy. As for my service in the Royal Navy, well, that was mostly in time of war, which was a tough time for everyone on sea or on land; but for me it was a wonderful experience, each ship a warm, tight community, with everyone working for the same end and purpose and all of us for one another's good. I can never forget the men that I met; the willing, wonderful ship's companies, cheerfully accepting any hardship in the common cause, for the good of the country.

Against all these many benefits and assets, I have to set one great disadvantage: the lack of normal home life. Wife and family have had to accept that the ship comes first; children have an itinerant father, and you find at times they are almost strangers. While I was away on one cruise, my seven-year-old wrote her first letter to me, carefully printed in pencil, with evidence of many rubbings out. It said: 'Dear Daddy, Please come home soon, you have been away so long, we feel as if we had no Daddy.' Each time one does get home on leave, life is lived against the clock. One's wife must learn to run things on her own because so often she must; and she has to be both father and mother to the children.

Somehow or other, I seem to have been fortunate in my life (and you need luck as much as accomplishment), because I have now come to realize that my life has been well rounded and fulfilled.

And if I sniff the breeze at times and square my shoulders, it is to be expected; for I have good memories of many good things, and there is always the future. A new life starts every morning.